JOURNEYS TO THE JAPANESE

Also by Morton and Lucia White

The Intellectual versus the City: From Thomas Jefferson to Frank Lloyd Wright

JOURNEYS
to the
JAPANESE
1952–1979

Morton and Lucia White

The University of British Columbia Press
Vancouver 1986

Journeys to the Japanese, 1952–1979

Canadian Cataloguing in Publication Data

White, Morton, 1917–
   Journeys to the Japanese, 1952–1979

   Includes index.
   1. Japan - Description and travel - 1945–
2.Japan-Civilization-1945–   3.
White, Morton, 1917–   4. White, Lucia.
I. White, Lucia. II. Title.
DS811.W494 1986   915.2'044   C85-091446-9

International Standard Book Number 0-7748-0231-6

Printed and bound in Canada
by John Deyell Company

To
Nick, Trish, Jenny, Livy, and Alex
and
Steve, Kate, and Joe

CONTENTS

PREFACE

In this book, which is based on journals, correspondence, and recollections, we record some experiences and present some reflections on roughly thirty years of association with the Japanese, primarily with scholars and their families. Most of our contact with them occurred while we lived and travelled in Japan during five visits there, some of it while they visited in the United States. We saw our friends in seminars and conferences, in the lecture-hall and the beer-hall, in their homes and in restaurants, in the city and the country, at work and at play. We watched some of them move from youth to the ripeness of age, and we saw their country rise from abject military defeat to the economic pre-eminence it now holds in the world. We were therefore able to observe Japan and Japanese life during a crucial part of this century. We watched it change in a period of turbulent and rapid transition; we also saw it maintain many of its ancient traditions.

Not being professional students of Japanese language, history, or culture, we have not written a scholarly work. Rather, we have presented some impressions and ideas of Japan which we hope will interest the reader who can find more scientific information elsewhere. Although our responsibilities and personal connections led us to spend a good deal of time with philosophers, students of American life, and their families, our frequent visits and our travels within Japan gave us an opportunity to see beyond the confines of the classroom. The reader will observe that we give more space to our first visit in 1952 than to any other visit. This is partly owing to our having been assaulted by a great variety of novel experiences on our first encounter with Japan, experiences that we were moved to report in the fullest journals we kept.

We wish to thank Rebecca Davies for cheerfully typing the manuscript.

ONE

The First Invitation to Tokyo

One day in November of 1951, Morton received a telephone call in his Harvard office from John Goheen, then professor of philosophy at Stanford University. Goheen extended an invitation that seemed impossible to decline. He asked Morton to visit Tokyo University in the summer of 1952 in order to conduct a seminar on American philosophy; it would be financed by the Rockefeller Foundation and administered jointly by Tokyo and Stanford Universities. The seminar would meet daily for four weeks, and the same schedule would be followed by four other American professors who would deal with history, economics, political science, and literature. Each professor's seminar would be attended by what Goheen referred to as "twenty mature Japanese students." The students who would attend the seminar in philosophy might not know very much about American philosophy, Goheen said in a letter, but he flattered Morton by saying that they would be "intensely interested" in what he might have to say. Some of them had already been pursuing studies of William James, John Dewey, and Charles Peirce, but, Goheen added, they were eager to hear something about analytic philosophy and other recent developments in the States. Referring to his own Tokyo seminar in the summer of 1951, Goheen remarked that he had given some attention to American philosophy in the colonial period, but that Morton should feel free to avoid that and to give special emphasis to nineteenth- and twentieth-century philosophers and philosophical movements.

Goheen went on to say that the seminars would be directed by two Tokyo professors, Hideo Kishimoto and Shinzo Kaji, about whom the reader will hear a great deal in what follows since they became very good friends of ours. They would lead the American professors through a schedule that Goheen outlined in a way that masked what was in store for us:

| June 30–July 4 | Orientation [sic!] |
| July 6 | Reception |

July 7– August 1	Seminars
August 4– 8	Round-table conference
August 9– 15	Rest and conferences at a provincial university.

Goheen also told us about a problem created by the fact that Japan was still occupied by American military forces. Not only would we have to apply for a passport but also for a military permit.

The permit, Goheen continued, was the touchy point, "as you can find out from my old friend John Fairbank" (the distinguished Harvard scholar who was then having difficulty entering Japan). Goheen added a remark that reflected the political atmosphere of America in 1952 as well as the fact that Japan was still occupied. He said that the American authorities would require both of us to get permits to travel abroad, and that we would have to show that accommodations were available for both of us in Tokyo.

In spite of the daunting schedule that Goheen described and in spite of the red tape involved in getting our military permits, Morton was thrilled at the prospect of going to Japan, and Lucia was equally thrilled when he broke the news to her. The financial arrangements were such as to make it possible for both of us to go. Morton would receive a salary of $1,500; he would receive a round trip air ticket from Boston to Tokyo; and he would also be supplied with funds that would take care of travel and living expenses in Japan. It should be borne in mind that in 1952 the American dollar commanded about 350 yen by comparison to the 250 or so that it is worth now.

Given the favorable exchange, we thought we could make the trip without going broke, but what would happen to our sons Nick and Steve, who would be ten and seven at the time of our trip in the summer of 1952? It was not easy to solve that problem. We would have loved to take them along but feared that it might prove difficult to do so. Even if we could have afforded to take them, we would have had to worry about transporting them around Japan, about their health, and about keeping them occupied. After much agonizing, we did something that they did not altogether love: we decided to install them in a New Hampshire summer camp with the improbable name of "Little Sir Echo." Morton's parents agreed to visit them regularly, and we vowed to them that we would make up for leaving them at home by taking them with us on our next trip to Japan. That trip was not to be very far in the future since our visit in 1952 was followed by another in 1960, when we kept our promise to the boys. After that visit there would be a third in 1966, a fourth in 1976, and a fifth in 1979. These visits and the frequent visits of our Japanese friends to the United States made it possible for us to write this book.

As soon as it was clear that we would be going to Japan in 1952, it seemed wise to learn something about the country, and that would have to be a great deal indeed. We knew nothing about it or its people except what we may have gleaned from eating in a Japanese restaurant in pre-Pearl Harbor New York—there was, as we recall, only one such restaurant then—and we probably did not know more than a couple of Japanese words. Therefore, Morton decided to attend a class at Harvard in introductory Japanese. It was given by his Harvard colleague and fellow tutor at Adams House, Edwin O. Reischauer, later to become U.S. ambassador to Tokyo. Morton attended the class dutifully for several weeks, but then he began to think that he was slipping behind his younger classmates. The woman who conducted the recitations would drill her students by asking them to translate the usual inanities of the first sessions of an introductory course in a foreign language—things like "the tree," "the river," "the mountain," followed by "the tree by the river" or the "tree on the mountain." All of this would be recited by the class in sing-song unison, and soon Morton began to fall behind his classmates in his chanting. So he wondered whether he was linguistically inadequate, too old, or just stupid, and therefore asked Ed Reischauer to tell him candidly which of these deficiencies might be preventing him from keeping up. In reply, Reischauer said he thought the explanation was entirely different. "You see," he said, in effect, "you are taking this introductory course only for the first time whereas some of your classmates have already taken it once or twice before." Morton did not know whether Reischauer's implied comment on the difficulty of Japanese was true or whether he was merely being generous to a dumb colleague. So Morton asked Reischauer whether he should go on trying to learn the language. Reischauer said "No," to put it bluntly, and may well have been displaying qualities that turned him into a diplomat when he added that it would be wasteful for one who was going to spend such a short time in Japan to try to learn so difficult a language. But whatever Reischauer's motives were, he discouraged his pupil from going on in the course. To this day the pupil regrets the fact that he heeded his former teacher's advice, especially because of the many visits that we made to Japan after 1952. How much more we would have learned about the country had we known how to read at least a bit of the language! In future years we tried to learn how to speak some of it and how to read it in the transliterated form called "Romaji," but we never really learned to read or speak it competently.

While telling about matters preliminary to our departure, we should mention another Harvard professor, Perry Miller, the distinguished historian of American thought and literature who, alas, is no longer alive. One night shortly after Goheen's invitation had come, we were dining with the Millers; and it emerged that we were going to Japan at the invitation of John Goheen. When Perry heard this, he remarked that he had once been invited by John to teach in the same program but had declined. We surmised from the manner in which Perry reported his refusal that perhaps he might accept if he and Betty were invited to come along in the summer of 1952, so we asked him whether he would and he replied with enthusiasm that he would. The next morning Morton telephoned this news to John Goheen, who was delighted to hear it. He immediately called Perry and asked him to teach the seminar in American literature. Perry accepted without hesitation, and, as a result, we were joined by two very good friends on our Japanese journey. Their presence in Japan was a source of very great pleasure to us; moreover, it was the beginning of a long friendship that included two other joint academic junkets in the years that followed.

Since we did not fly together in the days when Nick and Steve were children, only Morton joined the Millers on the flight to Tokyo from Boston by way of Seattle. Lucia went to Japan by way of California and Hawaii. Morton remembers a few things about his trip that may be worth reporting here. The plane was a Boeing Stratocruiser which carried what might be called a pouch underneath it. In that pouch there was a bar that Perry Miller visited very often. He reached it by way of a winding stair-case which he easily negotiated in the downward direction but which, for good reason, he had trouble ascending. Morton, on his only visit to the bar, chatted with an elderly army sergeant who remarked as he looked out the window: "If we drop into that water, we'll be frozen to death in a minute." That was not very encouraging to one who feared flying, nor was the descent into Anchorage. After leaving that bleak town, the plane stopped for a while at the even bleaker island in the Aleutians called Shemya. There the passengers were given sandwiches and coffee in a one-storey house that was virtually underground. To protect it from the howling winds, a trench was built around it so that the level of one's eyes as one stood on its floor was about the same as the level of the ground surrounding the house. Leaving Shemya with relief, Morton and the Millers headed for Tokyo. Soon after passing over the coast of Honshu, the main island of Japan, they caught sight of the waves rolling into it from the Pacific and they glimpsed some lovely green land beyond the coast. That welcome sight quickly disappeared and the next thing they knew their plane was enveloped in very dark clouds. They saw menacing strokes of lightning, and the plane began to experience turbulence of a kind that Morton had never experienced before, has never experienced since, and hopes never to experience again. The plane would drop for what seemed like miles in a second, and then it would bob up and down violently; it wobbled, groaned, and creaked. The Millers, who were experienced flyers, had enough sense to be worried. Morton, who had never been through anything like this before, was excited but too ignorant to be as worried as he should have been, partly because the blasé sergeant next to him was sleeping through the whole thing. Finally, the storm disappeared and the plane began its descent. Then, at last, it put down at Haneda airport in Tokyo.

The scene there was one of chaos coupled with extraordinary Japanese efficiency. Somehow, after having been examined by armed Japanese soldiers, armed American soldiers, and incomprehensible Japanese customs agents, Morton and the Millers were greeted by their Japanese hosts, who had managed to identify them without difficulty. They helped them pass through the various obstacles one encounters upon entering an occupied country, grabbed their bags, and whisked them into dark American automobiles that were owned by Tokyo University—yes, American automobiles, for those were the days before Japan dominated the automobile industry. The route from the airport to Tokyo was dotted with buildings that were mostly gray or white, crate-like and flimsy, with picturesque signs in bold Japanese characters. While travelling from the airport, Morton and the Millers were first taken through the outskirts of an industrial area where cars, bicycles, and people were racketing in both directions. Then they were driven through suburbs where clumps of trees and gray-green grassy banks appeared with pagoda-shaped luxurious homes behind high walls interspersed between the little rows of frail, modern, one-storey buildings. At last they arrived at the Matsudaira Hotel.

TWO

The Matsudaira Hotel

We were pleasantly surprised to find that the American professors and their wives would not be imprisoned in a downtown skyscraper but rather in a hotel on the outskirts of Tokyo. The Matsudaira Hotel, or "Hoteru," as we learned to say to the taxi drivers, was situated a few miles west of the central Maranouchi section of Tokyo on the edge of a quiet, moderately high plateau, which because of its coolness in summer is especially desirable for a residential island. To reach it we took off from the Shinonomachi railway stop and trudged across the unpaved bus turn-around, which was either so deep in dust or so interlaced with broad puddles that we should have liked to take to *getas* like the swooping, laughing children who used the wide roadway as a playground. For a block this road passed low-built, unpainted shops retailing such things as prize peaches, unrecognizable vegetables, Western-style clothing, and the Japanese equivalent of snacks—a bit of rice rolled in dried seaweed to munch with green tea. Most of these shops were adjoined by a room or two where the shopkeeper's whole family lived, and from what one could observe from the outside, their crowded lives proceeded in a surprisingly neat and orderly fashion. This small beehive of shop-homes ended abruptly where we turned right down a narrow road flanked by high plaster-covered walls. Behind these were unseen gardens, and some of the residences were occupied by English or American government attachés evidenced only by nameplates at the gates. Just before the road plunged over the edge of the plateau, a gate wide enough for a single car stood open, and we entered the grounds of the hotel to which we had been assigned, formerly the residence of a Count Matsudaira.

The white gravel driveway stretched on between lawns on both sides that stayed surprisingly green in the summer heat. Through the tangled trees a small wooden tea-house bower could be seen and beyond it, simple wooden tables and chairs were set at discreet distances between tiny fruit trees. One could drive straight across the stone flagging at the entrance of the one-storey stucco building and stop under the main peak of the curving gray-tiled roof, but this was done only by the V.I.P.s occasionally in very bad weather. Since the hotel was a semi-Japanese, semi-Western establishment, there was always a nice array of linen slippers on the broad steps of the foyer for the Japanese businessmen who frequently dined there en masse, but we visiting American professors and wives clung to our shoes as a symbol of our accustomed lives, and never fell into changing to the much more comfortable slippers.

The area of the foyer was commanded by a tiny central desk, presided over usually by a rather cocky, bright chap, whom we came to call Jimbo, and a pretty, young Japanese woman—both looking and acting, as far as we could judge, like typical American teenagers. Only their occasional gestures of gentle ceremoniousness reminded us of their true nationality. They carried on the hotel business in a vague and agreeable way and were always happy to chat in simple English and to learn more whenever we Americans were waiting in the narrow sitting room with the enormous overstuffed, broken-down chairs sheathed coolly in white linen.

Our bedrooms were assigned in order of academic rank at various intervals along corridors that made a cross-hatching of the one-storey building. There were several spots en route to the rooms where one could look through sliding windows down into a rivulet with carefully spaced boulders molding its course among greenery and occasional flowers; and the mild tinkling always soothed our heat-torn spirits in passing. The bed-sitting rooms were quite pleasant with furniture of a kind that was simple, unobtrusive, and casually assembled with a background of delicate yet lively colors and a tasteful print or two to deck the walls. Morton had first been assigned to a room opposite the kitchen, but the shouting of the boyish cooks and their playing French jazz on a gramophone all night finally drove him to protest so that on Lucia's arrival we were reassigned to a suite which boasted a built-in window seat. This occupied a whole wall of the main bedroom, which was neatly papered in a linoleum-like pattern of grey, bluish-tan, and green set off by a ruby-colored rug and curtains. Behind the bedroom was a high pink-tiled bathroom which had a wide floor that dropped down at one side an inch or two to form a convenient foot-bath adjacent to the tub.

An entrance hall beside the bath and bedroom protected us a bit from the sudden entrances of the maids and the procession of maintenance men, who one day appeared unsolicited to "correct Morris." This mission completely mystified us until we saw that the men all wanted to examine the numerous small holes in the walls, and we inferred that Morris was a mouse who shared our suite, and he continued to do so for three weeks until one day he was trapped in our coat closet. When the capture was reported, we were dismayed by being told by half a dozen members of a posse of men and maids that they "did not like Morris" but could not bear to dispose of him, and then they all fled shrieking and giggling down the corridor. It was only when Morton became ferociously adamant over the house telephone that a cook's boy endowed with stolid courage came and at last relieved us of unwanted "Morris."

We gradually came to realize that the Matsudaira was managed by a distant absentee owner and that our comfort was almost entirely in the hands of Jimbo at the front desk, the cook boys, Freddie at the bar, six little maids in blue uniforms, and four little waitresses in uniforms of daffodil yellow. The maids were graced with pretty names such as Fuji-san and Osaku-san, and they were invariably gentle, sweetly-smiling, and as playful as bright-eyed kittens. When they glided about ministering to our needs, we were invariably enchanted; but we never knew whether they would turn up to make the beds at all or to take the breakfast orders. Nevertheless, whenever we returned to the hotel entrance after a long expedition into the hot city, several of them would be clustered at the window of their joint bedroom, looking out as from a theatrebox, and they would wave and exchange monosyllabic banter with all comers. The maids did not speak much English, but sometimes they would give us bits of information about themselves to the effect that they spent their days off either at some American movie or on visits to their parents in the country. But we felt a much stronger current of communication with them because of their smiles and evident discussion of us than we did with the two reticent older women who were empowered with quite unknown responsibilities. And we had to be content with silent observation of the wizened grandmother of old Japan who—wrapped like a cocoon in her sombre kimono—occupied herself incessantly either with flower-arranging at the long sink in the sunniest corridor or in presiding over the hotel treasures of handsome screens, lacquer table services, and vases that were brought out for business association dinners from the safety of the mausoleum-like treasure house which stood apart in the back court.

While we remained at the hotel for almost a month, our lines of communication with the hotel personnel remained generally pleasant and were punctured only once in a while by irritating episodes. Besides our difficulties in getting rid of "Morris," there was one other domestic disturbance that resulted from our lack of tolerance of noise during the hours between midnight and sunrise, hours when we craved unbroken quiet. A central bath within earshot of the inner bedrooms was set aside for the use of the male hotel employees from midnight on, and they congregated there for a free-for-all of wrestling, singing, and splashing which would have registered more decibels than a small boys' swimming pool in the United States. It took constant reminders to mute this institution at all—the men simply were unaware that noise interfered with anybody's sleep, which also explained the all-night jazz innocently issuing from the kitchen.

Perhaps these laxities partly explained why our hotel was not as well patronized as the location and prices should have warranted in summer. Besides, there was its distance from the center of Tokyo, which meant at least a half-hour's trip; but this course was easy enough to travel, and occupants of public conveyances were never openly hostile to foreigners, but either indifferent or engagingly curious or helpful, wanting to practise their English whenever the opportunity offered.

The long-term guests at the hotel besides our university group were a few American businessmen, an outspoken and elderly but vigorous Korean, who was hoping to revive a fishing trade with American concerns, and a few reticent Chinese, who were not negotiating anything with Westerners—as far as we could judge. The transients were a large but remarkably unobtrusive procession of American G.I.s and British servicemen, some with Japanese girls, some vainly looking for them, and some aimlessly waiting to be shipped home or back to Korea, where, of course, a war was going on.

In fact, our life at the Matsudaira Hotel was sharply divided between becoming acquainted with the simple pleasures of a small semi-Western Japanese hostelry and our growing awareness of the horrors of the Korean war. These horrors were recounted to us in the hotel bar where a group of G.I.s who were about to be demobilized had set up their headquarters.

One of these groups of G.I.s was an air force technical crew with whom we drank for several hours one evening and shared fitfully shifting reflections. These men in order of their appearance were: Mike, a used-car salesman from New England; Jim, the senior officer of the crew, also a New Englander; George, a heavy-set, good-natured farmer from Pennsylvania; and his laughing, dark-complexioned friend Al, who also hailed from a Pennsylvania farm. Their opening gambit of conversation dealt with tips on the purchase of used cars: "Have the oil changed before purchasing any make (except Plymouth, which defies this diagnostic test) and you can tell a lot about the health of the motor by whether the oil pressure is maintained or not." This was Mike's formula, and the other chaps hashed it over. Then they went on to dream about super-cars and spoke yearningly of the Tucker with its rubber dashboard and pop-out glass which was advertised briefly in the western states by models that carried a large sign-board reading: "You have just been passed by a Tucker at 115 mph cruising speed." "Life would be just about complete if you owned a Tucker," young Al stated categorically, and everyone agreed except a nameless boy whose face was as unmoving as a block of wood and who never spoke throughout the evening. Mike gave the subject the *coup de grace* by adding bitterly that the Tucker manufacturers were squeezed out by the big companies, "who will dribble out its features one by one."

After a pause the conversation turned to Korea. Most of the men proposed quietly in one way or another that the U.N. pull out of Korea because, as one of them put it: "All the troops on both sides were engaged in turning nothing into nothing, and losing men doing it." The senior officer announced without enthusiasm and as though by rote that the Korean action was a conflict to defend a principle and to prevent the Commies from making a move somewhere else. In response to this, the others nodded, but they evidently felt in their every fiber that this view was very dim, distant, and abstract (and each said so privately afterwards). They shifted their attention uncomfortably and talked instead of the cruelty of the Koreans on both sides: how thefts from military establishments were punished by shooting, hanging, or tossing the culprit tightly bound into any river handy. By contrast the U.N. contingents punished thefts by having the offender stand holding a heavy stone over his head for several hours. Torture—yes, the officer Jim admitted, but it discouraged the crime, and the person could be set free quickly to recover.

Only a little about the fighting was allowed to intrude in words when a neat, sunny-natured boy, who was surely the pride of his family back in Arkansas, entered the bar and the conversation abruptly and with innocent candor. He had recently been caught one evening in an air raid at the front, and all his outfit could do in the absence of anti-aircraft artillery was to drink plenty of whiskey and hope not to be hit while they watched the show. But one of his buddies, a young boy new to combat, went to bed by himself and was stiff in the morning—dead from fright. The air force men slouched silently in their chairs for a few seconds, and then, to bridge the abyss of tragedy quickly, they returned to musings about the pleasures of driving any old kind of car, spending money, and just being with the folks at home. Farmer George sociably passed around a photograph of his wife, a sweet spindly young blonde behind harlequin glasses, and two eager-looking boys who appeared to be gazing into the future with friendly shyness. The conversation naturally turned to marriage, and Al blustered that he for one would avoid it as long as possible "so as not to have to be made over." The older farmer, detouring around this remark, counselled with simple finality: "All each person has to do in a marriage to make it work is to give a lot *all* the time."

On another evening a new group of G.I.s collected in the bar with us, and this time the Korean business agent, Mr. Kim, joined us for drinks and the opportunity to assuage his boredom with talk of his family and also to enlarge on reminiscences of his activities before leaving Korea. He was very lonely for his Korean wife, whom he had settled a few months earlier in San Francisco. He described her as a strict, old-fashioned kind of woman, who had shaped his children's characters well. His eldest son was studying law at a San Francisco college. There were several other children between him and a ten-year-old son, the apple of his father's eye, who had recently written him requesting permission to shine shoes at a neighbor's store. He had written: "Do not misunderstand me, father, for you have given us plenty of food, shelter, and clothing, but I just want to see how it feels to have money of my own." The father, though evidently proud of his children and their enterprise in a new country, was proudest and happiest because of their friendship and popularity with American children of different races. We were to understand that they had made many friends now with all kinds of children—all—white, black, and other orientals.

Mr. Kim gave us an eager recitation of his activities as adviser to the U.N. forces on transport problems. He was especially pleased with his contribution in assisting the army during Communist-led strikes. He reported that the Communists often did stunts to arouse the strikers, such as stealing bodies from the dissecting laboratories of hospitals which they dressed up in students' clothing and paraded on poles through the streets, announcing that they had been victims of U.N. brutality. He said that he had been an eyewitness in a communications strike when the police, charging up a staircase with tommy guns, were met by the embattled Communists head on. Just before the capture of the Communists, their leader threw his hands up in surrender. The struggle subsided for one long moment, and then with a sudden flash several of his comrades swung their axes high and sliced their leader in two. In another moment they themselves had surrendered sullenly. From this ghastly incident Mr. Kim concluded, "You never can tell what a Communist will do next."

On another occasion Mr. Kim went on to say that he himself was detailed by the U.N. command to break a railroad strike that was preventing military supplies from reaching the troops. His immediate superiors, American officers, had wished to send in South Korean police reinforced by American troops, but Mr. Kim had successfully argued that such a move would be very poor propaganda for the United States. He pointed out that this was one of many cases of the army's insistence on speed in putting down disorder and their neglecting opportunities for building up public understanding. He also observed that the United States personnel were able to reason very well when they had the facts, but that they too often assumed that they had the facts when they did not. "They tried to solve algebraic equations with too many unknowns," as Kim put it tersely.

In another burst of detail, Mr. Kim told how on a third occasion the South Koreans decided to help themselves to apparently abandoned military supplies. They wanted desperately to use anything they could convert into food and were painfully disappointed when they tried out nice clean-looking petroleum for salad oil. During another crisis, when not less than seven hundred barrels of petroleum had been spirited away by the Koreans, Mr. Kim persuaded the military that he should be allowed to try the discussion method before punitive action was taken. He went into the rice paddies himself and up and down the river sides with two G.I. escorts, who always insisted considerately that he be protected by walking between them. After a long search, the village headman was tracked down, and Kim, dispensing with his escort, talked all night with this chief, telling him that it was wicked for his people to risk their lives for a yard of cloth or a pitcher of oil, that the Koreans were not liberating themselves, and that the U.N. would do everything it possibly could to meet the needs of the wretched people. The village headman agreed to take these suggestions under advisement; this he did for three long days while the military grew more and more restless, but in the end supplies were returned in great quantities. Mr. Kim was earnestly apologetic for his people and explained that they were becoming more and more demoralized and cruel because of their experiences as a subject people. Earlier in their history, he pointed out, they were not at all distinguished for their cruelty, but now the atmosphere of war had transformed their characters and distilled in the people from the poisons of prolonged fear and rage—terrible *bitterness*. Suddenly Mr. Kim looked around at us with enigmatic intensity and asked whether we had seen the great Buddha at Kamakura. "No? Well, it is just like life—empty."

As the conversation ebbed away, we drifted out of the bar, walked in the dark garden, and then sat down on the two long sofas flanking the driveway entrance. Here Jimbo and a few of the house girls—as on previous nights—joined us to ask questions about English and resumed our drill on the pronunciation of the most necessary Japanese phrases. They were patient and good-natured teachers; each stumbling over a phrase provoked a silvery shower of laughter. "Ō-hayo go-za-i-ma-su," the accent must be shifted gently to "o-hayō" to say "good morning." And so on until we had run through the informal lesson and everyone triumphantly tossed "goodnight" back and forth: "o-yasumi-nasai," "o-yasumi-nasai." But when we had returned to our bedrooms, it was not often that sleep came quickly as the sound of laughter, jazz, and splashing baths kept our ears tingling long after we had retired. Finally another sound punctured the silky moisture of the summer air, the staccato tapping of the fire-watchers, who signalled with their wooden sticks in order to remind all householders to put out their fires. This conventional, steady, rhythmic sequence finally came to mean, like a cricket's chirping, an end of wakefulness and release into sleep for some of us.

THREE

The Japanese Philosophers in 1952

When Morton first entered the somewhat dingy classroom of Tokyo University where his seminar was to meet, he was utterly surprised to see all of the members of the group rise at a signal from a man whom we would call the monitor, bowing their heads as they rose. Taken by surprise, Morton automatically bowed in response, but since this was one of the earliest days of his stay in Tokyo, his bow was awkward and stiff. Besides, he did not like the idea of having his students rise whenever he entered the room, nor did he like the idea of having to respond with a bow. Consequently, he announced to the seminar at the next meeting that he would prefer them not to engage in this ritual during later meetings of the class. With this request the monitor and the students found it hard to comply, and so it took several meetings for them to rid themselves of their habit. Understandably, they felt uneasy about being asked to give up their traditional ways, and at times Morton wondered whether he was wrong in asking them to do so. Finally, the standing and bowing did disappear, and as time went on the seminar began to feel more like one in the United States—at least in some of its external features. In one respect, however, it did not resemble some of its American counterparts. The students did not read their own papers to the group as they might at Harvard. Instead, Morton—or White-san as he came to be known early in our stay—gave a prepared lecture to which the students were invited to respond by asking questions or making comments. This was not easy for them. For one thing, some of them were not very good at speaking English; for another, they were understandably diffident about speaking on a subject in which they were not highly trained. The whole idea of exchanging views with a professor seemed to go against the grain of the authoritarian educational tradition in which they had been raised; and since most of them had served in the Japanese armed forces, their habit of deferring to a person in authority had been very much reinforced.

Academically speaking, the group was quite heterogeneous. The list of attendants shows that the class consisted of university graduate students, assistants, instructors, assistant professors, and one full professor. They came from very different institutions of learning as the following list will indicate: Aichi Teachers College, Chiba University, Chuo University, Kagoshima University, Kanazawa University, Kyoto University, Niigata University, Osaka Municipal University, Tohoku University, Tokyo University, Tokyo University of Science, Tokyo Teachers College, Yamaguchi University, and Yodogawa High School in Osaka. Their interests also varied widely. Their general fields were listed as philosophy, education, and psychology, but, more specifically, they were interested in Dewey's theory of education, esthetics, philosophy of natural science, philosophy of mathematics, logic, semantics, Kant's philosophy, logical positivism, and Peirce's philosophy. Historians of American philosophy will observe that many of the students were concerned with topics that were of interest to American professionals in the fifties. At that moment young Japanese philosophers were trying to learn what many young American philosophers were trying to learn. The Japanese were trying to break out of the confines into which they had been forced by their elders, who tended to focus on German philosophy from Kant to Husserl. For the Japanese philosophers in Morton's class the most exciting ideas were associated with pragmatism, logical positivism, and analytic philosophy.

We had our first opportunity to have more personal contact with members of the seminar at a tea that was given about a week after class had begun. We had been invited for tea at 1:30. Morton's assistant, Mr. Ohmori, met us at the office of the Department of American Studies at Tokyo University and promptly conducted us to a reception room which contained a huge square table surrounded by two dozen high-backed ministerial chairs. The room was in bare Western style, finished in dark wood. The students sitting on three sides of the table were as varied in physiognomy as one would see anywhere—enormous individuality of facial structure and quite varied expressions. Some had short heads that were somewhat flat across; some had long, heavy black hair and broad brows; some had long, bald dome-shaped heads; some had their hair shaven down to almost nothing. They had bright expressions or dull or listless expressions and seemed quite ready to show approval, disapproval, or unconcern. These were not the poker faces that we are told about in some descriptions of the Japanese people. One American woman psychologist had announced to us categorically before our departure that the Japanese who spoke English never gave you the feeling that they were communicating with you. This was not our impression. Perhaps these students were very much the exception or perhaps we were deceived, but we did not think so.

The student in charge of the tea party, Mr. Kuwaki, led us to the head of the table so that he, Mr. Ohmori, and the two of us sat facing the rest of the students. Mr. Kuwaki rose and greeted us in rapid but somewhat broken English. He then suggested that as we drank our tea (which turned out to be coffee) and ate our cake and ice cream, we should go down the table and let each person tell something of himself. He began the proceedings with a long and somewhat disconnected account of his travel in Europe. He had gone there before the war, living mainly in Germany, where he had studied the ideas of Husserl. When the war came, he did not wish to return to Japan, and he delayed being called back by getting himself assigned to government work abroad. He travelled in Germany and Central Europe and finally went to Helsinki, returning to Japan only at the end of the war to renew his study of philosophy.

Another student, a tall man, with a long, narrow ascetic face and surprisingly round and bright shining eyes, told in rather meager English that he had only recently but very passionately become interested in philosophy after teaching some other subject. He explained that he was married and said that his only trouble was that his wife was not interested in philosophy. He had read in one of Morton's books that Lucia was a help in the preparation of it, and he thought this was such a happy arrangement. He wondered how this had happened.

When Lucia was given a cue by the interpreter to speak a few words, she explained that she was perhaps rather like the student's wife and had not been immediately interested in philosophy. She felt it to be over her head and, besides, was quite busy with children and housekeeping. Lucia explained further that she had only recently been reading in philosophy, especially about the analytic movement, which her husband had lectured on at Harvard during the past year. She went on to say that she believed that the Japanese showed that they were greatly interested and particularly gifted in learning and that as a people they could help tremendously in discovering the connections between science and life for which people all over the world were searching.

After Lucia spoke, several students responded to Kuwaki-san's request by explaining where they came from in Japan and telling us many other things about themselves. The only woman in the class, a round-faced, sweet-looking but plain person with tousled dark hair, said she came from a city noted for plain women and that she was studying social science and the elements of developmental psychology, which was then being started in Japan. Miss Sawa Murakami was about five feet tall, but rather plumper and more round-eyed than most Japanese. Her expression was downcast and somewhat phlegmatic. She said that her name means "swamp," and that for some reason her father had left off the usual suffix "ko" for a feminine name. She described herself as a schizophrenic and felt that all Japanese women were tyrannized by their men. She longed for the happy day when men would change their behavior, but she thought that there had been only

a slight change since the war. She believed that most Japanese women en-
vied American women because the latter were powerful managers of their
homes. The rest of her remarks were quite scattered. They had to do with
her profession and interests. Though a student of philosophy, she taught
educational psychology at Sendai University and belonged to a faculty of
one hundred, of whom only five were women. Four of those taught domestic science and gymnastics. The university had two thousand students and
prepared teachers for elementary and high school teaching.

The next person to speak at the tea was a young and vigorous fellow
whose steady magnetic smile alternated with infectious and boisterous
laughter. He told how he had spent the whole of the war in the navy working to develop the technique of training men to be human torpedos. He had
worked along the China coast and around the South Sea islands. He stirred
up a surprising groundswell of merriment in his fellow students with his
talk—merriment the sources of which were hard to understand. He gave the
impression of a boy explaining cowboy exploits with sheer delight in the
adventures and the noise and the violent, deadly activity.

A man who had been slumped in his chair looking utterly weary, and
sodden, and even dissipated suddenly rose. His expression was transformed
into an appealing and intensely serious one as he began talking. He
explained that he was very eager to learn philosophy but that he was
struggling to do so under some difficulty. His place of residence was
Hiroshima. His wife had to continue living there because of her work. He
lived in Tokyo most of the time during the summer of 1952 but managed to
return home once a month. He had been a teacher of mathematics for many
years and planned to return to his regular post in the fall.

After two or three other men had announced their names and the mean-
ings of them, another young man with peculiarly pointed features, broad
forehead, and oriental coloring presented himself to the class. He appeared
to be more southern European, perhaps Portuguese, than Japanese. His
English was fluent, and he turned out to be a university professor of chemistry. His smile was captivating as he told of the impression made on him by
an American professor of physiology who had come to Japan recently, had
visited the most primitive communities of Japan, and had concluded that the
only happy Japanese lived in those communities. This American professor
had also voiced a point of view that was similar to that of Gandhi, urging his
Japanese friends to rid themselves of all Western influences. The chemistry
professor then announced that he was puzzled about this problem, and he
wished to ask us Americans what we thought would make the Japanese
people happy.

Morton addressed himself to this last speaker and to the class on this
question, realizing that it was not ironic but genuine and deadly serious. He
said first that he could not give a formula in reply, and he urged the students

to beware of pat answers to the question whether they took the form of political, nationalistic, or religious slogans. He asked them to understand that simple as the question might seem, the answer to it would have to be discovered by long and painstaking work in many areas of study from which people were willing to bring answers that could be tested by experience.

After leaving this meeting with his more mature students, Morton went to another room in the university where he was to give a lecture to undergraduates. Each American professor had been asked not only to conduct a seminar for advanced students of philosophy but also to give a set of ten lectures to undergraduates from all over Japan who were participating in something that was called "The Integrated Studies Group." These undergraduates were all concentrating in American studies. Like their elders in the seminar, they were not expected to know English well enough to understand the lectures without the aid of an interpreter, a man who worked in the seminar as well as in the undergraduate classes. Unfortunately, he was not a philosopher but a trained theologian who was a follower of Reinhold Niebuhr. For this reason, he knew very little about the ideas presented in either the seminar or the class for undergraduates, and he was not sympathetic with what little about them he might have understood. Occasionally his interpretation would be corrected in the seminar by Ohmori-san, who, however, was always careful to make his corrections in the most polite and tentative way so that the interpreter's face could be saved. However, Ohmori did not attend the undergraduate lectures, which were a less advanced version of those presented in the seminar, and *there* the interpreter went unchecked. Fortunately, his freedom led to less misunderstanding of the lectures than might be expected because it turned out that the undergraduates were better at English than the advanced students were. Most of the latter, being older, had served in the armed forces where they had spoken no English, whereas the undergraduates, most of whom had been too young to serve, were able to pick up a good deal of English while speaking with members of the American occupation.

In fact, there was reason to believe that most of the undergraduates really did not need an interpreter. Nevertheless, since he had been hired to do a job, he could not be told to go away. So he droned on and on, translating sentence by sentence, even though at one point it became perfectly evident that such labor was not necessary. Morton told a joke and the class immediately responded, as he hoped it would, with much laughter. Probably it was his old standby—the one about the Japanese who, when told that Morton was not Professor Whitehead, said "Oh! I see. Professor White without the head." However, the poor interpreter remained oblivious to the fact that the joke had been understood by virtually the whole class, and therefore he dutifully translated it into Japanese. But once he translated it, there was dead silence in the room. Either the joke was not a joke in Japanese, or the class had felt, with reason, that they had had enough of it. The interpreter was not fazed by this demonstration that he was not needed. He remained until the bitter end, forcing Morton to wait patiently as each one of his sentences was put into Japanese. The interpreter also went on making mistakes, but an interesting device grew up to undo the damage caused by his mistakes. After the class Ohmori would conduct a secret meeting of the seminar students at which he would correct the official interpreter's mistakes without causing "loss of face."

So far we have said almost nothing about the more intellectual aspect of Morton's relations with Japanese philosophers, and it would be well to do so now, first by saying something about the subject of his seminar and then something about a couple of lectures given by him to more professional groups.

Although Morton had planned to teach the substance of his Harvard course in American philosophy, which began with the American reaction to Herbert Spencer and leapt through the philosophies of James, Royce, Santayana, Peirce, Dewey, and other American greats, he saw at once that John Goheen was right to encourage him to say something about analytic philosophy. The typical student in his seminar was mainly interested in what was going on in American philosophy in 1952. And so he began with a brief survey of the chief ideas then agitating American philosophers, as well as some indication of what he thought was true and what he thought was controversial in those ideas.

Mindful of his obligation to deal with the history of earlier American philosophy, he turned to the views of Royce, James, Santayana, Dewey, and Peirce. This, so far as he could see, was not insufficiently historical for his students; if anything, some of them felt that it was *too* historical. This heartened him greatly in spite of his interest in the history of American philosophy, for it showed that there was at least *some* tendency of younger Japanese philosophers to rebel against the traditional habit of attaching oneself to some Western national philosophy on which one would then become a specialist for the rest of one's life. The great bane of Japanese philosophy since the beginning of the Meiji era, according to many of the Japanese themselves, was the absence of any attempt at a direct, serious confrontation of the problems of systematic philosophy. The prevalent attitude was well illustrated by the fact that a philosophy student once introduced himself as a "student in the department of *Western* philosophy" at Tokyo University. He was not a student of philosophy; he was a student of Western philosophy. In the same way, his teacher would not count himself a teacher of systematic philosophy but a Kant-specialist, a Hegel-specialist, or a Husserl-specialist. The Japanese philosopher of 1952 viewed the philosophical world as a large map on which he had placed himself early in life. When he put himself in Kantian territory, that fixed him for life; from then on he had the responsibility not only of lecturing on Kant but of seeing life through Kantian spectacles and of presenting the Kantian position on any given topic. Occasionally, as in the case of the famous Dr. Nishida, there was an attempt to fuse Hegelianism with Buddhism, but usually slavish attachment to the great Western philosophers, preferably German philosophers, was *the* method of doing philosophy in Japan. Against this there had been two questionable reactions that Morton tried to combat. One was to attach oneself to an American philosopher, to James, or Dewey, or Peirce, just as one's father, so to speak, had attached himself to a German philosopher. The other was to treat American philosophy merely as an index of the American economy or the American character, rather than as a group of ideas to be studied critically. The first way illustrated the familiar Japanese tendency to imitate America; the second was linked with the tendency of Japanese Marxists to see Western philosophy as a form of ideology representing the interests of a social class.

In spite of being influenced by these questionable kinds of reaction to what their teachers had done, the students in the seminar were, on the whole, seriously interested in learning something about systematic philosophy. However, even when they were interested in more technical questions of epistemology, ethics, or metaphysics, they were somewhat suspicious of pure logical analysis. They seemed to feel a need to link philosophy with their daily lives, and this helped make Marxism attractive to many young Japanese philosophers. They thought that it would provide them with a total view of man and the universe and therefore with a platform from which to examine problems in different fields of intellectual endeavor.

A group which called itself "The Institute for the Science of Thought" was heavily influenced by the desire to make philosophy less remote and less abstract. It therefore encouraged the study of pragmatism, mainly under the influence of Shunsuke Tsurumi and his sister Kazukuo, whom we shall presently meet again. They were children of a Japanese politician, and both of them had been educated in the States—the brother at Harvard, the sister at Columbia. Their institute dealt with many different problems and announced itself in a fervid way as an opponent of traditional Japanese philosophy. For example, it studied what it called "Common Man's Philosophy," under which title it conducted investigations like "The Philosophy of Policemen" and "The Philosophy of Geisha Girls." Some of its members were actively interested in symbolic logic; others in the study of Peirce. And just before we arrived in Japan, they had published a collective volume on the philosophy of John Dewey. Morton addressed this group one day and participated in a day-long discussion of the topic "Some Controversial Points in American Philosophy." His talk, which dealt with technical questions in the theory of language, epistemology, and ethics, was discussed by a number of the scholars present.

One of the scholars, Professor Kuno, a self-styled pragmatist and translator of John Dewey, presented an extremely interesting picture of his own intellectual history. He began his career with great admiration for American philosophy, particularly for the philosophy of Dewey after the First World War. When in 1919 Dewey delivered his Tokyo lectures entitled *Reconstruction in Philosophy,* Kuno said, Dewey's influence was almost nil. Japanese philosophy was exclusively under the influence of German thought. Morton understood from the translation of Kuno's remarks that Dewey's influence grew considerably and that many Japanese philosophers regarded it, along with the New Deal, as an example of the liberal American spirit. Kuno said he had turned to pragmatism and liberalism because he was anti-fascist. He thought academic philosophy served neither science nor the common man. The mass arrests of 1938–39 and those of 1943–44, he said, marked a period during which he and his friends suffered for their liberal views. In his final remarks he spoke of what he had once admired in American philosophy. One object of his admiration was the Deweyan tendency to find continuity in things that seem discontinuous, the tendency to link philosophy with life and social issues. But, he complained, recent American philosophy had not been following this line of thought. He then made another observation which reflected a rather widespread attitude in Japan in 1952. He said that the Japanese were caught in the middle of a clash between ideologies and that if a war were to come, they would be the first victims of Russia. *Therefore,* he went on, they had a practical need to find continuity between seemingly discontinuous things, the implication being that the Japanese would have to adopt some sort of philosophical neutralism, some middle course between American and Russian thought.

It was difficult to know how prevalent this sort of attitude was in 1952, but it did not appear to dominate the thinking of a group of establishment philosophers whom Morton addressed on the first of July at the very beginning of our 1952 visit and therefore before he had any notion of the philosophical climate in Tokyo.

The real climate, however, was unmistakable. It was dreadfully hot and humid even in the early morning of that day. Morton entered the university car with closed eyes at something like eight in the morning and was driven to the Gakushi Kaikan, a handsome alumni club on the campus of Tokyo University, where he was to address a group of professional Japanese philosophers on the Jamesian subject, "The Right To Believe."

When Morton entered the lecture hall, he was greeted by someone who later became a very dear friend, Hideo Kishimoto, professor of the science of religion at the University of Tokyo. He had been a student of the late Professor James Haughton Woods of Harvard and was as charming a man as we had met in all of Japan. Kishimoto-san was short and round and almost always smiling and genial, looking amazingly like the great Buddha at Kamakura, which he always described to us as "the handsome one." But on this morning Kishimoto-san was not as gay as usual. He greeted Morton cordially but nervously and introduced him to a Professor Ikegami, professor of logic at Tokyo and, as Morton learned later, the Japanese translator of Husserl's *Ideen*. Professor Ikegami was an impassive, heavy-lidded man who reminded us of the main character in a Russian movie we had seen many years ago, a movie having to do with China. Professor Ikegami bowed formally, but he did not smile. He shook hands in the most diplomatic of ways. Morton felt something was wrong. At this point he hardly received great encouragement, for Kishimoto-san called him aside to say: "Of all the American professors *you* will have the most difficult task. Japanese philosophers of the older generation have great contempt for American philosophy. In fact they think you Americans have no philosophy at all." In response Morton gulped and gripped his manuscript. But he was soon to have another bit of less than helpful news. The interpreter came up to him after having studied his English manuscript for a few days and said in a very mournful tone: "It is very difficult, but we will try our best."

This served, if anything, to wake Morton up, and instead of feeling the drowsiness of a tropical morning after a hot night, he felt the cool damp of nervousness as he faced his friends in the audience. There were forty in all, and they were all seated when he entered. At once they arose and bowed when he came in, and he bowed self-consciously in return. He was introduced in Japanese, and as he listened, all sorts of things passed through his mind. But suddenly he saw a smiling face in the audience, the face of the only female professional philosopher in Japan, so far as he knew, and the only woman in the audience—Miss Tsurumi of the Institute for the Science of Thought. Morton had known Miss Tsurumi in 1941 when they were both graduate students at Columbia. She was then a rather lovely looking girl, but now she was a very handsome tired-looking woman, smiling warmly and helpfully in a way that he would never forget. He did not recognize her at once, for in between the shadow of the last eleven years had fallen, years which were awful enough for any Japanese, but particularly so for a female philosopher suspected of liberal and American sympathies.

During this lecture there were moments when the interpreter was completely baffled by what the speaker was saying, moments when the Japanese fell to arguing among themselves as to what Morton meant, moments when his prize jokes brought blank stares and his most serious contributions to philosophy brought incomprehensible smiles. At last it was over, and he sat down. But that was not all. The Japanese have a very different conception from the American idea of the desirable length of academic gatherings. Lectures of two hours are very common, and conferences of five hours are thought to be the obvious responsibility of any serious group, so Morton was now exposed to extended pawing by the lions. The first questioner was

Professor Ikegami, whose privilege it was to examine the witness first, being the chief philosopher of Tokyo present. Morton felt a bit as though he was taking part in a scene from *The Mikado,* with Professor Ikegami as the Lord High Executioner. The question would be put to the interpreter in Japanese and then translated for Morton. He answered it in English, and then it was translated back to Ikegami. This went on for a half-hour. The substance of the debate was exceedingly interesting, and Ikegami conducted himself like a gifted disciple of a philosophy Morton deplored. Complete understanding was never achieved, and there was very little philosophical agreement. Nevertheless, Ikegami's hostility seemed to diminish, and Morton imagined that the U.N.-like quality of the exchange was decreasing. Morton was angered somewhat by the fact that Ikegami asked for translation of Morton's words even though Ikegami knew English quite well — behaving as Clemenceau is said to have behaved at Versailles — but Morton's anger disappeared when it became apparent to him that Ikegami was sneering less than he had been at the beginning of the exchange.

The bout with Ikegami was followed by a few minor skirmishes with philosophers of lower rank and by some helpful exchanges. Then Morton was asked — after he had advanced an elaborate thesis on a specific problem of philosophy and after he had tried to defend it in detail — to give a survey of tendencies in American philosophy. At this point, with no little irony, Morton apologized for having delivered the wrong kind of paper, much as one might apologize for coming to a party with the wrong kind of clothes, but he was assured that this was just the kind of paper the Japanese philosophers wanted, only they wanted a little more. Their point might have been better expressed if they had said that Morton's paper was just the kind they had wanted, only they were now waiting for his second paper!

Adopting an ambassadorial attitude, he controlled himself and started to give an account of American philosophers in the manner of Jane's Fighting Ships while discreetly avoiding any discussion of the weights of dreadnoughts. This concluded, several Japanese philosophers proceeded to ask about which "Ism" White-san espoused. Since Morton had been making an effort in his paper to avoid this sort of ticketing of philosophers, he tried to communicate his attitude toward it through his interpreter. In spite of his efforts, however, he had to spend the rest of the time avoiding being identified with "Isms" of different kinds. At last he was allowed to escape amid much bowing and handshaking. A few perfunctory remarks followed the shuffling as everyone left the lecture-room. Outside, a striking looking gentleman came up to Morton and, speaking with a strong Oxford accent, asked "When are you going to let John Fairbank visit us?", referring to the difficulty John was having in visiting Japan that year. And, on the next day, Morton heard reports of his talk from some of the Japanese connected with the American Studies Seminar. One of them told him that the talk was a success, meaning that the Japanese philosophers had concluded that he *had* a point of view, much as they disapproved of it! Another told him that because of his success in presenting a philosophical point of view, they thought he must be a European!

Lest the impression be given that Morton never got further than this in his relationships with professional Japanese philosophers, something should be added about Ohmori-san, Morton's assistant. Ohmori-san was then a man of about twenty-nine or thirty who looked younger than that. He was extremely generous to us and one of the most interesting persons we have ever met in Japan, and he is now a dear friend. He spent one year in the States while studying at Oberlin College, where he was taught by a student of Carnap. During that year Ohmori learned a great deal about modern logic and epistemology. And in the seminar he was indispensable to Morton. Ohmori-san was (and is) more than an excellent philosopher; he is an extremely well-read and cultivated man. He began as a student of physics, after which he resolved to give up mathematical calculation—as he put it—for a life searching for the metaphysical principle of the universe. He reported that he quickly became aware that this was a highly dubious undertaking and fell into a tough, analytic way of doing philosophy, convinced that metaphysics was not going to provide the salvation of mankind and the solution of all his personal problems.

Many of the Japanese professors on the committee for American studies spoke very highly of him, and some of them correctly predicted a bright future for him. He himself was then very pessimistic about his future, chiefly because of the great philosophical gulf between him and Morton's powerful "friend" Ikegami. Professor Ikegami was not happy about Ohmori's Americanization, and it seemed in 1952 that the German philosophical atmosphere was not one in which Ohmori would be able to flourish. He felt this very strongly and often expressed regret about his decision to leave physics. Once again Morton could see the depressing effect of the lack of agreement and consensus in philosophy. In the America of 1952 a man with Ohmori's talent would certainly have landed a decent post in philosophy. Ohmori was justifiably bitter about the treatment he was receiving because of his views, disappointed with stupid professors who were unable to distinguish philosophical merit in the fog created by their own philosophical prejudices.

Ohmori-san reminded us a great deal of young American intellectuals in the thirties. Like many Japanese intellectuals in 1952, he was involved in the ferment of Westernization and was interested in socialist politics, read French novels, thought about existentialism, and was filled with despair. He was a scientifically oriented philosopher who read novels and poetry. He once thought of being a critic or a playwright, and he knew a great deal about modern French painting. He was a sophisticated man who was acute enough to see through some of the sillier American professors, and he was extremely sensitive to subtle things that escaped the notice of other Japanese connected with the seminars.

The constrasts within Ohmori's spiritual life and his professional problems in 1952 reflected certain tensions within Japanese philosophy as a whole, and those tensions were in turn affected by larger forces in the world. Almost since the beginning of the Meiji era, Japanese philosophy had been dominated by German philosophy, except for a brief flirtation with British thought, and this domination continued until the defeat of the Japanese and their German allies in the Second World War. That defeat had its effect on thinkers of Ikegami's generation, the generation which had sat at the feet of the Germans. Though the Germanophiles continued to lecture and write about Kant and Hegel, they were being subjected to intellectual pressure. On the one hand, pro-Russians were urging them in Marxist language to stand Hegel on his feet; on the other, American philosophers were urging them to discard Hegel altogether in favor of pragmatism, logical positivism, or linguistic philosophy. However, thinkers of Ikegami's generation were too old to exchange their German ideas for these newer ones. So they tried their hardest to stem the tide represented by the younger generation. But even the younger generation found it difficult to shift its philosophical allegiances dramatically. Members of it continued to read and to lecture on classical German philosophy while they tried to learn something about Marxist materialism and mathematical logic. They were in a somewhat confused state, pulled by opposing forces in different philosophical directions. Looking back at thirty years of contact with Japanese philosophers, one cannot avoid concluding that they have never resolved certain profound conflicts: first of all, the conflict between their Oriental inheritance and all Western thought and then, on top of that, the conflict over *which* tendencies within Western thought to follow.

FOUR

A Land of "Contradictions"

Although we were prepared on our visit in 1952 to discover that Japan was a country of "contradictions," to use a familiar cliché of those who deliver travelogues, it did not take us long to find out that the cliché was true. In 1952 any Westerner would discover this when he came to that intersection in downtown Tokyo where upon turning left he would see the then modern Nikkatsu Hotel with its bars, drugstores, doormen, flower shops, and liquor stores; and upon turning right he would see the Emperor's Palace, complete with moats and drawbridges. But even beyond possessing these features of the cityscape of central Tokyo, Japan was composed of at least two cultures living side by side. In seventy-five years she had tried to move from a feudal economy and society to a nation employing some of the most high-powered tools of modern industrialism. In 1952 Japan was still culturally divided—as well as a country with ancient buildings next to modern skyscrapers—and the division was illustrated by certain paradoxes in Japanese society. This cultural division was made remarkably plain when a businessman left his modern office in Tokyo and then, after removing his suit, put on his kimono after a ride on a packed train like the old Third Avenue L in New York. In the summer heat the same businessman could be seen removing his trousers and placing them on the baggage-holder of a long-distance railroad train so that he could sit comfortably in his underwear rather than in the Western clothing to which he was not fully accustomed.

The rapid industrialization of Japan's feudal society not only helped explain the paradoxes of personal dress and architecture; it also helped to explain certain economic problems faced by Japan during the aftermath of the Second World War. These problems were sketched by Professor Ohara, a Japanese economist who spoke at a conference we attended in 1952. Since industry was such a great factor in Japanese life, Professor Ohara strongly emphasized Japan's need to export its manufactured products. It had to export, he said, in order to live; therefore, in 1952 Japan was in a great crisis because of the decline in its exports. In that year, Ohara said, exports were half of what they had been before the war. The Japanese had lost their foreign markets, most notably their market in China; they exported almost nothing to the United States in whose political orbit they were; England was jealously guarding its markets in southeast Asia; and the Germans were underselling the Japanese throughout Asia. How, then, Ohara asked, was Japan to improve its foreign trade? It might try to keep its wages low, but he thought that was impossible as well as undesirable. It might try to rationalize its methods of production, but that would be difficult because it lacked capital. Furthermore, the war had destroyed much of its plant, and Americans were hesitant about investing in Japan. Under the circumstances, he saw nationalization of industry as desirable from an economic point of view, but he thought it was a political impossibility because of the attitudes of the American Occupation. All of this explained Japan's great desire to trade with China and why Marxism was so popular among Japanese intellectuals.

Economic and political conflicts were not the only effects of the rapid industrialization which had helped propel Japan into war with America and ultimately into defeat. The American victory created another sharp division in Japanese society by forcing its proud warriors to foreswear the use of arms. Japan's military tradition was still alive in 1947 when the American occupation forced it to adopt a constitution in which it renounced war. The first paragraph of the preamble of that document began with the following words: "We, the Japanese people, acting through our duly elected representatives in the National Diet, determined that we shall secure for ourselves and our posterity the fruits of peaceful cooperation with all nations and the blessings of liberty throughout this land, and resolved that never again shall we be visited with the horrors of war through the actions of government." The second paragraph began: "Desiring peace for all time and fully conscious of the high ideals controlling human relationships now stirring mankind, we have determined to rely for our security and survival upon the justice and good faith of the peace-loving peoples of the world." And the famous Article 9 of the Constitution read:

> Aspiring sincerely to an international peace based on justice and order, the Japanese people, forever, renounce war as a sovereign right of the nation, or the threat or use of force, as a means of settling disputes with other nations.
> For the above purpose, land, sea, and air forces, as well as other war potential, will never be maintained. The right of belligerency of the state will not be recognized.

We did not doubt that some Japanese were unhappy about this abject renunciation of war even though others *were* happy about it. To the latter it meant that Japan would not have to drain itself economically by supporting an army and navy; it meant that reactionary Japanese militarists would lose much of their power; it meant that Japanese women, who were strongly pacifistic, could rest more easily; and it meant that neutralist intellectuals could also rest more easily. Still, there was considerable Japanese resentment about being forced to renounce land, sea, and air forces—resentment which produced yet another conflict that could be traced, however indirectly, to Japan's industrialization and its consequent emergence as a world power. Article 9 turned it into a world power which could not defend itself—a paradox that did not sit well with many, even with some who knew the horror that war had visited on Hiroshima.

We reflected somberly on the paradoxes of Japan's attitudes toward war when we heard a Japanese philosopher lecture in Hiroshima on the Buddhistic way of life. As he quoted from the writings of Prince Shotoku, the pacifist-founder of Japanese Buddhism, we could not help asking ourselves: "How could Japanese militarism flourish in an atmosphere dominated by the values of Prince Shotoku?" But as soon as we asked ourselves *that* question, we asked another: "How could Western militarism flourish in an atmosphere dominated by *some* of the values of the Prince of Peace?"

Thinking about the various contradictions within Japanese society we could better understand the desire of Professor Kuno—the speaker who addressed the Institute for the Science of Thought—to use Dewey's philosophy as a tool for resolving some of the dualisms within Japanese social and personal life. This in turn brought to mind Dewey's reflections on the social role of German philosophy in the nineteenth century. According to Dewey, the Germans admired Kant because he seemed to justify the gulf between their philosophical ideals and their actual practice. Kant's view that the noumenal world of the spirit was governed by one set of rules while the phenomenal world was governed by another could easily be employed, Dewey held, by a people who wished to suspend their high ideals while they sought to build up their power in the world. Recalling this, we were led to wonder whether Japanese attachment to German philosophy had performed a similar role in Japan.

Since we were dealing with intellectuals who lived in a world divided by so many conflicts, we were often nervous about their reactions. The Japanese professors who formed the committee to run the seminar were, in the main, sympathetic to the United States, but many of the students and young professors were Marxists of one sort or another who either admired or feared Soviet power. This made them sympathetic to what was then called "neutralism." And, as a result, American professors often emphasized that they were not in Japan as emissaries or agents of the State Department but as scholars financed by the Rockefeller Foundation. Naturally, their association with the capitalistic Rockefellers also made them suspect, but somehow being a tool of the Rockefellers—if that is how we were viewed—was far less odious from the point of view of a Japanese leftist or neutralist than being an agent of the State Department.

Thus, while Japanese professors were poised on one tightrope, the American professors were poised on another one. They were aware of the delicacy of their situation in a country which was still feeling the effects of an occupation and of a crushing military defeat at the hands of American forces; therefore, they were often faced with a peculiar dilemma, as the following story may indicate. One of them was asked how he regarded some of the new modern buildings then rising in Tokyo and how he would compare them with some of the ancient Japanese structures that he had seen in Kyoto. He was asked this by a Japanese leftist who, the American professor reasoned correctly, would damn him whatever his answer might be. If he said that he preferred the new Americanized skyscrapers, he would be put down as an insensitive American barbarian, unable to appreciate the values of old Japan. But if he said that he preferred the old temples, he would be said to be patronizing the Japanese by implying that they were incapable of erecting modern structures, symbols of the new industrial world that Japan was entering. Honest professors who might be asked the same question said just what they thought; others, who were more discreet, were likely to say that they liked both kinds of buildings—that the old Japan was great in one respect whereas the new Japan was great in another. Needless to say, the discreet professors were labelled "opportunists."

Whatever conflicts, tensions, or contradictions might have been brought to Japan by modern technology, they did not destroy the traditional Japanese talent for self-conscious social activity nor the Japanese interest in artistic expression. These reminders and remnants of pre-industrial Japan were luminously evident during our first visit; and they continued to be so during the visits that followed. While the Japanese entertained us, we could not help comparing their efforts with our own similar efforts at home; and we were forced to admit that however good we might be at that sort of thing, the Japanese outdid us. We think of ourselves as hospitable people, and certainly many of us respond with a lively spontaneous interest when we meet strangers. We welcome them into our homes; ask them to family-style dinners; engage them to meet our circle of friends at luncheons, cocktail parties, or evening sociables; and go out of our way to help newcomers "get settled" in our communities. Such occasions take forms that express our own highly developed gregariousness, but our efforts in this direction paled by comparison with those of our Japanese hosts in welcoming us as visitors at the University of Tokyo.

There were, first of all, the university formal receptions, which were like all formal receptions; they did not offer too much opportunity to get around the language barriers. But since Lucia arrived in Tokyo ten days late and missed the first series of receptions, she received another kind of reception as an individual when the chief members of the American Studies seminar came out to the Matsudaira Hotel to pay her prearranged formal calls of inquiry about her journey and her special interests in visiting the country. It was a surprise to Lucia to discover that the wife of a visiting professor should be the object of special consideration, for she had expected that the American wives would remain very much in the background and find their own ways of occupying their time, especially in a country where women traditionally have participated so little in university life. However, our Japanese hosts, in deference to the American custom of including wives in the social life of universities, gave them an overflowing measure of acceptance.

For example, the Japanese asked a brilliant and tireless female educator, who spoke English fluently, to introduce the American women to the special traditional activities in which Japanese women excel—notably flower-arranging and cooking. The exotic flowers and the novel vegetables and fishes were exciting to behold, and upon being introduced to them, the American women made a child-like rediscovery of everyday objects which they, in their chase after the "higher things," were in danger of forgetting. For the flower-arranging classes an exquisitely tiny teacher preempted the hotel bar two mornings a week. After presenting her students with suitable and challenging vases of different shapes, she would bring in buckets of chrysanthemums, carnations, heather, and leafy branches to be arranged in several ways according to traditional rules governing the relative lengths of each flower and branch and the angles at which they must rise from the horizontal. Her students were amazed at what charming different creations could finally be achieved with such an economy of means. When their "arrangements" were finally crowned with the approval of the teacher, the students would proudly carry them away through the hotel corridors accompanied by the gentle cheers and laughter of the hotel servants.

For the cooking classes the Japanese woman educator had enlisted the help of the director of a domestic science school. At the school, teachers and two score adolescent girl students, coolly clad in light blue uniforms and white shirts, greeted the Americans at the entrance while they changed into slippers. They were conducted to an airy kitchen classroom simply equipped with work tables, a long sink, and several gas braziers; and here the school director, who was also one of the country's authorities on nutrition, explained how Japanese food adequately met human nutritional needs, with the one major exception of calcium since there was so little milk available in Japan. Then the American visitors were introduced to the mysteries of making, among other things, fish broth, spinach with sesame seeds, mashed broiled eggplant, tempura shrimp, tempura fish, and—surprisingly—tempura carrots, broccoli, and spinach. After the American women were initiated into the elaborate and graceful tossing together of the ingredients of sukiyaki, they were unanimously seized by an infatuation with the cooking utensils: long metal chopsticks, workman-like broad-bladed knives of various shapes, bamboo ladles, and kettles and sauce pans of a mellow, golden metal as light as aluminum. They hunted for these implements in the shops and found them abundant and cheap; they began to include them in collections of Japanese trophies which would brighten and add new interest to their more antiseptic and streamlined kitchens at home.

Flower-arranging and cooking were not the only arts that represented the old Japan. There were also the theatrical arts: Kabuki, Bunraku, and Noh. We cannot present a technical discussion of them, but we do want to describe an especially memorable evening when our Japanese hosts entertained all the visiting American professors and wives by taking them to the presentation of several Noh plays in the Meiji gardens at sunset. The gardens were crisscrossed by a maze of driveways and paths; and, as a result, our drivers got lost and wheeled around a dancing platform, weaving between hurrying packs of people. We finally took to walking, entered to the left of the shrine, and were led into a front section of seats. We had heard a rumor that we might have to stand, but this turned out to be false. Our guides, Kishimoto, Goro Mayeda, and Motoo Kaji, arranged us in our seats and then introduced us to a Shinto priest whose son had just married one of the emperor's daughters. He was a serene, pleasant, kindly old man dressed in quiet robes.

We had a few minutes to look around before the performance. The stage was built out from the central shrine. The platform, along which the musicians, raconteurs, and actors entered, extended from the left back of the central stage a few feet, then turned at a right angle and extended some fifteen or twenty feet to a curtained backstage area. On the ground beside both the right and left ends of the stage stood three high wrought-iron braziers filled with twigs. Grouped around each one was a large neatly stacked pile of clean cedar logs. Huge crowds packed all sides and the back standing room of the theater, and the audience was very quiet, only occasionally starting a buzzing and jostling as they tried to get a more comprehensive view. Our own view was rather poor because we sat on ground level. Just before the start of the performance, about a dozen U.S. Army personnel appeared, accompanying General Mark Clark; they sat in the front rows across from us, but they were about six rows further forward. The entrance of Clark was a signal for an invasion of news photographers with flash bulbs which made explosive pops like Roman candles. At the last minute attendants carrying long lighted torches came down the middle aisle and set the bonfires ablaze.

For the first play—which was about the Spirit of Iris visiting a prince who was resting at an inn—a corps of musicians dressed in slate-gray kimonos with butterfly shaped sleeves occupied the back of the stage and the right hand side. Those on the side sat with their profiles toward the audience and did the chanting in level recitative, sounding something like Gregorian chants but without much range of tone. In the center two special drummers were prominent; they carried on frequent interludes of a set rhythmic pattern, tapping two small, thin drums of rather flat timbre with their right hands as they uttered a low growling exclamation and then a growl that ended in a very high hoot like that of an owl.

Meanwhile, the actors moved onto the stage with quiet uprightness. Sometimes they made long recitative speeches, and at intervals the musicians carried on the story. The only part that required active motion was the dance of the Spirit of Iris, played by a masked man who represented a Chinese dream woman in gorgeous red and gold brocade kimono. One of the specially arresting gestures of this dance consisted in jerking the arms so that the sleeves swung up and around the forearm. Then with another jerk the sleeve was unwound. Our Japanese women friends kept pointing to the actors' feet because they had a strange walk, putting down heels first and advancing each foot only four inches at a time.

The second play, a farce, was hilarious. The mountain-climbing priest always lifted his legs high and twirled his beads as he frantically tried to cure his possessed brothers of seizures of "too-hooing," which occurred with wonderfully increasing frequency. The priest's costume had a domino appearance with large white chrysanthemums spaced out on the back and front of a dark gray short kimono. The other costumes were also magnificent—brocades of the most lavish embroideries, many done years ago. Those who played warriors wore giant pale blue pantaloons, floor length, and a broad thick butterfly bustle across their fannies.

In the third play, these warriors engaged in a stylized battle with a spider. This play commenced with a pale, beautiful, lean-faced man sitting on his bed with a regally scarlet kimono draped over one shoulder. After he had sprung up once to chase the spider with his sword, the second act started with a wonderful green-thatched mound being carried in by four actors dressed in the same dark drapery material. They placed the mound in the middle of the stage just before three warriors entered. After moving with lumbering caution around and about, the warriors managed to dislodge the drapery and discover a gleaming white spider web standing inside. The web contained a bloody red mass which suddenly sprang out through the web and appeared full height with wild red hair flying. Its face was covered by a golden mask with a weird grin and flashing eyes that changed expression in the changing light; it wore a gilt brocade kimono and menacingly danced among the warriors, from time to time spreading a web of wreathing vaporous tentacles. At the end of the fighting, it was cornered with its back to the audience, and then it suddenly keeled over toward the audience and subsided flat on the stage.

All this occurred to the accompaniment of rhythmic drums and low, undulating chants and screaming flutes. Even after the performance, we heard powerful drums being played far off in the gardens and came to realize that they had been throbbing all evening. At first we had thought this was another element of the performance, but while going home that dark night through the pine avenues, we came upon a circle of light and there saw a small raised stage like a bandstand where festival dancing was still going on to the droning accompaniment of those drums.

As we left the Meiji Shrine, we went along in a wave of hundreds of Japanese spectators. Along the avenue we saw several men carrying lighted lanterns of medium size which were orange, red, blue, and lavender. Kishimoto and Motoo Kaji soon got hold of some of them and conducted us with ceremonious gaiety in and out of the lanes until we finally caught up with the university cars. Entering the cars, the Millers, Kishimoto, Goro Mayeda, and we all decided to go off to dinner at the Forbidden City, a Chinese restaurant that was accessible to the Shinanomachi section. It was close to ten o'clock at night, and we sat at the corner of a balcony overlooking two vacant boulevards and a highway, hoping to be cooled by delicate breezes that had sprung up. There we dined and talked late until the feline Chinese hostess began to hover around us and chatter after all the other patrons had departed. Kishimoto and Mayeda finally went running off into the darkness to find another elusive taxi for themselves after having pushed the Millers and us into one that they had previously caught at the restaurant door.

We have tried in this chapter to present our impressions of tensions and conflicts that we saw in the Japan of 1952, but while we were observing what we thought of as disparate elements within Japanese life, our Japanese colleagues were noticing certain contrasts within ours. This was evident in a speech by President Tadao Yanaihara of Tokyo University delivered in perfect English at a ceremony to welcome the American scholars. First, he remarked on the fact that almost a century had passed since Commodore Perry had come to Japan in 1853, hinting in a not very subtle way that while Perry had forced his way in, we American scholars were coming with olive branches after the nightmarish "War of the Pacific." Yanaihara, we reflected, was indicating to us that we too could be belligerent and peaceful by turns.

Then he reminded the Americans that our restrictive immigration law, which had shocked the Japanese so much, was now being revised to permit Japanese to enter our country, albeit in small numbers; also that we were at last permitting the naturalization of Japanese nationals living in our country. This was his way, we thought, of telling us that we could be mean as well as hospitable to foreigners. Materially and spiritually, he went on to say, the wounds that Americans had inflicted on the Japanese were being healed. During the Occupation, Yanaihara continued—while, it should be remembered, the Occupation was still going on—"there were a number of fair, unselfish and fine Americans who . . . assisted in the democratization of Japan." On the other hand, he said, as he added an antithesis to his thesis: "not all Americans were of this type . . . even the most unselfish had to conform to the requirement of the Occupation administrator."

Yanaihara was also candid in his assessment of American scholarship. He acknowledged that Japanese-American contact had been close in the previous century, "but frankly speaking," he added, "American academic influence has been less than that of Western European countries." The Japanese, he said, had adopted their method of study and their modern thinking from the European tradition, "perhaps . . . because the sciences in the U.S.A. were still in the process of development." This remark was kindred to that of the Japanese philosopher who thought that Morton was a European because he had a philosophical point of view. It was also reminiscent of a tendency on the part of many Japanese scholars to regard their American colleagues as fellow-neophytes who were obliged to sit at the feet of Europeans just as they were.

In a sense, therefore, the president of Tokyo University was reminding the American visitors that they came from a country which had its barbaric as well as its civilized features. They could be warlike as well as peaceful, and their scholarly accomplishments could range from the mediocre to the distinguished. He was as patronizing to the American scholars as he supposed that the American scholars might be to the Japanese. He could not, of course, view America as a country which combined elements of *feudalism* and modern industrialism, for he was, as it happened, an economist by training. Yet, he could certainly argue that America had only recently—by Japanese and European standards—entered a period in which it could claim to be able to tell others about its achievements in philosophy, history, political science, economics, and literature. "We are very grateful," he concluded with a touch of irony, "that these prominent Americans, not connected with politics, business, or journalism, have come to Japan to introduce American studies to us and at the same time to become acquainted with our way of life and our ideals." Plainly, Yanaihara was a proud scholar and a courageous one. He expected us to treat our Japanese colleagues as equals and not as enslaved intellectual captives. If we saw Japan as a land of contradictions, he was reminding us that our country was equally so.

FIVE

From Tokyo to the Hinterlands

Although we were based in Tokyo, our schedule in 1952 called for some weekend travel as well as for a two-week trip away from Tokyo after classes were over. During our weekends we went first to Nikko and then to Mount Fuji and the Five Lakes; our two-week trip took us to Karuizawa for a "round-table conference' and then to Hiroshima, where we participated in "rest and conferences at a provincial university." All of this gave us a chance to abandon steaming Tokyo. And let no one think that we exaggerate when we say "steaming Tokyo." Never before had we encountered anything as hot and as humid as that city in the summer. For nights on end we tossed and perspired in our beds after spending days baked in an unbearable sun. Needless to add, there was no air-conditioning in the Hotel Matsudaira nor in the classrooms of Tokyo University. Occasionally we would slip away from our American friends and colleagues and would take dinner in one of the dining rooms in Frank Lloyd Wright's Imperial Hotel or in the restaurant on the top floor of the Nikkatsu Hotel, places where we could find some blessedly cool air. We were so exhausted by the heat of Tokyo that any trip away from it seemed to herald welcome relief even if that was to be purchased at the price of attending conferences after giving too many lectures. Of course, we did not realize how hot Hiroshima would be, but the other places did afford relief from Tokyo's sultriness as well as some glimpses into aspects of Japanese life that differed sharply from those we had encountered in Tokyo.

Very early one morning a procession of university cars brought the American delegation to the central railroad station of Tokyo, where we boarded a train for Nikko. We were led to reserved seats at the front end of the neat little electric express in which there was a small glass cage for the engineer and his assistant. The Tokyo professors in charge of the trip were Kishimoto and Shinzo Kaji; and they were accompanied by Kaji's nephew Motoo and by Miss Kiyoko Takagi, who dispersed among us to explain our route. Meanwhile, the canned music started as soon as the train did and sang

Viennese waltzes all through the trip. There was a long stretch of travel through the fringes of Tokyo beside gray canals, across small bridges, and between small gray factories alternating with wooden match box houses. Along the muddy by-paths beside the railroad track children and workers were hiking in a continuous procession.

Soon the little rice paddies began to appear, first tiny and separate, then running together in larger areas with high mud "dike-walks" separating them. The rice was well along, about fifteen inches high. We could see small patches of corn and soya beans or some other large leafed plants or vines near farm houses. These houses were screened by thick hedges of a large glossy-leaved bush that was neatly pruned into shape and extended right up to the eaves. Everything in the houses was quiet, for everyone was already in the rice paddies or on the way there. People were working in pairs or in small groups. The women wore striped, dark, tight-fitting blouses; they also wore kerchiefs over their heads. The men wore similar clothing. Both men and women wore something resembling puttees around their calves while their feet were left bare. Often the women had babies strapped to their backs. All cultivation was done by hand with a small forked implement. The sight of the broad jade green paddies dotted with people nursing the rice along and assisted by flocks of slender white cranes was lovely to look at.

After perhaps twenty-five miles we saw in the distance the shadowy shapes of irregular hills. When we came up to them we found that they were covered with heavy growth, much evergreen, and giant bamboo. Other neat patches of hillside had been stripped of trees and replanted with bright green grasses. Reforestation had been carried out in a painstaking manner, and, as a result, most woods looked beautiful though there were areas of neglected uplands and forest as in any other country. We got off the train at Nikko high up in the mountains, a town something like a Swiss resort village with trinket-filled wooden shops stretching down the streets. On both sides of the street there were deep gutters in which clear brooks raced each other downhill. We proceeded by bus to a house of the Zen Buddhist priests, where the head priest, bald-headed, benevolent, and dressed in a simple dark kimono, bowed us into his domain. Here we were shown through the series of reception rooms where representatives of the emperor and descendants of the shogun are received. The rooms were made of exquisitely colored screens with flowers, butterflies, a red sun, and a black moon and milky way, and—to distribute the pattern—tiny squares of bright color applied in a kind of collage. There were very elegant cloud effects made by dusting various shades of gold or white or gray paint across surfaces of natural wood or paper; and, of course, the place was beautifully matted.

Luncheon was served in an open porch floating among the branches of giant cedar trees overlooking a misty mountain scene. Tiny doll-like children of the priests cavorted in the garden below while the priests themselves were having a meal. After lunch we toured the rococo lacquered temples; we were guided by priests and surrounded by hundreds of tourists, workers, and schoolchildren. Inside the shrines priests chanted while the devotees threw money into a large wicker tray. In a central chamber of carved teakwood a stone in the ceiling marked the place where the shogun's representative used to kneel. The Deities' Court was decorated with heavy lacquer walls of gold chrysanthemums on a black ground; and on an altar-like arrangement a golden, coiled object caught the light and shadows from so many angles that it appeared to be in motion. In one of the shrines we saw the temple dancers, handsome maidens with mask-like expressions, who performed a tensely serene sword dance accompanied by drums, flutes, and bells. They were dressed in white kimonos and red bloomers.

Leaving Nikko, we drove to a funicular with a slope of forty-five degrees in order to ascend to another height and then made our way to Lake Chozenji. Here we were installed in a charming Japanese inn where each couple had a paper panelled room and partitioned porch overlooking the expansive silver lake set among the cone-shaped green mountains around which vaporous clouds moved all evening. Here we joined together for a Japanese dinner, sitting on cushions around the room. Young women in kimonos served noiselessly and rapidly as they kept the saké flowing. Everyone laughed all the time. Kishimoto played the host. Kaji-san became browner and smiled more and more with each thimble-sized cup of saké, and finally he went to sleep.

We retired after visiting the Japanese-style hole-in-the-floor toilets and washing in yellow metal basins at the soapstone hall sink. Outside the windows was a little garden where rumpled cocks were picking up seeds. When we returned to our rooms, we found our beds made of fine light mattresses. They were very comfortable though hard. Each pillow was about the size, shape, and consistency of a ten-pound bag of sugar. The next morning we took a double bath in the deep wooden tub. For breakfast, Lucia had sour bean soup, abalone, and horseradish, cucumbers and rice with a side dish of gelatinous, paper-thin slices of seaweed while the unadventurous Morton had scrambled eggs.

After breakfast we took our ease. Then we walked to Kegon Falls, a long veil-like stretch of water that plunged at terrific speed because it was part of a steeply descending mountain stream. We explored the lakeside of Chozenji and rode past villas of French and Belgian diplomats. We saw newer villas under construction. Only their roofs were finished, and their frameworks were made of the peeled trunks of trees. The workmen were taking a little time off for a picnic nearby, but we gained the impression that every day was a work day in the Japan of 1952. After our walk we took lunch in the European Lakeside Hotel, where six English businessmen or soldiers on leave were chatting with their pretty Japanese girls. After lunch, we headed home to Tokyo.

Our next excursion from Tokyo took us by train and bus to Fujiyama and the Five Lakes. We made our headquarters at Hakone, and as usual had a whirlwind tour of two days that was as exhilarating and exhausting as our other periods of "rest" between classes. The most interesting part of this trip took place during a conversation in the bar of the Yamanaka Hotel at Hakone, where we gathered for drinks with our Japanese hosts. One of them talked rather freely about his experiences in the two or three months immediately following the surrender in September 1946. He had been asked by the Director of Education to act as the liaison person between the Department of Education and GHQ. He explained that he had announced his point of view to both sides, saying that he could always be relied upon to tell the truth but not necessarily the whole truth since he felt obliged to keep confidences. He reported two incidents which vividly illustrated the problems associated with the postwar transformation of Japan. One was the problem of withdrawing pictures of the emperor in full military regalia from all Japanese schools. GHQ thought that all these pictures should be summarily confiscated. Our Japanese friend objected that this would be deeply resented, and finally GHQ delayed action until he could enlist the efforts of the Director of Education. After some reflection, the director cleverly devised a solution: he announced that the pictures were to be replaced by a recent picture of the emperor in civilian dress. The principals of the schools were asked to turn in the military pictures, but when they did, the crafty director never produced any replacements.

The second incident concerned a prominent national Shinto shrine in Tokyo which was attended mainly by veterans. GHQ had decided that it should be closed because the direction of it had been usurped by a band of naval officers. Our friend had visited this shrine and discovered that everyone officiating there was in uniform while the priests remained in the background. He told the officers that the shrine would be closed, at which point they were all terribly hostile to him. He felt himself that the closing of the shrine would enrage all the Japanese people because it was dedicated to mourning dead soldiers. He finally suggested a compromise: all persons officiating at the services should be clothed as civilians; and when he had convinced the Japanese of the efficacy of this arrangement, he returned to GHQ. The tolerant American officer who was to decide whether the shrine was to be closed agreed to visit a huge festival at the shrine. When he appeared, lo and behold there was no trace of military people in control, and the priests were officiating as usual. Our friend was not sure whether he had done the right thing or not, but he thought that he had prevented a violent reaction of the Japanese people against the Occupation.

Our friend often felt in this postwar period the extreme uncertainty of his relationship with anti-Americans of the left and the right. So much so that he had quite frankly discussed with his family the possibility of armed men entering their house, binding him, and taking him away forever. His sons unsuccessfully urged him to flee to the United States with his family.

Our trip around Mount Fuji carried us away from this gloomy report. We drove in a bus to a rather ordinary European-style hotel by the lakeside near the mountain. The town was being blasted by constant jukebox jazz. Streets were lined with curio shops, bicycle stands, and corrals of riding-horses. Hundreds of young Japanese hikers streamed back and forth along the dusty roads carrying tall climbing sticks, dressed in shorts, and wearing split-toed rubber-soled shoes for rock climbing. The sport of hiking and mountain climbing was a German import. On the dirty beach beside the town were many rowboats for rent and the lake was alive with rowers and light-rigged sailboats as well as racing motor launches. Since this was a sports center, almost everyone in sight was young. Occasionally, a large U.S. Army truck rumbled and lurched along the main street beclouding everything with dust. From the lakeside Mount Fuji rose up in a handsome dark cone with slight white streaks of snow in the crevices near the broken-off top. During most of our stay Mount Fuji was veiled and unveiled many times by misty clouds. She was most spectacular in early morning when her lava slopes were a rich bloody red and gentian violet against a pale blue sky broken only in a few places by long irregular streaks of snow. Since we woke up around 4:30 A.M. because of the public jukebox concert, we decided to get out of our room and rented bicycles so that we could ride to the other end of the lake. At that hour there were plenty of Japanese cyclists and a lone American minister, looking overblown with a hangover and clutching his Bible. When we returned to town, our friends were engaged in a rapid crossfire of photography on the beach and in the hotel garden before breakfast.

We experienced our first hair-raising adventure on the lake when we were taken for a motor boat ride. The boat was barely big enough to take the whole party, and we squeezed into the covered cabin while the Japanese sat on the after deck and the boatman struggled with cranking the engine. We kept on drifting, and ten or fifteen minutes elapsed with the engine giving no sign of life and fumes accumulating rapidly. Finally, everyone was persuaded to put out cigarettes, but just as they did, a towing boat arrived bearing a mechanic who wanted to come on board with a candle-lit Japanese lantern. All of us violently protested and shoved him away. Eventually, we got started by towing and went skimming about the lake. Most of us were sitting on the roof and stern deck as we watched the stars and sang catches of songs.

On Sunday the bus took us first to pick up President Yanaihara, who had come to the country accompanied by two very pretty young secretaries. We drove on through the green covered volcanic hills around to the second lake and took a large barge-like motor boat for a spin. The water was a wonderful blue, like a star sapphire, and the mountains a rich slightly yellow green with horizontal strips of cultivation along the lake rim.

Our visits to Nikko and Mount Fuji were made on weekends; but once the long hot month of July was over, we were led to the mountain retreat called Karuizawa, where a very large conference was held on two grand themes: "The American Occupation and the Future of Japan" and "The Problems of Freedom." Not only did the American professors, the Japanese professors, and various assistants attend this conference, but also a number of distinguished Japanese scholars and intellectuals who had no connection with the seminars. The conference was held in a pleasant hotel from August 4 through August 8. Our notes and journals show that the attendants managed to combine a great deal of pleasure with arduous discussions of such topics as education, the economic situation, Soviet-American relations, social reform, the problems of population, freedom of the press, academic freedom, freedom and women, the anti-subversive law and the loyalty oath, as well as freedom and the feudalistic tradition.

We came to Karuizawa after boiler-room heat in Tokyo, where we had to drag our mattresses onto the floor to get a breath of air. As the train headed for the resort town, it climbed up to fantastic mountains that were covered with vegetation. They were fascinating in shape but not in color since the greens were so little differentiated in mid-summer and the foliage was so overshadowing. But when they became veiled in cloudy grays of different thickness, their forms stood out, and this produced the effects created by so many masters of Japanese painting on screens and scrolls.

During the first days in the cooler climate of Karuizawa, we were treated to the pleasures of several initiatory social occasions on which all sorts of episodes enhanced our acquaintance with Japanese life. One such occasion was a grand dinner party for the whole group when small tables and cushions were set about the large lounge between the raised fireplaces. At each table a charcoal burner was placed in the middle, and all the materials for sukiyaki were ranged around. At our table the official chef was Goro Mayeda, while Miss Tsurumi and Mrs. Kau were the actual presiders over the frying pan. Mr. Kau, Morton, and Lucia gobbled portions which were produced so fast that only the briefest pauses intervened between bites and drinks of saké. Even so, these pauses were filled with amusing jests about philosophy while we drank to the refrain of "andriaihaku" or "without regard for the far-fetched consequences," as it was translated. All of us roared with Homeric laughter while our friends at other tables kept wondering what we were up to. When Mr. Kau began to boast about how much he liked raw eggs, all the extra eggs were broken into the saké-flavored sukiyaki, and he was allowed to gobble them up one by one while they were only half-cooked.

After supper when the rug was rolled up, Miss Tsurumi, dressed in a handsome gray and black kimono with a strikingly embroidered obi colored with lavender and orange-red flowers, danced a kabuki dance. It went with a story of how a young girl had wooed a priest, and how, when he felt obliged to repudiate her love, he had shut himself up in a huge bell. When she pursued and caught up with him, she wound a serpent around the bell, whch turned into a hell-fire that finally melted the bell and reached his skeleton. Miss Tsurumi danced with marvelous grace and with a control that seemed too great to be exciting, but she told us later she had used too many facial expressions and that her face should have been even more controlled and completely mask-like.

Another afternoon we went to Miss Tsurumi's for a special visit. We retreated to her father's study, a huge second-floor room which was bowered in trees. In the center of the study was a stone and cement fireplace with a pipe extending up through the roof of the little bedroom over one corner of the room. We talked at random about the meeting of the Institute for the Science of Thought and about the fact that a Communist member had objected to their receiving a grant from the Rockefeller Foundation even though the foundation had never tried to influence the direction of their research. Miss Tsurumi showed us woodcuts from a country school of sixth-grade children who had told her about some of their "life experiences." She also told us about diaries of factory girls who made daily entries over a two-year period. She related the story, later repeated in the conference, about the country school teacher whose parents would still beat her when they were irritable. On top of that, they had arranged a marriage for her which she had decided to accept without knowing the man in order to escape spinsterhood. The teacher had never had any impulse to strike back, but Miss Tsurumi allowed that she herself would have never resumed a relationship with anyone who had struck her. She pointed out that the teacher was in charge of a large class in her school and that her abject surrender to her dictatorial parents was typically Japanese. Later, on the way home, we talked about large rural families whose tiny sporadic income was supplemented by the earnings of children who were sent to work in factories or in houses of prostitution. We then raced back to the hotel just in time for the afternoon conferences. Morton attended the one on economic problems where he heard the talk of Ohara reported in an earlier chapter, and Lucia went to one on educational and psychological problems.

The latter, which was chaired by Perry Miller, started out with a continuation of a subject which a Professor Maia had opened at the general morning meeting: the importance of understanding depth sociology. Professor Maia had urged there that just as it is extremely difficult to understand an individual without penetrating the semi-conscious and unconscious activities of his personality, so it is very superficial to approach a society without consideration of the "depths" of social feelings and habits which lie underneath surface social behavior. He declared at the opening of the smaller conference that Japan could be regarded only as a surface-democracy whose depths were undemocratic. He discussed this idea in connection with his observations about child development, observations which he had made as a child psychiatrist and researcher in psychology. He pointed out that children brought to his clinic invariably looked at the mother before answering any questions and always seemed to be seeking her approval in each reply that they made. He felt that the physical and social structure of the home helped to account for this excessive dependency. The home was usually very tiny, so that parents and several children all occupied one or two rooms. Most frequently, the family circle was composed of parents, children, and the husband's parents; and sometimes it included other unmarried members of the husband's family or of the families of his brothers. Within such a group a feeling of family rather than of individual privacy was likely to develop. And the basic reason, he thought, for this kind of family structure was economic. The large family circle simply could not afford to break up into separately housed smaller units composed only of members of the immediate family. He believed that in this kind of group the child's personality remained undeveloped and that the woman's personality remained so, too. Her early training made her defer to men and boys at all times; and later, after marriage, she was put in the position of deferring to her mother-in-law. He mentioned, but did not discuss in detail, the other part of the picture: the fact that the man was much more dominant in Japanese society than he was in Western societies like the United States. Maia concluded by saying that there was a great need to democratize the family before political democracy could possibly flourish in Japan.

When this meeting shifted its focus, other members of the conference made remarks about the newly organized system of education in Japan, the main feature of which was the 6–3–3–4 arrangement of the years respectively devoted to elementary school, middle school, high school, and university. While there had been a great increase in the number of universities since the war—from fifty to about two hundred—there was still a great shortage of teachers to serve on the faculties of normal schools. University students were said to be interested mainly in economics, English literature, and political science, but they appeared to have little interest in education, agriculture, and natural science.

Several participants in the discussion were disturbed about what they regarded as backward trends in education. They pointed out that the Japanese system, which had been greatly influenced by university education and especially by German education, had the tradition of keeping apart from life, a trend which they thought was very reactionary in its effects; and that unlike educators in the United States, their educators had come to form a caste. Some of the Japanese participants strongly favored the idea of limiting their students' political expression in extra-curricular political clubs, believing that such clubs would divert their energies from solid work. The participants were rather astounded to hear how freely United States students were allowed to organize into political clubs. Several Japanese questioned the idea of offering students so much opportunity; part of their fear of students' organizations was in reaction to the students' revolutionary tendencies. Other members of the group, however, felt that the students' interest in political life should be encouraged and allowed expression so that they could become more mature in their reflections on politics and in their political activity.

Because so many members of this group seemed so deeply concerned with very fundamental questions such as "What kind of life shall Japan make for herself?" one became aware of their deep anxiety about their society as a whole. They often seemed to be asking for very general answers to questions of this sort, to be seeking a philosophy or creed. All this reflected the chaotic period through which they were living as well as the widespread sense of helplessness among the intellectuals. A few asked for specific proposals of action based on the American experience, but in view of the enormous difference between the Japanese and the American social situation, the Americans at the meeting found it impossible to answer their questions. Their needs were so enormous that one could see clearly why religious solutions or quasi-religious solutions such as communism might be accepted most easily. One wondered whether their problems could be dealt with in other ways; one also wondered whether without such credos, formulas, and rituals the Japanese would be able to dispel their general anxiety quickly. In spite of this preoccupation of intellectuals with cosmic questions, the ordinary people we met seemed to have an enormous capacity for active, tireless work in rebuilding the physical structure of the country—for example, hospitals and houses in Tokyo and the whole city of Hiroshima. The people engaged in these acts of concrete physical reconstruction and in the fields of social welfare and nursing seemed to be far and away the most satisfied people in their everyday existence. And yet the university people and the intellectuals in general seemed to express the basic fears and questions of their society in emphasizing that the occupation had left Japan in a terrifying "moral vacuum," to use the words of Kishimoto. This situation was said to be similar in many ways to that of post—war Germany; it was also said—and very frequently—that Japan was in desperate need of psychiatrists. In reponse to these comments prominent leaders such as the Americanist Takagi and President Yanaihara argued that the Japanese needed Christianity more than anything else. But since the material and institutional substructure of Japan's society had been so pulverized, one wondered whether its people could gain much from general theological or philosophical ideas unless they could be embodied in educational or other institutions that would help organize community life.

The idea that the Japanese needed more Christianity stimulated one of the more unusual exchanges during the conference at Karuizawa, an exchange in which Perry Miller and Morton expressed some differences on the role of Protestantism in fostering freedom in the West. It was unusual from the point of view of the Japanese because they expected that the American professors would likely keep politely silent about such disagreements. For this very reason, both Perry and Morton thought that it was a good idea to bring their differences out in the open, showing the Japanese that their American colleagues were not conspiring to impose a single American ideology and that Americans valued open intellectual debate. These differences went back to the time of Morton's arrival at Harvard in 1948, when Perry and a number of other Harvard professors were expressing great admiration for the views of Reinhold Niebuhr, the well-known Protestant theologian. Many of them professed to disagree with him in theology because they were atheists, but they also held that this did not interfere with their admiration for his liberal political views or with their great respect for his ideas about human nature, ideas that were allegedly distinguished by their realism, which, they said, showed that Niebuhr was a deeper liberal thinker than John Dewey.

It should not be thought that a formal contest took place between Miller and Morton at Karuizawa. The occasion was rather one when Miller delivered a talk to which Morton responded as a member of the audience. Being an historian of ideas, Miller concentrated in great measure on the role that Protestantism had played in the history of freedom, a role which he contrasted with that played by pragmatism and utilitarianism. The latter two philosophies, he thought, were less spiritual and more commercial than Protestantism in their impact; he asserted that "the Western crisis of spirit," as he called it, was too deep to be dealt with by advocates of what he termed "pragmatic utilitarianism."

Morton began his reply by distinguishing between the historical question upon which Miller had concentrated and the question whether Protestant theology could, in 1952, provide a philosophy that would help us understand and foster freedom in society. While concentrating at the beginning of his remarks on the historical question, Morton admitted that Protestantism had played a great part in the historical development of the idea of freedom, but he added that it had also expressed itself in less salutary ways; for example, in the puritanical suppression of natural impulses, in fostering the idea of thoughtless obedience, and in encouraging theocracy. Then he remarked that utilitarianism had also expressed itself in both conservative and liberal political directions. Thus Hume, who could be called a utilitarian in some degree, was a Tory; but John Stuart Mill, the avowed utilitarian, was a liberal. For this reason, Morton emphasized, the question of how different philosophies or theologies had been used in the past was not fundamental for those who were seeking a guide to political action today. However liberal or conservative in its effect a philosophy might have been in one set of circumstances, in another set it might easily play another role. In his concluding remarks on the historical question, Morton urged Miller to resist labelling pragmatism and utilitarianism as commercial and unspiritual philosophies by comparison to Protestantism. He reminded Miller of Max Weber's views about Protestantism's encouragement of capitalistic virtues and also of the spiritual aspects of the thought and character of the pragmatic William James.

Leaving history, Morton turned to the relevance of Protestant theology to the problem of contemporary social action. How, he asked, can it help to adjudicate between conflicting social values? Only, as Niebuhr himself indicates, by adopting what would be called a pragmatic attitude. What, then, he also asked, is the virtue of defending a theology that rests upon *mystery* as a basis for pragmatic politics of the sort that Niebuhr encouraged as a high official in Americans for Democratic Action (ADA)? It is sometimes said in reply to this question, Morton went on, that Protestantism provides a correct picture of the human predicament. But does it do so without qualifications? Has it provided many clear and constructive solutions to personal or social problems? Morton doubted that it had. Moreover, he felt that the psychoanalyst Erich Fromm, whose then-popular book *Escape from Freedom* Miller had cited favorably, would be more likely to appeal to Freud for practical guidance than to St. Paul, St. Augustine, Calvin, Luther, Cromwell, or Reinhold Niebuhr.

Reacting to something else that Miller had maintained, Morton said that the effectiveness of Protestantism in galvanizing men emotionally depended in great measure on getting them to accept the Christian mysteries. He wondered, therefore, how Professor Miller, who did not agree with Niebuhr's mystery-filled theology, could find that theology emotionally effective. Morton warned against what he called vulgar pragmatism concerning ideas and said that as a philosopher and teacher he could not conscientiously espouse a doctrine which he did not believe, even though espousing it might encourage his students to fight for his own values. As a matter of fact, however, he doubted that Christian theology would be able to lead the world to freedom. It might, he said, serve as the foundation for another Crusade but not as the basis for a world that was united, peaceful, and free. This, he believed, would require a more universalistic ethics than that of Protestantism.

The response to Morton's remarks was mixed. They appealed to many Japanese scholars who were not Christians but, understandably, not to those who were. As if he were serving as a witness to the truth and for Perry Miller, President Yanaihara announced that his Christian belief had carried him through the darkest days of the war, whereas other Japanese sided with Morton and praised him for his outspokenness on so delicate a subject. In general, the airing of the disagreement between the two Americans had the effect desired by Perry and Morton; it showed that the visiting professors were not in league, not eager to impose one ideology on the Japanese.

In addition to commenting on Perry Miller's talk in Karuizawa, Morton presented one of his own on the problems of freedom. Like his colleagues, he was obliged to be as clear as possible in order to overcome the linguistic barrier. He never underestimated the intellectual powers of those who listened to him, but he felt obliged to avoid technical philosophical language as much as he could without, however, being condescending to his Japanese audience. Perry Miller was a little less concerned about condescension, so he followed a somewhat different course that could sometimes have a hilarious effect. Perry, a charming and delightful man, who was well over six feet tall, would often put his arm around a tiny Japanese scholar and talk a sort of pigeon English to his intimidated companion: "You come here at five. I be here. You be here too. We be together. Understand?" In reply the Japanese would sometimes merely nod, even when he was able to speak perfect English. He would decline to use his English in order not to embarrass Perry. Morton was incapable of speaking that way, but he did try to speak as clearly as he could, especially when he was being interpreted by a Japanese professor of English who knew no philosophy. With this in mind, he presented a philosophical talk on freedom in which he sought to be comprehensible without talking down.

Morton began by saying that, from a philosophical point of view, there were many problems connected with freedom but that he would talk about only a few: the fundamental ethical problem, the fundamental logical problem, and the fundamental problem of what might be called social technology. The fundamental ethical problem, he said, might be stated by means of the simple sentence: "Is freedom good?" or, in other words, "Is it good to be free?" About the answer to this question, he went on, there would probably be little dispute among those listening to him, but certain disagreements would be likely to arise once they asked "What *is* freedom?" This question would constitute a logical problem since any search for a definition constitutes a logical problem. Finally, he said, a problem of social technology would be raised when we asked how to attain and preserve freedom.

After making this distinction, Morton went on to consider the view that freedom is the absence of restraint. Although he did not spend too much time on this topic, he remarked that many western thinkers had distinguished restraints in politics, in religion, in the intellectual life, and so on and that by making such a distinction they hoped to distinguish the freedoms called political, religious, and intellectual. Morton went on to say that these different freedoms can sometimes be in conflict. This was recognized, he said, by philosophers who appealed to the myth of a social contract. According to them, we accept the restraints imposed by government in order to eliminate the restraints that murderers and robbers might impose on us. In this way we come to see the need for weighing the value of the different freedoms and therefore of different kinds of restraint when they are in conflict. We may think, for example, that it is better to suffer the restraint imposed by a police force than the more objectionable restraint imposed by a criminal.

Taking this point of departure, Morton tried to connect his philosophical remarks with certain historical developments. He pointed out that many liberal thinkers in the West had come to think in the early years of the twentieth century that while religious and political freedom had been won, the resulting victory was in some degree hollow because it was not accompanied by economic and social freedom. Socialists and liberals joined in a crusade against wage slavery, soft-pedalling the importance of "mere" political freedom, which they came to describe as purely formal freedom. This has been called the Age of Confidence that preceded the Age of Anxiety, the growth of totalitarianism, both fascist and communist, and the Second World War. Fascism erased many precious freedoms, and communism destroyed political freedom in the name of a so-called "higher freedom." Stalin, Morton said in 1952, had betrayed the tradition of freedom as understood by democratic thinkers, and he had helped to discredit political liberals who had emphasized the importance of economic freedom while using language unfortunately resembling that used by Stalin.

Stalinism, Morton continued, had helped to encourage the growth of McCarthyism in American domestic politics and MacArthurism in American foreign politics as well as attacks on liberals like Holmes and Dewey. Then Morton declared: "I wish firmly and unequivocally to speak out against McCarthyism and to denounce this effort on the part of the bigoted and the confused . . . . Although I believe that Stalinism is a great threat to the world, I do not believe that it is the greatest danger to our social welfare in America. On the contrary, I believe that McCarthyism is, for it seeks to destroy social reform in the name of a dishonest defense of liberty. This does not mean that I think that America is in a state of anti-Red hysteria. It is emphatically not in spite of McCarthy's efforts to whip up such hysteria."

Morton's talk had been delivered at a meeting entitled "The Problems of Freedom"—one of the two main themes of the conference. On the other theme, "The American Occupation and the Future of Japan," the Japanese naturally took center stage. One of them worried about the arrival of fascism after the Occupation ended. He likened Japan to a wayward child when the stern school master has left the room. In his eyes the Occupation had been a combination of the idealistic approach to life and willingness to play politics, and this was the view many Japanese scholars took. In various ways, he said, the Occupation prepared the way for the return of reaction, and recent publications showed the trend. Some were concerned with exposing the Occupation's trials of military men, some with the virtues of

Tojo's war memoirs, and some with glorifying the "thought-police." These books, the speaker said, were read sentimentally by the Japanese people. Furthermore, the so-called Anti-Subversive Laws revealed a reactionary trend. Military personnel were reassuming positions of high reponsibility; many reactionaries trained in the old tradition were also filling such positions; and many Japanese thought that secondary schools should be allowed to hang military portraits of the emperor in prominent places. It was the speaker's opinion that such developments, along with the poverty of the country, might well encourage the arrival of fascism.

Finally, there were two Japanese speakers on the subject of freedom and the Occupation: Professor Maia and Shigeharu Matsumoto. Professor Maia noted that the effects of the Occupation were "more or less good." He repeated his earlier claim that although the surface institutions of Japanese society had become more democratic as a result of the Occupation, the depths of people's personalities in general remained undemocratic from the force of early conditioning in the authoritarian Japanese family structure. During the discussion it was agreed that certain bureaucrats had defeated much of the Occupation's educational policy that was *good on paper*. Shigeharu Matsumoto's view was that the Occupation was infinitely better than any other in history and that this paramount fact should always be remembered. On the plus side he mentioned the constitution, the codification of criminal and civil laws, the improvement of court procedures, and the introduction of anti-trust laws, labor laws, welfare laws and education laws, as well as land reforms. The great question, he added, was whether these paper reforms would have a lasting effect. Moreover, he said, basic political problems had been created by the pacifistic Article 9 of the constitution, and the national sovereignty of Japan was always threatened by the presence of American troops. Matsumoto thought that the general questions of how democracy might be perpetuated in Japan were more than anything else psychological, namely: How can people grow up with democratic feelings? How can good leaders be developed? How can the differences between the American and Japanese temperaments be reconciled? And the general defect of the Occupation, he continued, was unanimously felt to be a consequence of its having no clear idea of the New Japan and of its having no clear idea of the nature of the Communist Party.

There were several occasions between the discussions of these troubling problems when we had glimpses and side-glimpses into Japanese social and personal life. The Matsumotos, a striking couple, were hosts at an afternoon tea and cocktail party. They were both unusual Japanese, so they deserve a word of description. He was an extraordinarily handsome man with the noble countenance of a ruler, an impressively tall and muscular figure. He looked rather Chinese to us and perhaps came from this strain. He was a lawyer by training and had been educated abroad. When he spoke English with grace and deliberation at the general session, his calm face lit up with a varying play of expressions—whimsical humor and penetrating decisiveness being most prominent. He seemed quite at ease in talking before the large general sessions, unlike many of the Japanese participants, but in informal talk he seemed curiously more diffident than his colleagues who were shy before an audience. His wife, who was also broad-faced and beautiful, had a direct, engaging manner. She had also studied abroad, and the story was told that when she and her husband started walking side by side in the streets of Tokyo after their marriage, she was frequently stoned. This couple belonged to a large vacation colony at Karuizawa where some ten or fifteen families held land cooperatively and ran a central clubhouse where meals were served and a central nursery school cared for the small children of all member families. The cottage of the Matsumotos was charming and simple, hidden among pines and maples and offering a narrow view of the valley and gently rising mountains. We sat around a large rectangular living room and circulated to talk with the various Japanese, who carefully divided themselves among us. Mr. Matsumoto told about some of his hopes to bring Japanese theater productions to New York and to circulate Japanese films, for he was the head of an intercultural program being financed by an American foundation. He had decided upon this job rather than to become Japanese Ambassador to the U.S., it was said. He also chatted about wonderful vacations they had had in these mountains in the snowy seasons and how they had lived here at times during the war in very cold weather which would have seemed to us insupportable in such a frail house but which, as he told about it, seemed enchanting. His wife asked numerous questions about women's education in the U.S. since she was thinking of sending her daughter to Swarthmore to study psychology after she completed her work at Women's Christian College in Tokyo. Lucia was especially curious about the daughter, and we were soon to have a passing glimpse of her. Before that, as we were trailing down the slope in front of the house, a couple of roly-poly children (about two and four), very charming in brilliant colored sweaters, came dancing out from behind the pine trees. They were quite irresistible, and we caught them up in our arms in turn and talked with them. They showed no sign of being startled or afraid but smilingly conveyed that this was exactly what they would expect of everybody—to be cuddled and loved. Their delighted equanimity in response to the attention of adults was what we had observed often about young children on subways and the public thoroughfares of Tokyo. Maybe their expecting universal affection was the result of what Professor Maia had warned us was in reality underdevelopment and agreeable passivity, but it was infinitely beguiling to the stranger.

After leaving the tiny children, we finally met Miss Matsumoto. She explained that she would ride with us in her father's Cadillac to pick up Miss

Tsurumi, who would be joining us for dinner at the Matsumotos. Miss Matsumoto was very beautiful, with straight black hair parted in the middle, its long locks tied back and streaming over her shoulder. One would have judged her to be about fifteen from manner and dress, and Lucia thought her amazingly precocious while she was assisting the Tokyo University organizers of the conference. Actually, like so many Japanese, she was older than she appeared. She sat in the front seat with the driver and Nakaya, the Tokyo University professor of history, a handsome, very nervous Japanese. Miss Matsumoto began directing the driver through a maze of side roads. Her manner appeared imperious, and as it quickly became evident that we were lost, she became more and more adamant, urging the driver to rush off on foot one way, to rush back, to turn the car around and drive back to another crossroad, and so on. We were in a flat valley thickly overgrown with brush. The mountains were out of sight and the sky so hazy that the sun was botted out. We must have wandered for three-quarters of an hour and were completely dizzy from the frantic searching. Now and again during our zig-zagging Nakaya would rush off impulsively and disappear, but in the end he and the driver between them closed in on the Tsurumi grounds and, after wild shouting, he appeared with the calm and collected Miss Tsurumi. During the episode we sensed the panic of our hosts at having plans go awry and supposed that loss of face was involved in their not having the situation completely under control. In general, the entertainment of guests was planned so subtly that it seemed to happen spontaneously and to proceed without the slightest flaw.

We turn now to another extended trip that we made after classes were over in Tokyo, a trip to Hiroshima that we started with trepidation because of this city's central place in the history of horror. The trip of the American scholars and their wives to Hiroshima in 1952 commenced when we boarded a small ship at Kobe on the Inland Sea. On the trip we spent only one night on board ship. Each couple occupied a simple cabin equipped with a couple of couches, a couple of chairs, and a wash basin. The small ship was spic and span, and not very crowded with passengers.

What was most remarkable about the trip was the appearance of the Inland Sea during daylight hours and at night. The day when we took ship at Kobe was exceedingly calm, and the surface of the water in all directions glowed softly in delicate shades of opalescent pink, blue, and gold as the sunlight shifted, and the grayish purple mountains along the northern and southern shore and the pyramid-shaped islands made a distant border along the horizons. The atmosphere of the Inland Sea was quite different from that of the Mediterranean, for the Mediterranean is often a much more brilliant color, deep azure mostly, with snowy crested waves sometimes streaked with patches of vivid, translucent green. In contrast to the high and exciting color of the Mediterranean, the Inland Sea seemed like an endless stream of delicate water that finally dissolved into expanses of liquid pearl at sunset. And at night the water was a deep velvety black, shot through with phosphorescent spangles where the ship made its trail.

Our only stop during the daytime was at Takamatsu on the island of Shikoku. There a high mountain rose up sharply a short distance from the dock, and at the base of this mountain there was a convenient funicular which allowed us to ascend to the top with astonishing alacrity. Our Japanese hosts were delighted by the enthusiasm of the American professors and their wives, all of whom were on board the funicular car. From a lookout at the top of the mountain, we could see the shimmering sea stretching east, north, and west—an expanse that was broken here and there by hazy, grayish-blue volcanic shaped islands at irregular intervals across the horizon. After a long time admiring the famous view, we returned to the funicular only to find that it had broken down. Perhaps the electricity had failed. There were frantic attempts to make the machine work again, but without success—so the whole group was forced to clamber down the steep slope, stumbling over the rocks and staggering along a broken path to reach the ship before the appointed hour for sailing to Hiroshima.

It had been arranged for the American scholars and their wives to stay at a Japanese inn just outside Hiroshima, perched on a peninsula jutting out into the Inland Sea. There we were joined by President Morito of Hiroshima University, who invited us to go swimming as a refreshment. A few of our number joined him for this swimming party during which we splashed around for an hour or so. Now, when so much has been reported about long-term effects of radiation, one cannot help wondering how much of it had remained in the Inland Sea in 1952. Needless to say, mankind knows something about its effects on the people of Hiroshima, enough, we hope, to prevent anything like those effects from occurring again.

One of the more troubling and dismaying episodes at the very beginning of our visit to Hiroshima was Morton's being asked: "Professor, what do you think of the atom bomb?" The question was bluntly put by a smiling Japanese newspaperman who carried a camera that he clicked incessantly at the railroad station while taking pictures of all the arriving Americans. Morton cannot remember his exact answer to the question, but he can certainly remember expressing his horror and disapproval of the bomb. Those feelings were made more intense when the time came for us to trudge around in the dusty streets of Hiroshima; and they reached their climax when we were brought to the center of the blast, the forlorn spot occupied by a tower in the midst of the rubble. Nearby we saw a sign that sickened us. It read: "Atomic souvenir" and was placed over a shop that sold objects bearing that singular designation.

We arrived in Hiroshima during a period of almost intolerable summer heat, but we were asked to stand in direct sunlight for what may have been an hour before the university photographers had finished taking their group pictures. "Just one more prease!" was repeated over and over again by those indefatigable cameramen as they snapped away. This heat was a tiny price to pay for the hellfire that our country had visited on this woebegone city.

It must be remembered how recently that hellfire had fallen from heaven. The university was making a desperate effort to revive itself—the figure of the phoenix was used constantly—and we were all given a copy of the following letter, written a year and a half earlier by the president of Hiroshima University to presidents of universities all over the world:

Hiroshima City, Japan
25 January, 1951

Dear Mr. President:

In my capacity as President of Hiroshima University, situated in the center of Hiroshima, which is world-famous as "Atom-Bombed City" and designated by the Japanese Diet as "Eternal Peace Commemorating City," I am sending letters to a large number of universities all over the world. We have chosen to include your university especially in order to ask for your help in our great task of reconstruction here.

Since I came to this university in April last year, I have been making every effort to rejuvenate it to be a peace-university, as a spiritual and cultural center of a peace city.

Permit me to dwell a little on some of my own personal matters. Immediately after the cessation of hostilities, I gave up my academic career and entered into political life. I participated in establishing the new constitution of Japan as a member of the House of Representatives and as chairman of the Political Research Committee of the Socialist Party. I was actively engaged in the drastic reform of the Japanese educational system, as Minister of Education in the Katayama and Ashida Cabinets.

It was mainly for the following two reasons that I resigned as a member of the House of Representatives and from my political party in order to be president of this university.

1. I was firmly convinced that the establishment of a New Japan depends fundamentally upon the education of youth, namely, the nurturing of a new people. With the beginning of the Meiji era, Japan launched upon a remarkable revolution in the fields of politics and industry, but she has never had a renaissance and reformation in the strict sense of the word, as those experienced by the European peoples. Japan needs, above all, a spiritual or human revolution that will make the foundation of our new constitution solid.

2. In order to establish a peaceful city, nothing is more important for

the Hiroshima people than to cherish peaceful thoughts, together with a will to realize permanent peace. This will be supported by the ever-present memory of a bomb devastated city, which was as grave and eloquent a tragedy as we had ever known. Especially do I think it necessary when I recollect that Hiroshima was one of the chief military centers since the middle of the Meiji era. Therefore I believe that our university has the important responsibility to be a spiritual center for the city. To fulfill this responsibility is extremely urgent, but it is difficult to attain, in view of the present situation at home and abroad.

Materially and spiritually, the establishment of a peace-university is a herculean task, just as it is to keep the world in lasting peace. The citizens of Hiroshima City and Prefecture, supported by the National Government and Civil Information and Education Section, GHQ, SCAP, are co-operating in this enterprise. But on account of the stringent circumstances in Japan since the surrender, the work is slow to progress.

Apart from this, I think it is a very significant project per se for many universities in the world to co-operate in the establishment of a peace-university in a city that is often supposed to be the Mecca of the world-peace-movement. It is for this reason that I should like to ask for your assistance in the reconstruction of our university. And this co-operation may not amount to much from the economic point of view, but it will be of deep significance, from the spiritual point of view, in contributing to international understanding and the permanent peace of the world. This will be of benefit not only to the students and professors of the university that receive it but also to those of the universities that offer it.

I know, however, that universities in any country are not always provided with ample funds for their own support, so that I want to place more emphasis on their moral assistance and encouragement rather than material contributions.

If you would accept one or both of the following two suggestions, it would be greatly appreciated.

1. I have a desire to establish within our university, an institute for research into international peace problems. As an initial stage for this program I want to collect books and periodicals concerning peace problems. This is also a gigantic task for Hiroshima University which, during the war, completely lost its central library and its contents. I wish for your help in this work. I should be very pleased if your university would send us one book, or pamphlet—the more, of course, the better—considered valuable by your university or of note in your country.

We will inscribe on them the name of your university in memory of your goodwill and keep them permanently in the university's "international-peace-library". The reading of these books, indeed, the very existence of this library, I believe, will undoubtedly create and promote an atmosphere of universal friendship, spreading peace commensurate with the peace-university.

Our university consists of faculties embracing literature, politico-economics, education, sciences, engineering, and fishery and stock-breeding. If, therefore, your university has any extra books in these fields of studies and could spare them for us, in addition to the books concerning peace problems, it would be greatly appreciated.

2. I would like to ask for your co-operation in the "verdurizing" of our university. I was surprised when I came to Hiroshima for the first time after the war to see the half-built university buildings standing on the bare, desolate ground destitute of a single tree with green leaves, just as the other parts of the city were. So I have worked out a plan to "verdurize" the university campus, and turn it from a burnt, red-rusty hue to a fresh green color. Not red, symbolizing struggle and blood-shed, but green which is the color of growth and hope, I believe, should be the color of our university. I would like to ask for your help in this program, too. When it is realized, thousands of students studying within this campus—there are 4,500 students in our university—will observe that the tree under whose shade they are taking their rest was sent through the goodwill of "A" university, the avenue along which they are walking was planted through the gifts from "B" and "C" universities, and that the hedge covered with pretty flowers is a symbol of "D" university's friendship, and new inspiration for international fellowship may result. Won't this be more powerful than thousands of words or a series of speeches to cultivate a peace-loving spirit in the minds of the students? Bearing such a dream in mind, I beseech you to send us a young tree that characterizes your country or your university. Under the present conditions, however, it might be difficult somehow. Should it be impossible, some seeds of the tree can take its place. We will do our best to sow and nurture them. If even that is not possible, we could procure a young tree here in Hiroshima at your discretion and expense. In this case, you would need to send us a sum of money amounting to three American dollars for one tree and a sign showing the name of its donor. If the species of the tree is indicated, it will be a help. If the tree you indicate can not endure the climate and soil of Hiroshima, will you allow us to select a substitute according to the advice of our professors who have specialized in horticulture? The tree you may donate will long be remembered by the sign attached to it with the name of your university in addition to that of the tree.

In view of the critical international situation, I want to step forward in the direction of the slogan, "No more Hiroshimas," and beg your assistance in establishing this university as a peace-university as well as a spiritual center for the Atom-Peace-City.

With very best wishes for the prosperity of your university and the diffusion of a peace-loving spirit, I hope a friendly liaison and spirit of cooperation will be inaugurated between your university and ours.

Very sincerely yours,

Tatsuo Morito
President
Hiroshima University

The above letter, we think, conveys a good deal of the spirit of the Japanese we met in 1952. It was made up, among other things, of intelligence, industry, efficiency, determination, dignity, and—we wish to stress this—friendly feeling toward us. During the Second World War another picture of the Japanese had been conveyed by those who spoke of infamy at Pearl Harbor, but it was obvious that the subdued and atom-bombed Japan of 1952 was very different from the Japan depicted on war films—the Japan of brutal soldiers, sailors, and *kamikaze* airmen. Our associates in the academic world were, for the most part, decent, generous people who later became our life-long friends. We were therefore deeply moved as we bade them farewell at the end of our stay in 1952. After we mounted the steps of our plane, we sadly waved back to the twenty or thirty men, women, and children who waved to us. We could still see their fluttering handkerchiefs from our window as we taxied away to the strip from which we were to take off, and we felt very forlorn when we thought of the thousands of miles that would soon separate us from them—forever, as we mistakenly thought at the time.

SIX

Preparing to Revisit Japan in 1960

We enjoyed our first trip to Japan so much that we tried to arrange a second one at the first opportunity that presented itself to us. When, in the fall of 1958, Morton was informed by the Center for Advanced Study in the Behavioral Sciences in Palo Alto, California, that he had been appointed a fellow there for the academic year 1959–60, we immediately began to dream of visiting Japan in the summer of 1960 after the term at the Center would be over. We thought that since we would be three thousand miles closer to Japan than we would be while at home in Cambridge, why shouldn't we try to travel directly from California? This time, however, we thought it would be great fun if our sons Nick and Steve were to come along with us. By 1960 they were eighteen and fifteen and had developed a great taste for travel. Since we had promised them in 1952 that they could come to Japan "next time," we made great efforts to keep our promise.

Such efforts would involve raising a considerable amount of money; transporting and supporting four of us would not be cheap. After extensive correspondence, the newly formed Center for American Studies in Tokyo agreed to make some funds available, but additional funds would be necessary if the whole family were to make the trip. Fortunately for us, the Harvard-Yenching Institute, then directed by Ed Reischauer, made a grant to Tokyo University that would supplement the contribution of the Center for American Studies, and therefore the trip became possible for the whole family once we scraped together other funds of our own.

Much of the correspondence with Tokyo University, where Morton would teach once again, was carried on with two of the most charming Japanese scholars known to us, Hideo Kishimoto and Shinzo Kaji. After meeting them in 1952, we had seen them often in Cambridge because they had frequently come to Harvard in the fifties, had visited our home, and, like other Japanese who had come to Harvard in that decade, had become good friends of the family. Alas, they are no longer alive. Kishimoto died of cancer after a very long and courageous fight about which he wrote a book that was widely read and greatly admired in Japan. In reading our correspondence with him, we recently came upon a sad paragraph that vividly reminded us of his up-and-down struggle with his disease. "During my trip," he wrote in March of 1959, "apparently I was carrying cancer again in a mole on the left side of my head. On my return to Japan, I went to hospital, and had it dissected. Watching the result of the operation for about six weeks, now the doctor thinks the cancer was successfully localized, and I shall be safely living for good."

Kishimoto-san did not live "for good," but he was remarkably good to us in the years we were privileged to know him. He was full of wit and vitality, and with Shinzo Kaji did an enormous amount to foster understanding between Japanese and American scholars during the period after the Second World War. Kaji was for many years a professor of economic history at Tokyo University, and at one time served as secretary to a Minister of Education. He was an expert on the working of the Japanese bureaucracy as it affected visiting American scholars in Japan. Both Kaji and Kishimoto possessed great administrative ability, and together they formed a remarkable team. They were the ultimate sources of practical wisdom for all scholars concerned with American Studies in Japan. We shall always remember their kindness to us and always cherish our friendship. They had a great deal to do with our wanting to go back to Japan in 1960.

In singling out these two elder statesmen, we must not forget others who made us eager to return, for example, Kinuko Kubota and Shozo Ohmori. Ohmori managed to overcome the philosophical prejudices that seemed to threaten his academic career in 1952 and now is one of the major philosophers of Japan. Miss Kubota is a remarkable woman who has risen high in Japanese academic circles and also in the world of international politics; for a while she was a member of the Japanese delegation to the United Nations. She is also the subject of a funny but possibly apocryphal story involving Princeton University. Being a specialist on American politics, Miss Kubota wished to attend that institution of learning shortly after we came to know her in 1952. So she applied, the story goes, without realizing that in those days Princeton did not accept female students. It seems that the Princeton authorities responsible for admitting advanced students or foreign scholars were ignorant in their way. They did not know that "Kinuko" is a woman's name. So Kinuko was duly accepted by the bastion of male chauvinism that Princeton then was, and to the ultimate surprise of the authorities, she arrived in 1953, expecting to register and commence formal academic work. Naturally, many faces were red, but all faces were saved by some academic stratagem that allowed Miss Kubota to stay on in Princeton and pursue her research. As it happened, Morton was a visiting member of the Institute for Advanced Study while Miss Kubota was studying in Princeton, and so we came to know her very well. In later years, after her rise to fame, she would remind us that she had served as a baby-sitter for us in 1953 and as a "dog-sitter" for the Perry Millers, who, as it happened, were also at the Institute that year.

Whereas Miss Kubota was one of our closest friends among the Japanese Americanists, Shozo Ohmori was our main link with Japanese philosophy. Like many of his compatriots, Ohmori had visited Harvard during the fifties and had kept up a correspondence with us from Japan. And so, once the arrangements for our 1960 trip had been completed, Ohmori wrote a very touching Christmas letter that read:

Dear White-san:

Merry Christmas and Happy New Year. After so long a silence, I feel difficult to find words to start talking, and I also feel that when I start I probably cannot know how to stop talking. But I just want to say this: 1960 is a really happy new year for me, providing me 2 months of being together with you. I am just waiting.

Shozo Ohmori

Please send my and my wife's greeting and best wishes to Mrs. White, Nick and Steve.

By the time we had received this letter in California, almost all of the arrangements for our trip had been completed. Nothing remained but the transfer of money into our pockets, and even that was accomplished before the end of April 1960. Little did we know, however, that politics and international relations might cast a shadow over our preparations.

The shadow was the result of all of the events connected with a new Japanese-American Defense Treaty and a planned visit to Japan in June 1960 by President Eisenhower. Historians and journalists have written much about the excitement surrounding the treaty and the visit, but the story that directly influenced our behavior was told by a Japanese friend who wrote to us at the time. It was this friend who, along with others, persuaded us to come to Japan and not be deterred by the feared aftermath of the so-called "Hagerty incident."

On June 19, 1960, Eisenhower was to arrive in Japan; he was to do so on the very day on which Japanese ratification of the treaty was to take place. The details of the treaty need not concern us, but it is necessary to report our friend's view of the Japanese reaction to it. For a year, he said, strong opposition to it had been brewing among socialists, intellectuals, labor unions, and college students who opposed a fresh acknowledgment of certain commitments to the United States because they feared that such commitments might involve Japan in a war. On the other hand, our friend wrote, a large number of Japanese were quite indifferent to the whole thing.

May 19, which preceded Ike's scheduled arrival by a month, was a crucial date in the Japanese ratification of the treaty. If nothing were done about the treaty on that day, the Diet would have automatically adjourned and ratification would have become impossible. Therefore, some members of the Socialist Party tried, through the use of physical force, to prevent the chairman from opening the session of the Diet on May 19. They tried to keep him in his own room. He in turn asked police to push the Socialists out of the way, and with the help of the police managed to get to the rostrum. When he got there, the Socialists were not yet in their seats, but, nevertheless, Prime Minister Kishi took what our correspondent called an "unbelievable step"—he asked for a roll call on the treaty while the opposition was not in the room. In the absence of the Socialists, the Liberal Democratic Party voted affirmatively in just a few minutes, and the treaty was overwhelmingly accepted.

On the next day, May 20, Japan exploded. Even people who usually paid no attention to politics were indignant about the prime minister's action. Kishi, our friend commented, had been for some time the object of a certain amount of distrust; he had been a member of Tojo's cabinet and a war criminal. But what he did on May 19 converted whatever underlying distrust of him there might have been into outrage and animosity. The issue of the treaty itself receded into the background, and Kishi himself became the issue. People demanded his resignation; enormous demonstrations took place; two big general strikes were called. Kishi, however, underestimated the intensity of national feeling and stubbornly persisted in the notion that it would die down in a few weeks. He announced cavalierly that it was all the work of leftist agitators and that the majority of the Japanese people were on his side, a view that was apparently shared by the American ambassador to Tokyo, MacArthur (not to be confused with General MacArthur).

Eisenhower's scheduled visit was, as we have said, to take place on June 19, which was just one month after Kishi's action, an interval of time which had great political significance. According to Japanese parliamentary rules if a resolution is passed in the Lower House of the Diet, it automatically becomes law in one month should no action on it be taken by the Upper House. This made it clear, our correspondent said, that Kishi had timed Eisenhower's visit so that it would coincide with what Kishi had expected would be automatic ratification of the treaty. His opponents reckoned that this would strengthen Kishi's position, and they therefore urged that Eisenhower's visit be postponed. Kishi refused, and in his refusal he was supported by the Liberal Democratic Party and by big business circles in Japan.

Now the story reaches the "Hagerty incident." James Hagerty, Eisenhower's press secretary, flew to Tokyo some time before June 19 to assess the situation. Our correspondent reported that this was probably viewed by the Japanese Communist Party as their chance. So far, he said, college students under the party's influence "had been quiet and well-behaved," but now they saw an opportunity to lead a mass movement in an anti-American direction. They came in droves to the airport, mobbed Hagerty's aircraft there, and prevented about fifty socialist members of the Diet from talking to him. The situation was chaotic. Japanese who were opposed to Kishi and the treaty became anxious about Japanese-American relations and continued to press Kishi to postpone Eisenhower's visit, but Kishi continued to refuse.

Then, our friend wrote, another dreadful thing happened in this chain of disastrous events. Some leftist college students—not Communists, our friend emphasized—broke into the garden of the building in which the Diet met, "and naturally a small war between them and policemen started." A female student was killed in the stampede, other students were seriously injured, and many policemen were hurt. And this finally led Kishi to call off Eisenhower's visit. In the aftermath of the girl's death, most universities and colleges closed down. Teachers and students gathered to protest. President Kaya of Tokyo University issued a statement in which he asked the politicians to do something about the situation, and he was publicly reproached by the Minister of Education. Anti-Kishi forces once again demanded the premier's resignation and he again refused. His opponents laid all the blame on him, and he laid it all on leftist intrigue. Our friend wrote: "We are now in the biggest political crisis since the end of the war."

He said that on the next day the funeral of the dead girl would take place, adding that he was sure that it would proceed peacefully. Although he expressed fears about a demonstration that was scheduled for the evening after the funeral, he concluded his letter by assuring us that the targets of Japanese hostility were Kishi and the treaty, not the United States. In buses, in department stores, in the university, he said, there was no feeling against individual Americans. Finally, he said that we should not worry about coming, that he hoped we would not change our minds about coming, and that the seminar would be attended by more than thirty people.

Other Japanese friends and colleagues also urged us to come. We had written Shinzo Kaji to ask him whether the Hagerty incident should prevent us from making the trip, and he immediately wired that we should come as scheduled. Professor Takeo Iwasaki of the Tokyo Department of Philosophy wrote to express his regret about the situation but insisted that there was no anti-American feeling in Japan, only "Anti-Kishi-Governmental feeling." He went on to say: "You need not have the slightest anxiety about coming to Japan with your family." Our friend Ohmori wrote in the same vein, and so we finally decided to make the trip. We delayed our departure for a while because Morton's father had become seriously ill. However, as soon as we were assured by his physician that it would be all right to leave the States, we followed the advice of our Japanese friends and left for Tokyo on July 3.

Professor Iwasaki would be in charge of the seminar. He mercifully wrote that the class would meet only three times a week for a period of four weeks, a schedule that was far less onerous than that of 1952. Iwasaki, with characteristic precision, remarked that in 1952 Morton had met his seminar "twenty times" and that the diminished workload in 1960 would be similar to that which had been assigned to Morton's Harvard colleague W. V. Quine in the summer of 1959. As in 1952, however, there would also be a "Specialist Conference" to be addressed "two or three times," and, for good measure, "some public lectures for the students in the University of Tokyo." When Morton read about this assignment of duties and thought about the heat of Japan in July, he swallowed hard but continued to believe that a family trip to Tokyo would be worth the sweat and the exhaustion!

The title of the seminar would be "The Language of History," and it would deal with certain problems in the philosophy of history. As in the seminar in 1952, Morton would do most of the talking. Therefore, the seminar would in effect consist of twelve lectures, each lecture being followed by a brief period for questions and comments by members of the audience. The outline of the seminar would follow that of a course Morton gave at Harvard on "The Nature and Function of History"; in subject-matter it would resemble that of his book, *Foundations of Historical Knowledge*, which was later published in 1965. One of his main motives in giving such a seminar was to show that the tools of analytic philosophy could be applied to problems more typically treated by European than by American philosophers. Another motive was his desire to address problems that were of concern to the many Japanese philosophers who were under the influence of Marxism and in this way to show the relevance of logical analysis to problems that were thought by the Japanese to have great political significance.

All of this was described in a letter to Iwasaki, where three modes of historical discourse were mentioned as constituting the main concerns of the lectures. First, the discourse of those who produced so-called speculative philosophies of history, for example, Marx and Toynbee. In lectures on this kind of language, the following problems would be treated: the notion of law in history (which would require discussion of the notion of scientific law); the relationship between the speculative philosophy of history and metaphysics; the problem of free will as it affects historical thinking; and the notion of a fundamental factor in history, for example, the economic factor as conceived by Marx or the idea of challenge-and-response as conceived by Toynbee.

The next mode of historical language to be treated was that employed by historians who made explanatory or causal statements without necessarily accepting grandiose speculative theories such as those advanced by Marx and Toynbee; for example, an explanatory statement like "Japan became a maritime nation after the beginning of the Meiji era because it had to import foodstuffs." Some of the problems to be discussed while considering this mode of discourse would be: the role of generalization in this sort of explanation; the relationship between such an explanation and social science; and the question whether this sort of explanation requires a special method that distinguishes history from other disciplines.

Finally, narrative discourse, the telling of a story, would be the third main subject. Here the major problem would be the need for selection and the attendant question as to whether such selection is guided by values and preferences of the historian, values and preferences which cannot be objectively supported. Here the idea of *historical relativism* would automatically become a major concern. By the time this third topic had been discussed, the lectures would have treated the three great problems of fact, law, and value in historical thinking. Morton thought he sounded like a nineteenth-century German philosopher when he used these impressive words, but, of course, he would be using them in the surgical, deflationary manner of a logical analyst, thereby showing the Japanese that Anglo-American philosophy was not confined to discussing trivia by any standards.

After spelling all of this out to Iwasaki-san, Morton added that he was prepared to deliver three lectures to the so-called "Specialists." The lectures were entitled as follows: "Pragmatism and the Scope of Science," "Moral Judgment and Human Freedom," and "Some Problems in the Philosophy of History." Looking back at what he attempted to do in those four sultry weeks of 1960, Morton wonders how he could have managed to do it. Fortunately, the task of delivering lectures to undergraduates was forgotten by his Japanese colleagues. It is hard to think that he would have survived the summer if they had not disappeared from the agenda originally prepared by his generous, but intellectually voracious hosts.

SEVEN

Revisiting Japan in 1960

So far we have confined ourselves mainly to preparations for our trip; it is now time to say something about what we found when we got to Japan in the summer of 1960. We arrived there in a broad-winged Pan American jet, a plane which had by then replaced the Stratocruiser as the main vehicle whereby tourists were carried to Japan. It was about seven o'clock in the morning of July 4, and a warm sun had already risen at Haneda Airport. As we walked toward the immigration building, we caught sight of Nobushige Sawada, a professor of philosophy at Keio University in Tokyo. We had come to know him well in between our two visits because he had studied at Harvard during this interval. He was a handsome man who could easily be taken for an Italian. He greeted us warmly, as did the other two members of our faithful welcome committee, Iwasaki and the ever helpful Ohmori. All of them had turned out once again to greet us after having also come to the airport on the previous day. Unfortunately, we had mistakenly sent word that we would arrive on the third day of July because we had taken the word of a travel agent who had failed to reckon with the dislocation produced by the International Date Line. We arrived quite safely anyway and proceeded through customs easily. The inspection was smooth and even perfunctory by comparison to the chattering confusion of 1952. The Occupation was over, and, accordingly, the atmosphere was much less martial. Fewer uniforms and fewer guns were in evidence; we felt much less nervous. Our welcome committee invited us to enter a big black limousine with jump seats and baggage rack. We did so and were transported into Tokyo by our hosts.

The streets were of the same interminable gray. We saw gray paving, gray dirt, and gray buildings that were single-storeyed shops, double-storeyed shops, or concrete factory structures. The road from the airport was as depressing and filthy looking as it was on our first visit, but when we said this to Ohmori—to whom we could speak quite candidly about such matters—he assured us that Tokyo had changed a great deal in other parts.

Once again we were treated to the exciting and frightening experience of Japanese traffic, fortified, however, by the size of our powerful, big automobile. The traffic raced along in the usual frenzied fashion, accompanied by the playful-sounding beepings of horns. There appeared to be many more cars on the highway—mostly small compact sedans that used gas economically.

After travelling for perhaps half an hour across urban stretches, we dashed up a little hill and entered a winding driveway to International House, which was to be our Tokyo residence. It was built during the period of our absence and, in some degree, represented the growing affluence of Japan. It was then a modern three-story building of gray concrete piers and glass panels set on a hillside with a pleasant garden of lawn and trees along one side. When we entered the handsome lobby, we were impressed by the speed with which four weary travellers were taken care of. Once again the reception desk was manned by very young people (or so they seemed to Western eyes) and many of them. We speculated that the low cost of labor led to *over*-staffing and to the formation of bureaucracies, even in relatively small outfits like this hostelry. Thus, when beds were turned down before dinner, they were turned down, we observed, by a team of *two* young men. We were, at the time of that first encounter with International House, not sure what kind of an institution it was. We had the impression that it was some sort of intellectual center, but later we saw parties of businessmen there all the time as well as elaborate wedding parties. There was a Rotary Club sign at the front door on the day of our arrival; it was probably announcing a meeting. However, we also saw some unmistakably academic people in the lobby of this hybrid institution.

As soon as we had gone through the rituals of registry, our hosts left us to rest up from our trip in the pleasant, modern, and ultra-simple study-bedrooms that are characteristic of International House. In those days, they all had a distinguished Japanese print or two on the walls. In the room we occupied there was a scene of a snowy village against a series of peaked, snow-covered mountains. The artist was the famous printmaker Utamaro. Among the other furnishings in our room there were, in addition to lamps, two single beds with good firm mattresses backed up by a joint head panel; three or four modern chairs of wood with upholstered backs and seats; a coffee table; and a couple of bed tables. The wood in all of these pieces of furniture was light in color. They were tastefully contrasted with a combination of handsome coverings: plain navy blue floor-length curtains that could be pulled across the whole side of the room; shoji screens that could be pulled to cover the glass windowpanel; and sliding screens to keep out insects.

When our curtains and shoji screen were open, we could see the grass-covered smooth roof of the central dining-room below us. Beyond that we saw a garden with a stone lantern at the edge of a little valley that was surrounded by low bushes. To the left of the lantern a sand path wound up the hill toward a tiered stone shrine set among pine trees. Behind this, and stretching across the whole length of the hill, was a screen of carefully trimmed trees. We were to observe later in the evening that the bank of smaller trees just above the garden was palely lit by some system of reflected light while the taller more distant trees remained dark at night. This garden, we were told later, remained as it had been before the war, when the land belonged to the estate of a Baron Iwasaki—not to be confused with Professor Iwasaki, who was no relation.

As we had arrived at the airport at seven in the morning, lunch was our first meal. After lunch and naps, we decided to go on the town in the evening. We invited Shozo Ohmori and his wife to come out to dinner with us, and he replied that *he* would be glad to come. His wife, he said, was busy with the "enfant terrible," his second child. We did not doubt that the need to baby-sit served to keep Reiko Ohmori away from our party as it might have in the States, but we wondered whether another, more Japanese factor might not have played a part in the situation. It was not expected or required that a husband take his wife to social parties, especially those to which he had been invited by foreign friends. Here Ohmori was acting very "Japanesey," as Hideo Kishimoto used to say when joking about the traditionalism of some of his colleagues. This "Japanesiness" also emerged when we invited both Ohmoris to join us on a two-week tour of Japan after the end of Morton's seminar. Ohmori spoke of the Japanese wife's great responsibilities—the children and the dog—when dismissing the idea that she should join us. And he was probably more Western and Americanized than any Japanese we knew. His paradoxical behavior was also evident in his persistent refusal to accept our invitation to call us by our first names and to allow us to reciprocate. Many other Japanese had relented on this issue, but not Ohmori, whom we came to think of as a sort of *samurai* beneath the skin—and not so deeply beneath the skin.

Well, the *samurai* was not too Japanese to take us to a French restaurant when we asked him to pick one out. It was called the "Wagon D'Or," and it sat on the top floor of a ten-storey skyscraper in the Shibuya district. We were able to begin with a martini made of Gordon's gin and with I. W. Harper Bourbon—something that struck us as new by comparison to 1952, when it was normally impossible to buy such drinks in most restaurants. The headwaiter took our orders in good English, another surprise. Some things, of course, remained the same. The usual large bottles of Japanese beer—Asahi and Kirin—were available and there were the familiar pickly, old, and tired-looking hors d'oevres. However, we were served excellent steaks, and so we were restored and developed enough strength to go walking after our meal.

Shibuya was then a very trafficky center with chaotic streets and many tall commercial buildings. We also saw a large, expensive-looking movie theater that showed American films. We walked down the side street of beer halls and *pachinko* joints, where we passed an odoriferous canal. It was between ten and eleven at night, and when we asked Ohmori whether it was a dangerous neighborhood, he said: "Notorious but not dangerous," leaving us with some doubt about what he meant by "dangerous." In any case, it was the electrically lighted, dazzling Orient of a hot summer night that we saw—countless scurrying people, enormous Times Square-like advertisements blinking madly, coffee shops, bars, clothing-shops, screeching brakes, overhead elevated trains, heat, wet sidewalks, and drunks. The average age of the swarming pedestrians seemed extremely low and, by comparison to 1952, there were fewer women—almost none—in traditional costume. Ohmori explained the absence of kimonos by pointing out that they were very expensive.

On our first day, however, we were unable to see startling differences between '60 and '52. The same heat, noise, politeness, dirt, electrification, desire to be Western and efficient, and awful smells at various points in Tokyo—sometimes from food, more often from worse. And we detected no anti-American feeling in the crowds in Shibuya, though we thought that a man spat in our direction when we came out on the street near International House. Apart from this incident, Ohmori's views on this score had been confirmed, but, of course, we would have other opportunities to test them. The boys seemed to enjoy Tokyo immensely and were excited by the pleasant prospects there. They found it no hotter than Boston in the summer!

The next day—really our first in Tokyo—broke through a pearly gray mist. Pale circles of blue appeared at 6 A.M., followed by a heavy blanket of gray clouds for a couple of hours, and then moistly warm air enveloped the city as we started our fifteen yen bus ride to central Tokyo. That summer we were able to get 358 yen for a dollar, which gives some idea of how cheap that bus ride was. And if the price does not make clear how cheap things were for an American visiting Japan in 1960, surely the following figures will. The price of a double room with shower in International House was $4.95 a day and a single room cost $3.30 a day; so the four of us paid $11.55 a day for our lodgings in three rooms.

Upon reaching central Tokyo, we got our bearings by rediscovering our old haunts of 1952, the Nikkatsu and Imperial Hotels. We also found what was still labelled "Avenue A"—it had been called that by the Occupation—as we walked near the Imperial Palace and Hibya Park. We saw many more ten-story buildings than we had seen in 1952, a great deal of construction going on, and many more cars. The scaffolding for the new buildings consisted of heavy wooden poles bound together, and while the construction went on, hordes of youthful people made their way around the dangerous construction sites. Very little power machinery was used, but the materials, steel and reinforced concrete, looked quite modern. Every kind of structure was being built or rebuilt during this boom: office buildings, roadways, sewers, and subways. But not many residential houses were under construction even though the need for them was very great. There were enormous numbers of laborers who wore oddly shaped knickers and long-sleeved shirts along with their hard hats.

We saw only a few women in kimonos and the traditional footgear as we marched about the Ginza, and there were many elderly women crouching along the walls while carrying on a brisk business shining shoes for men. We went to the arcades of the Nikkatsu and Imperial Hotels to shop for American soap and then plunged into the waterfall-cooled doorway of Takashimaya's department store to seek other necessities. We taxied home amid the swiftly cavorting traffic and found that the cab drivers would still honk mercilessly at people on bicycles. The cyclists often seemed to be in the outside lanes between two streams of automobile traffic, often as not steering with one hand while carrying a bundle or even a tea tray with the other!

Soon after our taxi had brought us back to "I. House," as some Japanese called International House, we welcomed Iwasaki in the lobby at about 6:30 P.M. His round, up-curved eyes looked very grave, but a tiny smile was on his lips. We had invited him to dine with us, but to our surprise and pleasure, our old friend Shinzo Kaji also appeared in the lobby at about the same time. His face lit up brightly upon seeing us, and he looked much less tired than he did when he visited us a while back in Cambridge where he was guiding the baseball-loving sage, Nyozekan Hasegawa, on a tour of the States. Unfortunately, however, Shinzo—who, unlike Ohmori, was always happy to be "on first-name basis" with us—was very thin and his hand shook violently as he lit his many cigarettes. We knew him as what the Japanese called a "strong drinker" and feared that his habit was seriously affecting his health.

Seeing Kaji, we told him that Iwasaki-san was joining us for dinner and that we would be delighted if he would also join the party. Shinzo replied that, alas, he had already eaten and therefore could not join us. Just after Kaji left the bar, where we were all having drinks, we informed Iwasaki that we had not planned to eat at International House and so wondered whether he would be good enough to recommend a good Chinese restaurant. At this point we immediately saw the difference between the worldly, practical, economist Kaji and the shy philosopher Iwasaki. The latter became alarmed, as he invariably seemed to become—we came to see this more clearly later on—when he had to make decisions. He indicated, very politely, that it would have been wise to have raised this question while Kaji had been with us, since Kaji was an expert on such practical matters. We said that we were very sorry, but that we were sure we could rely on his judgment. Iwasaki smiled and shook his head in modest (or perhaps immodest) disagreement; we were not sure whether he was loftily setting himself above such matters or modestly proclaiming his ignorance about them.

As chance would have it, Iwasaki and the four of us came up to the lobby from the bar in the basement and who should we discover in the lobby but Kaji making a telephone call at the reception desk. Iwasaki was terribly relieved and rushed to him at once, imploring him in Japanese to recommend a Chinese restaurant. Kaji rose to the occasion. He took charge as he swept his innocent junior colleague aside, and for the rest of the evening Kaji *was* in charge. Whatever other plans he might have had were forgotten and he determined to see that we got what we wanted. This was typical of the way in which we were treated by our Japanese friends through all of our years of visiting their country. Kaji grandly declared "I will arrange" as he shook his head up and down and gave us his beguiling smile. Picking up the receiver he had just dropped, he proceeded to call a restaurant he described as excellent. When we asked about Ting's, which we had known in 1952, he dismissed it as having become inferior. Instead, he ordered a cab which transported all six of us to something called "The Royal."

Upon our arrival at the two-storey restaurant, we were greeted by a long-faced, sinister-looking captain, a round-faced pretty woman dressed in Chinese clothes, and a bevy of bowing, chattering waitresses. As we ascended to the upper floor, where our private dining-room was, the girls and their hostess-leader chanted in high voices: "Arrigato gozaimashita, arrigato gozaimashita" in a steady, sweet tone. Why they said "Thank you" in the past tense before we began we could not quite understand; probably they were thanking us for coming.

As soon as we were seated, a procession of waitresses, including one with long black braids, quickly entered our room and placed a series of dishes on the lazy Susan in the center of the table. One of the dishes was a large plate of cold hors d'oeuvres with a prehistoric chill and appearance; it was an arrangement of chicken, pork, pickled celery perhaps, and a convulsed mass of what looked like transparent spaghetti that turned out to be jelly fish. It was not very good, and when chewed, it made little snapping reports in one's head. This was followed by delicious shrimp in red sauce that clearly had fresh chopped ginger in it; then thin slices of abalone steak with flat mushrooms and tiny spring pea pods; Peking duck for white puffy roll-sandwiches; a delicious soup and rice; then green tea. There were also purple "thousand year old" eggs to begin with and, in the soup, tiny, hard-boiled plover eggs.

Throughout the meal we drank quantities of beer, which, in combination with so much food and lingering jet fatique, made us very sleepy. And as we became sleepier, we became more and more silent. Iwasaki rolled his eyes in fright, getting drunk on the quantities of beer he was quaffing. He said very little except to remark on the business of the seminar. He mentioned that he had been in China twice, once in wartime, and then said in answer to a question of Lucia's that he had been born in India, where his father had served as a diplomat.

Kaji, as usual, was full of charm and information. He told us things about Japanese grammar. He said he would arrange to get our books from the express agency that had transported them from the States, would take us to a baseball game, and would even accompany us on a trip to the country for a few days. "Last time," he said, "you saw the Japanese city-side; now you must see the country-side." Kaji did not eat; he merely kept us company. There was some discussion as to whether the meal was authentically Chinese or whether it was influenced by Japanese cuisine. Nick was doubtful about a suggestion by Morton that the meal was not *echt* Chinese.

After we came downstairs, Iwasaki unfurled his umbrella as he left us at the restaurant door while Kaji hailed a cab. We dropped Kaji off at his home and then proceeded to International House.

After many preliminary conversations with Iwasaki about the mechanics of the seminar, Morton was obliged to carry out the difficult task of getting hold of the books which had been shipped from the States. They had been sent by International Railway Express, and we had been led to believe that they would be delivered to us at International House. However, we were mistaken. Apparently we should have declared them to be "unaccompanied" when we entered Japan. For this reason Morton had first of all to return to Haneda Airport to have his revised declaration registered. Second, he would have to go personally to Yokohama to pick up the books unless he was willing—as he was not—to hand his passport over to the express agency so that they could pick up the books. On this double trip to Haneda and Yokohama, Morton was accompanied by Nick and the faithful Ohmori.

Ohmori served as chauffeur, being the owner of what Morton described in his journal as "a tidy-looking auto called a Dat-Sun." Little did he know that this oddly named sort of car of which he had never heard before would almost destroy the vaunted American automobile industry in less than twenty years. Moreover, it was Ohmori, the son of a banker, who predicted in 1960 that Japan would soon be one of the world's leading industrial nations. If Ohmori had had enough money in those days to invest in Japanese industry—especially in the Japanese automobile industry—he might well have become a millionaire. Well, he was not a millionaire on July 7, 1960, when he squeezed Nick and Morton into his tiny Datsun and drove them the thirty miles or so to Yokohama. He drove it very well indeed, considering that he had been a driver for only two months. And, it might be added, if he had told Morton how recently he had started to drive,

Morton would not have dared to allow himself and Nick to be passengers. Be that as it may, the trip was not only safe but extremely interesting.

Nick and Morton were treated to a view of a great industrial part of Japan. They saw mile after mile of belching chimneys, electrical plants, chemical plants, and God knows what other kinds of plants that stretched along Tokyo Bay in a manner reminiscent of Chicago, Pittsburgh, Gary, Indiana, and parts of Philadelphia. Many of those plants were constructed after the massive bombing of Japan during the Second World War, and, according to Ohmori, they were instruments of what he was already calling Japan's economic recovery. Like Germany's, that recovery was the result of instituting new industrial techniques after old plants had been levelled. Of course, it was not without its human price, for we saw the usual dust, rust, and filth of an industrial center. We also saw drunks wandering in danger across the main road, as well as some wretched scavengers. On the way back, trucks barrelled along as they emitted their filthy exhaust. For those who did not care about the price of "progress," this represented a happy change from 1952, when Professor Ohara had painted so dismal a picture of Japan's economy in his talk at the Karuizawa conference. After all, Japanese technology was now on its way to becoming what was commonly called "Number One" at a later date.

Talk with Ohmori of Japanese industry soon led to talk of Japanese politics. He was opposed to the Security or Defense Treaty with the United States, though he admitted that the Socialists had made a dreadful mistake in trying forcibly to prevent the convening of the Diet for discussion of the treaty. But he also thought that Kishi's introduction of police into the Diet had been an even greater error. In his candid way, moreover, he granted that many Japanese who were opposed to the treaty could not present any alternative way of defending their country, stripped as it had been of a serious defense force. He acknowledged a curious sort of helplessness in the situation and added that the Socialists lacked the confidence of the people. He also reported that the intellectuals were 95 per cent opposed to the Kishi government after May 19, the day on which he produced his "sneak-vote" while the Socialists were out of the chamber. The political sympathies of the intellectuals might well be explained in part by their economic circumstances. Ohmori, for example, was earning $100 a month as an assistant professor of philosophy at Tokyo University.

When Morton and Nick returned from Yokohama, they found Lucia and Steve at I. House, where they had been spending the day in more sedentary pursuits. Steve had been playing chess with himself while Lucia wrote letters and studied some Japanese. Upon being reunited, we had cool drinks in the garden of I. House, where we also had an excellent supper that cost only $7.00 for all of us, whereas the meal for five at the Royal Restaurant had cost $25.00. Perhaps, we mused, that was because the Royal was purveyor to the Chinese Embassy.

On the trip to Yokohama we learned about Ohmori's views on Japanese-American relations, but he was not our only source on this complicated subject. We also learned directly about the reactions of a much more exalted figure in Japan and a much more influential figure in Japanese-American circles, Shigeharu Matsumoto. In 1952 we had met him at Karuizawa; by 1960 he had become director of International House and a prominent politician-scholar who was said to be very pro-American. He was very active in pro-American circles and a central figure in many projects that involved travel by Japanese and American intellectuals to and from the States. His position as director of I. House gave him an unusual opportunity to meet visiting Americans and to have close contact with the American Embassy.

Matsumoto, according to his own description, was in "the middle of the road" politically, so he felt free to criticize both the conservatives and the leftists. He criticized leftist professors for using "two standards," one in their academic thinking and one in what he kept calling their "strategic" thinking. We gathered that by using the word "strategic" he meant to imply that some leftist professors were inclined to support whatever they conceived as a "progressive force," no matter how such support conflicted with their academic standards of truth and moral integrity. Hence, he said, some of them encouraged the student demonstrators, expressed sympathy for the Socialists, and failed to see how the Communists were using so-called progressive sentiment in Japan.

Matsumoto's willingness to criticize political conservatism emerged in his remarks about the American ambassador. In a long conversation with us, Matsumoto described some difficulties he had had with Ambassador MacArthur. His account was of great interest if only because it showed that even an avowedly pro-American Japanese could have problems with the embassy in those confused days after the Hagerty incident. Matsumoto first related a story involving President Kaya of Tokyo University. Kaya had frequently implored or warned his students not to disrupt their work and not to engage in disturbances. But then the death of the female student during one of the riots prompted Kaya to make a statement in which, by implication, it was thought, he called upon the Kishi government to resign. This statement was given great publicity whereas his earlier statements were not. Moreover, this statement was interpreted by the ambassador as signifying hostility to the United States, and so he "asked" Kaya to resign from his membership on the committee that administered the Eisenhower Scholarship. Matsumoto was chairman of that committee, on which Professor Y. Takagi, the "dean" of American Studies in Japan, also sat, along with the American who headed the Fulbright Commission and a few others whose names we did not get. The Eisenhower scholar was given funds to permit travel abroad, mainly to the United States.

Matsumoto regarded the ambassador's treatment of Kaya as "outrageous." Yet he said he had "swallowed" it because he felt that if a fuss had been made about it publicly and the Japanese people had learned of it, a national uproar would have taken place. Since he was too interested in cordial Japanese-American relations to allow this to happen, he decided not to fight Ambassador MacArthur on the issue.

The Kaya incident was not the only one to produce friction between Matsumoto and the ambassador. It seems that the committee had decided to award a scholarship to a Japanese from Keio University, who, although a devout Catholic, had been persuaded by the Quakers to become a pacifist. On his application the candidate outlined his views concerning a number of matters and was led to say, among other things, that he was opposed to the Security Treaty. The committee had felt that he should not, to say the least, be penalized for his candor, and they selected him for the award. But the ambassador "vetoed" the selection. When we asked whether the ambassador had the formal right to veto it, Matsumoto said he did not know. In any case, he added that on this issue he was going to resist and that he was going to raise the question of the ambassador's right to veto the committee's recommendation.

Whether Matsumoto did resist or raise the issue we never discovered. But it was plain that he disliked the ambassador, who, therefore, must have had virtually no friends or admirers among Japanese intellectuals and scholars. Yet there was no doubt that the intellectuals had great political power in the Japan of 1960. After all, *students* had forced the cancellation of Eisenhower's visit, and Matsumoto went so far as to say that if the economy had not been in such good shape, the students might have fomented a revolution after some of the events surrounding the Hagerty incident, the antics of Kishi, and the death of the co-ed.

Although we found Matsumoto quite formal and reserved, we never doubted his intelligence or his influence in circles likely to be sympathetic to America. Moreover, he was usually very convincing when he commented on Japanese politics. For example, he shrewdly remarked that some leftist professors were under a kind of spell or psychological pressure to move together on issues like the Security Treaty and that it was rare for any one of them to stand up against the prevailing opinion of their colleagues on such matters. On the other hand, Matsumoto showed that his position really was in the middle of the road when he spoke of the Conservative "tyranny of the majority." (It should be remembered that the word "Conservatives," confusingly enough, referred to members of the Liberal Democratic Party.) Matsumoto definitely did not approve of Kishi's railroading of the treaty through the Diet in eight minutes even though Matsumoto was much more critical than Ohmori had been when commenting on the Socialists' interference with the parliamentary process.

One final story about Matsumoto's dealings with Ambassador MacArthur. He had been one of three Japanese intellectuals—the others were Y. Takagi and Koizumi, former tutor of the crown prince—who had asked for a thirty-minute audience with the ambassador in order to say why they felt that Eisenhower should not make his visit at that time. Instead of listening to them, Matsumoto said in consternation, the ambassador lectured them for twenty-five minutes. Takagi was reported to have said that he had never been so humiliated in all his life and that he had been treated far more cordially by Ambassador Grew just before war had broken out between Japan and America, when Takagi had visited Grew to present "the Japanese case." Matsumoto added that the ambassador called the State Department after his meeting with Takagi, Koizumi, and Matsumoto, to say (falsely) that Matsumoto had changed his mind about Ike's visit and that he no longer opposed it. In any event, at some point in this sequence of events, Matsumoto, Takagi, and other Japanese intellectuals cabled Eisenhower and asked him to delay or cancel his visit.

About ten days after this talk with Matsumoto, Morton wrote in his journal: "Today I met Henry Rosovsky, a Berkeley economic historian who specializes on Japan. We chatted pleasantly about friends we have in common and then began to talk about the [political] situation . . . he has loaned me a translation, made by someone else, of President Kaya's celebrated statement." The statement follows:

At a Turning Point
A Chain Reaction of Corrupt Politics
by
Seiji Kaya
President of Tokyo University

I am pleased that President Eisenhower's visit to Japan has been delayed. As the uneasiness of the students arises from undemocratic action, if there were only some prospects for alteration in the situation I believe that their feelings would also undergo some change. I would very much like to see the student movement return to a peaceful state. However, a prerequisite for that is a return to the rules which have been broken, and this would restore the confidence of the students in politics. I should like the politicians to save the current situation, keeping this in mind.

I am a natural scientist, and looking at the student movement since May 19th I feel very keenly that it is in the nature of a "chain reaction." In physics even if there is a stimulus a chain reaction will not occur without adequate "cause." The methods of Zengakuren are violent. There is also the opinion that it is moved to action by Communism, and it may be true to some extent that there is Communist influence in Zengakuren. But in the absence of a broadly based discontent and uneasiness a "chain reaction" of this magnitude could not be brought about by mere agitation. And even if it did we would be able to end it.

The basic "cause" of the chain reaction lies in politics outside the universities. And the only thing that can remove that "cause" is politics which will save the situation. One thing I wish to say to the students is that I hope the student movement is at a turning point.

It should be evident by now that Japanese academics were not living in an ivory tower during the hectic summer of 1960. And yet our Japanese friends had been correct in predicting that American civilians would not be subjected to animosity in spite of the political furor surrounding the visit of their president. This was obvious on the occasion of one of Morton's talks to "specialists." On July 9, he gave such a talk at Keio University in which he outlined the lecture he was to give in his seminar. Professors Nobushige Sawada and Minoru Murai, his former students at Harvard in the fifties, had cordially asked him to come to Keio and to speak to a small group consisting of members of the Department of Philosophy and their advanced students. We met in a stately, musty, wooden panelled room whose plaster ceiling had medallions on it for decoration. Over the fireplace was a gloomily fascinating portrait of Fukuzawa Yukichi, who helped to found Keio University and a copy of whose famous autobiography was presented to us. The audience sat on sofas at the side of the room, but their behavior reminded us of Haydn's *Farewell Symphony*; every few minutes one of the professors would depart—perhaps for an appointment, perhaps not—until there were only ten left. One of those who stayed for the whole performance was an elderly gentleman, about five feet tall, bald, and very stocky. He alternately frowned and scowled while the corners of his mouth turned down further during the lecture. He disappeared precipitately after the lecturer's last word, so neither of us ever did learn what was affecting him.

Before the lecture had begun there was some tense sociability. A charming Keio professor of philosophy named Matsumoto—not to be confused with Shigeharu Matsumoto—tried to keep some conversational banter going before the talk. After all of the social hemming and hawing, Morton began his talk. He spoke of his desire to expand the philosophy of language into a study of more than the language of physics and mathematics, thereby preparing the way for what he had to say about the language of history. Then he gave a thumbnail sketch of the course of lectures he was about to give in his seminar. In spite of the Haydnesque departures mentioned earlier, enough people had remained to prevent embarrassment for all concerned, but the only one of them to speak was a young logician who had been trained in Paris and whose questions showed considerable intelligence.

At about five o'clock the session was over. It was followed by light applause in the room and by crashing thunder outside, where a torrential rain was falling.

Apparently the lack of extended discussion after the lecture did not signify lack of cordiality on the part of the Keio philosophers. After bringing us back to International House, they returned in a couple of hours in order to bring only Morton—or perhaps both of us—to a dinner party which turned out to be very jolly. But first a word about the ambiguity of the invitation. Lucia and Morton had *thought* that she had been invited until it became evident that Mrs. Sawada and Mrs. Murai would not attend the dinner. American women would often be invited to parties to which Japanese women were *not* invited, but this gesture was made only in deference to American custom. So Lucia decided not to go, whether or not she had been expected to go. However, when Sawada arrived at International House, he asked where Lucia was when he saw Morton waiting in the lobby alone. Whether this was politeness that masked relief we shall never know. He expressed sorrow about Lucia's not being able to come—we don't remember what excuse she gave.

When the scholars assembled at the restaurant, it was obvious that if Lucia had come, she would have been the only woman in the house apart from the waitresses. It seemed perfectly clear that this place was "for men only." Its male chauvinism seemed as religiously observed as its vegetarianism. Once the gentlemen had removed their shoes and entered, they were ushered by the proprietress into a lovely dining room that faced a garden. It seemed as though they would be eating on a low porch and that they would be devouring their cooked vegetables while looking at uncooked vegetables in the garden. Fourteen or fifteen different kinds of vegetables were served, and they were prepared in an astonishing number of different ways. Morton had never eaten a meal like it and has never eaten one like it since then. Sawada, Murai, the French-trained logician, and a Mr. Kiyooka—a descendant of Fukazawa and the author of a text-book called *Japanese in Thirty Hours*—royally entertained Morton for what seemed like thirty hours as they served him beer, saké, and indescribable food. There was even some philosophical discussion during the evening, and questions were asked which could well have been asked immediately after the lecture. Morton could not avoid the feeling that his Keio friends preferred to discuss philosophy in the alcohol-drenched atmosphere of a garden.

The mood of this *Symposium*-like gathering was very different from that of the seminar. There the lectures produced a lively response. As might have been expected, the few Marxists in attendance reacted unfavorably to some of the things said in criticism of Marx's philosophy of history, but any Marxists who did attend were not very orthodox. Had they been so, they would have been much sharper in their criticism. As a matter of fact, *very* orthodox Marxists—members of the Communist Party, for example—could not be expected to attend a seminar conducted by someone whom they would be bound to call a lackey of the capitalists. As a result, the exchange between Morton and the moderate Marxists was polite and profitable. In the eight years since 1952, Japanese philosophers were showing the effects of their contact with American philosophy. Their questions were clearer and more pointed; they had been trained to good effect in logic and the philosophy of science. They respected currents of thought which the older generation—Professor Ikegami's—could not fully understand or appreciate. And this made Morton feel that his own small contribution to international understanding—in philosophy at any rate— was not without effect.

The job of lecturing to the seminar on the philosophy of history and to the specialists on other matters was more than enough to keep Morton busy. The lectures stimulated much more active discussion than their predecessors had in 1952, and this was very encouraging. By 1960 Japanese philosophers had not only become more familiar with the method of philosophy used by American analytic philosophers; they no longer seemed as docile as they had been. They asked more questions, registered more objections, and in general seemed more confident. No longer did they rise and bow when the lecturer entered the seminar room. All of that academic ritual had disappeared in eight short years; the excessive deference and obeisance that had been so disconcerting in 1952 was a thing of the past—or so the lecturer hoped.

EIGHT

A Miscellany of Experiences in 1960

Although philosophy, politics, and economic change
were of great interest to us in 1960, our lives were filled with a variety of
experiences that were not easily accommodated by those august categories.
We travelled, marvelled at monuments and art-objects, visited homes gaped
at people in the streets, walked, rode in automobiles, and enjoyed ourselves
in restaurants and inns. We talked with old friends, tried to make new ones,
and strove to capture what was interesting about Japanese life, whether traditional or significantly different from what we had seen in 1952. But although some of the things we saw and felt in 1960 were obviously connected with social, political, economic, or intellectual changes of the sort we
have already mentioned, others were not. They were interesting or enjoyable for their own sakes and not because they illustrated some kind of
phenomenon that a sociologist, economist, political scientist, or an-
thropologist might discourse about learnedly.

One sort of pleasant experience that was obviously connected with a
changing economy was that of visiting the houses of some of our friends.
They now seemed better able to entertain us and also less self-conscious
about doing so. The eight years during which we had seen some of them in
Cambridge had turned them into friends who were prepared to welcome all
four of us to their homes where we could see how they lived. Shinzo Kaji
was quick to have us to his place.

When we got there after driving through a street barely wide enough to
admit our taxi between high wooden walls, he apologized for the fact that
his house was so hot. All we saw of it was a narrow foyer, a garden about
ten feet square, and a tatami-matted room of about the same size with a low
table set for six, an upright piano with several figures on top, including the
head of the Venus de Milo, and a *tokonoma* in the corner. Mrs. Kaji served a
wonderful Chinese dinner. The Kaji children, all very handsome, were introduced to us. Two daughters, who were twenty-three and twenty, were
studying psychology at a university; two sons—Tako and Shaji—were six-

teen and twelve. Fireworks were brought out, and all the boys set them off in the garden. Shinzo, getting pleasantly high, brought out his vibrating electrical pillow, which each of us tried in turn while lying in the little corridor. Shinzo's brother-in-law unexpectedly arrived with his wife and joined the party. He was an electrical engineer who was then president of some university near Tokyo. After a couple of glasses of Suntory whiskey, he chatted happily and tried the vibrating pillow. One of the Kaji boys played some sweet arias on his flute. Then Shinzo suddenly appeared in his cotton kimono, rolling the sleeves up around his shoulders and tucking its skirt up short to the middle of his thighs. When it came time for us to leave after a happy evening, Shinzo and Shaji led us through the dark alleys to find a cab on the main boulevard.

Another evening of entertainment at a Japanese home occurred early in our 1960 visit when we were invited for dinner by Shozo Ohmori. By prearrangement he picked us up at I. House in his trusty Datsun and drove all four of us to his small home in one of the suburbs where he lived with his classically handsome young wife, Reiko (whom we already knew), and two tiny little girls of four and eighteen months who spent most of the evening quietly playing with a large collection of toy animals, happily occupied without intruding at all in the conversation of the adults.

The evening's entertainment took place in the Ohmoris' small living room, which was furnished with a comfortable, modern, upholstered "living room set" and simple side chairs that brought us together quite cozily. The other guest was another young professor of philosophy from Tokyo University, Makoto Yamamoto, who was at that time a very robust, vigorous, and entertaining bachelor, and who became a good friend in subsequent years. The dinner that Reiko Ohmori had prepared was quite an exquisite one, showing her skill in the highly developed Japanese domestic art of cooking. All the dishes of this dinner were carefully arranged with attention to colorful matching of the food and the serving dishes so that the diners were treated to food that was as pleasing to see as to taste.

With such stimulating fare the philosophical conversation of Ohmori, Yamamoto, and Morton became very animated. Then everyone tried playing Beethoven in turns on the upright piano, Morton performing *con spirito* the one Beethoven sonata he had ever learned to play. To finish off the musical interlude Ohmori played part of a Chopin waltz—Chopin is a great favorite with Japanese pianists—and then he concluded with a delicate performance of Beethoven's "Moonlight Sonata." To complete the evening's entertainment after the little Ohmori girls had been whisked off to bed, Reiko Ohmori passed around photographs she had taken of a number of her flower-arrangements that had won prizes in the last couple of years. She also let us see several illustrated folios of different styles of flower arrangement from the Sogetsu Art Institute of Tokyo, a very modern institution which offered instruction in the non-traditional school of flower arranging and sculpture. It surprised us to learn that there was no instruction at all at the Sogetsu Institute—at least at that time—in the art of painting.

During the middle of our 1960 visit we were entertained at the homes of two other professors of philosophy. First we made a visit to Sawada's in a handsome, hilly residential district southwest of Tokyo known as Freedom Hill (there's a novel about this section called *Mrs. Freedom Hill*). Here almost every house has a high wall around it and its garden, and the section has abrupt, short hills. We went first to see the Sawada's house, which he had described as "small and dirty," but it didn't fit the last half of this description. As far as we could see, the house was completely enclosed in a tiny garden. After viewing the garden, we had cold green tea served in a study large enough to seat six—with the Murais joining us. Sawada's children, all very handsome (two girls twelve and ten, and two boys nine and four, the latter Arthur, born in the U.S.), kept appearing from behind the curtain of the main room. After a brief stay we went on to the house of the Keio philosopher Matsumoto.

The Matsumotos had arranged to give the dinner party because their house was bigger, set beside a pleasant lawn garden. We were entertained again for a few moments in Mr. Matsumoto's library—lined with books and many pictures of Christ since Matsumoto is a devout Catholic. Then we were swept into the larger living-dining room, which contained only western furniture, several twentieth-century French paintings, an upright piano, and a large refrigerator. Mrs. Matsumoto appeared, buxom, gracious, smiling, and extraordinarily amicable. Though she said little, we were told that she spoke English very well and had been born in France, the daughter of a diplomat. She kept gracefully disappearing and reappearing through the curtain of the kitchen door, ushering in delicious courses of food, "home cooking international style" as Mrs. Sawada explained.

Mr. Matsumoto began the conversation by speaking in pleasant tones about very painful events. First he told about having been stung by a bee on the "contrariwise side" of his hand the day before, so that his hand and forearm were badly swollen. Then he told about his having been a faculty-elected member of the Board of Trustees of Keio University, in charge of academic questions before he ruined his health. He struck an awkward note when he explained that his guest Sawada, as representative of the teachers' union, had been his opponent in many discussions and that it was Sawada's victory over him in all the battles which had destroyed his health. He concluded his series of unhappy tales by pointing to a large painting of French railroad workers—three of them grouped in a way reminiscent of Cézanne's card players—and explained that this was by a well-known Japanese artist who had committed suicide in Paris. After this macabre tale, much light talk and joking began at the table. We were surprised but also pleased by the sudden change in atmosphere. We observed that Mr. Matsumoto spoke about sorrowful and happy events in exactly the same benevolent tone of voice and without showing any visible sign of his changing emotions.

When dinner was over, we went to see the garden. Mr. Matsumoto showed us the ancient stone lantern of Buddhist design with a tiny figure of Christ at the base, and the unusual square gold fish pond with pottery stools and table beside it. The three Matsumoto daughters were introduced; they were about twenty-nine, twenty, and eighteen—the only son of about nineteen was away mountain-climbing. The girls were all easy-mannered, gay, and Westernized—they had attended Catholic schools. Picture albums were shown of the eldest daughter's marriage to a bank official. It had been a very elegant affair in a Tokyo Roman Catholic chapel, followed by a reception at the Imperial Hotel. We were also shown some pictures of this daughter with the Japanese crown princess, who was a classmate and friend. This Matsumoto girl had been educated in New York at the Manhattan Convent of the Sacred Heart. It was clear that the family was quite wealthy and had many prominent connections, including the then chief justice of Japan, who was a relative of Mrs. Matsumoto; Mr. Matsumoto was the son of a prominent Tokyo lawyer.

After lingering in the garden a while, we were wafted back to the living room for music. Nick and the oldest daughter were persuaded to play a Viotti violin and piano sonata duet. Then, while the older people sat about sipping tea, the younger people took turns on the electric guitar at the dining room table. After a final round of photograph-taking, we were sent back in a car to International House.

In reflecting on our visits to the homes of Japanese academic friends in 1960—which had been a new experience for us since we had not been entertained at any of these homes in 1952—both of us were surprised at how relaxed and enjoyable these visits were. From descriptions given to us by American social scientists and by Japanese academics themselves, we had expected relations with our hosts and hostesses to be less easy, since some of our informants kept describing them as "rigid," "introverted," "tradition-bound," and "always mysterious." Of course, liberal offerings of liquor probably eased conversation somewhat, for getting drunk was not disapproved of in Japan. Whereas Japanese women would smilingly wave away hard liquor and would usually stop drinking after downing one tiny cup of saké or a little sherry, most men would not hesitate to drink all evening, beginning with beer and saké at the meal, and then moving on to beer and whiskey afterwards. However, the relaxed quality of these evenings at home was produced by more than alcohol. Our friends were generally at ease in small family-sized groups which included their young as well as their teenaged children. All of them would encourage us to take part in pleasant, relaxing, and diverting activities that we were able to share with them. No doubt they thought out such activities in advance, trying their best to arrange those that would not depend on our being able to speak Japanese or on their having to exert themselves too much in speaking English.

Speaking English provided no great problem for one of our more unusual acquaintances, a Japanese physician who had many international connections. Dr. Ono was a Tokyo otolaryngologist to whom we had been given a letter of introduction by a mutual American acquaintance, the late Beverly Kunkel, professor of biology at Lafayette University and a former teacher of Dr. Ono before the Second World War. We had a conversation with Ono which was unusual in several ways. It dealt with some of his firsthand experiences during the war, kinds of experiences to which none of the Japanese academics had referred either in 1952 or during 1960. Dr. Ono's remarks about his wartime life as a doctor in Tokyo were brief but memorable and affecting.

While dining with Ono at International House, we noticed that everyone—guests, waiters and waitresses alike—knew him and that because we were his guests, we were given a great deal of attention as well as extremely solicitous service. Very early in our table talk and without our prompting, Dr. Ono got onto the subject of hardships during the Second World War, when he saw severe malnutrition among his patients; they became "spongy" and bloated, he said, from lack of protein. He himself, when he was occasionally free from his professional duties, would make hurried trips to the country outside of Tokyo while carrying some of his family's valuable art objects—such as kimonos or pieces of lacquer or ceramics—to exchange for a small sack of potatoes or some other item of essential food. In the country he would also collect dandelions for salad or for wine-making. Food was rationed, of course, but often it was impossible to get the rationed articles at all.

Ono went on to talk about medical practice in Japan, which was controlled by a National Health Service. Every patient was entitled to receive medical care for a small fee, the only fee he would pay until the condition for which he consulted the physician was cleared up. Because of these low fees, Ono reported, bright young people were avoiding medical practice and going into business and engineering. In the light of this we could not understand why Dr. Ono himself looked so prosperous, how he could have just bought himself a new house in a very exclusive section of Tokyo, or how he could be planning a round-the-world tour to attend conferences in Vienna, Venice, Paris, Stockholm, London, and Chicago. On this trip Ono would be looking into foreign cancer research. He reported the view—about which we came to hear later in the States—that the closer a cigarette is smoked down to the butt, the more dangerous it is; but he went on to say that measurements of cigarette butts in France, Germany, England, Canada, and America showed that although American butts were longest, Americans had the highest rate of lung cancer. Dr. Ono speculated that it might be the type of paper rather than the tobacco that caused cancer because pipe and cigar smokers do not appear to be especially susceptible to cancer. And since he was interested in high-power photography for taking pictures of lung tissue, he hoped to look into this technique while in Chicago, where, he said, it was especially well developed. Ono struck us as being a highly gifted man who personified the intelligence, industry, and efficiency we had come to associate with the Japanese. We were especially happy to think of those qualities being used in medicine rather than in military science and also happy to be in touch with at least one medical scientist while we were seeing so much of philosophers and historians.

The informal evenings we had spent with our friends in 1960 were very welcome indeed. For one thing, they permitted our sons to enjoy some social life and even to meet some Japanese young people; for another, these evenings gave us more opportunity to become better acquainted with our Japanese friends. During our visit in 1952 we were so much involved in the formalities of conferences, lectures, and professional meetings that we could not easily penetrate the masks that people wear on such occasions. In 1960, however, even our trips away from Tokyo were less formal and more personal.

Our first trip from Tokyo was to Mashiko, a town famous for the design and production of ceramics. On an appointed day at 8 A.M. all four members of our family met Iwasaki and the driver of a brand-new Chevrolet at the front door of International House. We joined another group at Tokyo University and divided up in three cars. Shinzo Kaji, Professor Festinger, a Stanford psychologist, and Mr. Aoka, a ceramics merchant, went in the first car. A young Chinese student named Lin drove the second car, in which Steve, Nick, the younger Kaji daughter, and Takeo Kaji rode. Lucia, Morton, Iwasaki, and Mrs. Kaji travelled in the third car. For some reason, perhaps because Mr. Lin did not know the route, all three cars moved in a tight procession on the narrow, crowded highway. This tightness was made more hideous for us because the Chevrolet in which we rode had a left-hand drive though Japanese cars must keep left, and Iwasaki never gave any sign of objecting to our driver's pulling out when trucks were coming at us in the right lane. Morton sat in the rear on the right-hand side and was petrified because he saw those oncoming trucks before the driver saw them. We managed to survive all this and got to Mashiko, about seventy-five miles northeast of Tokyo. It is situated in lush farming country filled with rice paddies, patches of soya beans, pumpkins, and tobacco. Above all this there loomed shapely hills upholstered with vivid green grass, patches of cedars, and tall bamboo. On the top of the highest hill in the region, which commanded a sweeping view of hills and farmlands, we visited a Japanese restaurant near a Shinto-Buddhist shrine that housed a god "who snatched out the tongues of liars." It had innumerable steps approaching it and a small shrine on the side where childless couples could pray for the blessing of children; if their prayers were answered, they would make payment by contributing red cloth for the idols' suits of clothing. One of the pagodas at the top of this hill was three hundred years old; and the gate-like pagoda housing the huge, fierce wooden statues of Buddha's guardians was a five-hundred-year-old treasure.

Next we visited the establishment of Hamada, the world-famous potter. His place consisted of three enormous farm houses which had been moved from up-country by floating the gigantic supporting beams down on spring floods. Goodness knows how the huge thatched roofs were transported or whether they were rebuilt. In one part of this vast building Hamada and his second son were turning out pitchers and mugs on potters' wheels. Another part contained a long kiln reclining like a bulbous snake on the side of a hill. The pitch of this structure was very important, Hamada said in excellent English, for determining the heat distribution in the kiln; the exact heat was judged by peering into the furnace through round holes with stoppers in order to see the color of the flames. Hamada took us to the main house, which contained ceramic treasures from all over the world, paintings, and fine pieces of furniture. He discoursed about his work interminably, mostly in Japanese; and he ordered his servants to bring us some sickly-sweet, enormous dung-colored cakes. Steve, who was sitting near a pail and large cistern full of water, kept looking as though he was going to toss his cakes surreptitiously into the pail or the cistern! Hamada finally presented all of us with mugs, saying that he refused to sign them. Apparently he did not want people to have his products merely because they bore his name; he wanted them to appreciate his art.

After leaving Hamada's place, we navigated a narrow, winding track through rice paddies and came to a dead-end in another potters' settlement which was run by a relative of Aoka. It looked as though an earthquake had hit it. The buildings were ramshackle; haphazard piles of dusty utensils lay around on a hillside; some of them were ground into the earth and others were perched on boxes and niches on the sides of sheds. We were given some things for nothing, and we bought several dishes and jars.

After a long drive, we finally arrived back in Tokyo. On the way we caught glimpses of a policeman carrying a delicate Japanese lantern, of a girl in flowing kimono riding on the back of a motorcycle, of fireworks celebrating a summer festival over the canals and moats of the city. And since it had become a ritual that we should dine together before parting after such an excursion, we were taken to a tiny restaurant in Kaji's neighborhood. There we were fed delectable baked eel and rice in square red lacquer-covered "casseroles." All of us were exhausted and saturated with dust from the roads, great stretches of which had been under construction. In a tiny room of the restaurant the TV was broadcasting a baseball game full blast; a little boy and girl were gaily tiptoeing around; a third child slept peacefully while curled up in a blanket in front of the TV.

Our next vacation from Tokyo took us back to Karuizawa, the scene of so much intellectual excitement in 1952. This time, however, we visited the country home of our old friend Goro Mayeda, who, like Ohmori, was a very Westernized easterner, a deracinated Japanese who nevertheless loved the Japanese countryside.

We commenced our trip to Mayeda's house by taking a taxi from International House, and the Tokyo taxi had become such an indispensable mode of transportation for us that it deserves special comment. In 1960 a taxi ride was still quite cheap, and there were many, many more cabs than in 1952. Because they also went faster than they did in 1952, we were even more terrified of riding in them than we had been. Bicyclists, pedestrians, women, and small children were honked at violently and given no quarter by drivers; pushcart operators were crowded to the curbs. Drivers would speed wildly up the middle of the road between traffic lights and jam on the brakes violently at intersections. But they could also be very genteel. One day we rode in a handsome, blue, eighty-yen cab which had unusual refinements—a glass vase filled with chrysanthemums attached to the dashboard and a small damp towel with which the driver frequently mopped the perspiration off his brow, neck, and ears. Lucia would often find herself exhausted after these taxi rides because of the tension they produced.

So much for the Tokyo taxi. The one we entered on our way to Karuizawa brought us to the Tokyo railroad station at about 9:30 A.M. The station was occupied in an orderly way by countless people: large numbers sat on newspapers on the floor. There were several processions of teenaged campers, little girls in white hats and middies with black skirts and red knapsacks, and processions of mountain climbers in heavy boots. We noticed a noisy, offensive couple whose clothing made them appear to be Americans, but overhearing their conversation, we realized that they were French.

Our train took three hours and a half to climb into the mountains, going through long stretches of farm country covered with rice paddies, then gradually ascending into the spectacular mountains that look like black icicles standing upside down. On the sides of the railroad track every flat inch was carefully cultivated, and the sides of the brooks filled with crystal clear, rushing water were often neatly lined with boulders. The soft foliage of the cedars billowed on the lower hillsides while the heights were swathed in layers of gray mist, which persisted overhead all weekend so that we could not see how splendid the country was. After going through the twenty-seven tunnels very slowly on the cogged railway at the end of the trip, we were once again struck by the fact that in the farm country and in the rugged mountain stretches of the Karuizawa region one always sees somebody—often many people—in the landscape. There were farmers cultivating the rice or bicycling along the narrow tracks between the paddies, children waving outside a shack, motorcyclists buzzing around hairpin curves, a troupe of butterfly hunters with long nets, and always various trainmen, passengers, and loiterers in the stations.

When we arrived at the Karuizawa station, Mayeda was there waiting for us. He took us by bus to the Hoshino Hotel, a long rambling place that turned out to have a new addition with very pleasant Japanese style rooms decorated in refreshing taste—coffee tan walls, shoji screens at both ends, and on one wall a shelf which was not oblong but tapered down to the wall. The cabinets were covered in chocolate and silver rice paper in our room, and in the boys' room by a section of rice paper decorated with butterflies and grasses. Of course, there was tatami on the floors. After we had rested, lunched in our rooms, and bathed in the short and almost yard-deep coral-tiled tubs, Mayeda took us—by a somewhat indirect route—to meet his wife and year-old son, Fumio, a name, he said, which has the same meaning as the Latin word "ars."

On the way we visited an elevated Buddhist Temple and monastery near Mt. Asama. The monastery was having a new dormitory for students built on the revenue the bishop had realized by selling all the cedars felled in the previous year's hurricane. The garden was under repair, but the bishop proudly showed us one lily plant that had over a hundred buds. We climbed down the flight of steps and walked through an avenue of cedars past a deep, icy pool where there was a half-immersed statue representing the Virgin and a Buddhist female deity combined. Then we walked through the village on its main dirt street. At one corner was a large farm house with a thatched roof, surrounded by a trellis-hedge carefully trimmed and a screen of various evergreen trees. Because of the appearance of this place, we could tell that it belonged to a wealthy farmer. After leaving it we saw one storey, mud-plaster farms clustered together on both sides of the thoroughfare. An open stream rushed along a stone-lined channel at the road side. As we strolled along, we met ox carts; one of them was drawing a sewing machine, of all things.

After meeting Mayeda's wife, a slender shy woman, and their exquisitely formed quiet boy who was just learning to stand, we witnessed a novel kind of student demonstration. A couple of dozen children, boys and girls from six to about fourteen years old, had collected in front of Mayeda's farmhouse. They stood silently at the entrance path for about an hour while we had cold drinks, corned beef, cheese and cucumber open sandwiches—and Mayeda very pleasantly passed his plate of cookies to them. He explained that they had never seen foreigners before and that they admired teachers enormously; their province, it seems, was noted for having the highest standard of education in the country. As little Fumio watched them, he became quite expressive, demanding tomato juice, playing peek-a-boo under the table, and juggling empty match boxes.

By contrast to our visit to Karuizawa in 1952, when we had been told for days about the profound social crisis into which Japan had been plunged in the aftermath of the Second World War, this visit provided us almost exclusively with rest and relaxation. Karuizawa, one of the most famous recreation centers of Japan, was filled with quaint looking but sturdy and productive farms, artistically designed inns, and energetic people who worked against a background of spectacular mountain scenery. The setting gave us an opportunity to become better acquainted with Mayeda and his wife. The brief time we spent with them increased our growing sense that the scars of the war were being healed and that Japanese-American relations were being established on a basis of mutual respect and mutual enjoyment. Goro Mayeda was especially well endowed to bring about this feeling of reconciliation. He had been sent abroad as a young student by his family during the war so that he could devote himself to studying European languages as well as the classics. We gained the impression that he was a linguistic genius, and we knew that he was a wonderfully humorous and gentle scholar who was as much at home in English, French, and German as he was in Japanese. He was one of the most distinguished New Testament scholars in Japan.

In the course of our visit at his home in Karuizawa in 1960, Mayeda recalled with amusement that he had been the chief Japanese academic negotiator in 1952 who had arranged with the National Railway Company to get an extra second-class car on the train from Tokyo to Karuizawa. This accommodated the visiting professors of American studies and their Japanese opposite numbers. Mayeda said that the railroad company stoutly maintained that no train should carry a disproportionate number of second-class cars by comparison to third-class cars. To deal with this problem, Mayeda proposed adding only one extra second-class car, but the railway officials objected that this would make the train too heavy and pull it down the mountain. Since he had travelled very often on this line, Mayeda knew it was "technically possible" to pull an additional car on the line, but to conciliate the officials, he proposed adding an extra engine. Still, the disproportionate number of second-class cars remained, so he finally suggested dividing the extra car between second and third class passengers and thus was able to conclude his arrangements to everyone's satisfaction. He told about all of this with wide grins, giggles of laughter, and various cluckings of his tongue; then he suggested with more giggles that Morton should draw the appropriate metaphysical conclusions from this story.

After our visit to Mayeda's place at Karuizawa, we were taken—on the next weekend—to the home of a Japanese whom we had once met in the

United States. He was the well-known retired Japanese journalist Hasegawa, who had reached the venerable age of eighty-four and who lived in a very fine country house near Hakone, a house purchased for him by his many friends and admirers. Shinzo Kaji, being a friend of very longstanding of whom Hasegawa appeared to be especially fond, conducted us to this sage. Upon our arrival we were ushered into a library completely filled with books and boxes of manuscripts, a library which Hasegawa called his brain. He looked, if anything, younger than when he had visited the States; and in traditional costume while perched on a high, rattan-backed chair, he served each of us tiny cups of "young" green tea from a tiny Ming teapot. His niece and a sturdy woman-helper in Western dress assisted. Hasegawa spoke rapidly and clearly and was rather critical of the Japanese for being, as he saw it, a practical people incapable of theory. On the other hand, his interpreter Kaji told us that Hasegawa was devoted to Japan, preferring to live there while candidly criticizing his fellow countrymen. He was often sought out for advice by men of affairs who had become devoted to him when they served on a magazine he had edited for ten years; according to Kaji, they came to trust his opinion because his candor was not malicious. Over a fine Japanese lunch Hasegawa told a joke: when asked who had most authority in Japan, he once replied "the photographer—even the emperor obeys him." After lunch the old sage showed us his long-bow and his arrows and explained that he still practised the sport of archery for exercise. A photograph of him in his archery costume was very striking in bringing out his resemblance to an American Navajo Indian.

Another visit away from Tokyo brought us to a country inn that proved to us that this very special, traditional place of entertainment was still flourishing. Perhaps even before the eleventh-century descriptions in *The Tale of Genji* by Lady Murasaki, the Japanese country inn provided a kind of refreshment wonderfully soothing to the spirits of weary travellers. Late one Sunday afternoon we arrived at one of the most charming of these Japanese inns, owned by the Imadas at Miyagino. We saw three small separate houses, in the first of which we were welcomed with tea and unprepossessing gray gelatine cakes filled with sticky-sweet red bean paste. We were rather drowsy and all lolled together in the little room while Shinzo Kaji and Steve played Japanese chess. A fine large bathroom adjoined the living room, enclosing a natural rock bath-tub fed by a steaming hot spring and a large deep marble bathing tank with a seat submerged on one side. For this type of bath you stand on a drain-board, soap yourself first, and rinse by pouring water from little wooden tubs and dippers. Then you plunge in and soak in the main tubs which have water changing in them continuously. We took turns performing the rites of the bath for a long time before dinner. At this establishment the baths were immaculately clean and enjoyable. Shinzo said that at such a resort people always bathe morning and night and usually several times a day. However, mixed bathing, even in this district which was notable for it, was gradually decreasing in 1960.

Husband and wife Imada had been arguing for a long time about where we should sleep, but finally moved us up to the main new house where we could all sleep in a series of fresh and apparently airy rooms. We had a most pleasant supper, after which Imada and his wife brought out a koto and some handwritten manuscript music. They proceeded to play and sing several songs as the wind freshened and the stars came out. When bedtime came, we had the devil of a time retiring because our hosts kept shutting up the screens until we were pretty effectively boxed in from the breeze; then they brought extra pillows and bath towels to cover our feet in case the quilts were not long enough. Rather than prolong these attentions, we stopped asking to have the screens opened even though it meant doing without the eagerly anticipated breezes. In the morning, after more bathing in spring water, we walked into the garden precariously on our getas in order to see a small bit of Mt. Fuji, a faint reddish layer beyond the side of a neighboring wooded hill. Imada-san was already hurling water from a huge dipper at the bushes and rocks of his garden to keep things feeling and looking as cool as possible since the day already promised to be sultry. We had breakfast together—Nick still going strong on the large and varied Japanese breakfast of pickles, rice, soybean soup, and fish and seaweed—before we took the train back to steaming Tokyo.

Our final excursion in 1960 turned out to be a grand tour which combined an expedition around new territory. It included the Ise Peninsula, sightseeing at the Mikimoto Pearl Farm and the Ise Shrine, and finally a welcomed stop at the home of the Matsumuras, friends of Shinzo Kaji. This excursion was carried out with split-second timing even though we covered more territory than we had ever covered on any previous trip. We proceeded from Tokyo to Yagi, a remote village in the Kansai district. First we took a crack express train, riding in reserved seats to Nagoya on the private railway line as opposed to the publicly owned one. We were made very comfortable by its reclining seats and air-conditioning, and also by individual transistor radios which had special car attachments so that everyone could tune into his own favorite program—no general music, then the only music available on Pan American Airlines. Also, in spite of the narrow-gauge track, the ride was smooth and fast; we arrived exactly on time. On our train we had to order lunch from the waitress and sign up in advance for one of the three sittings. When lunchtime came, we had excellent steaks and a full-course dinner, skillfully served, the only drawback being that the system of serving forced one to finish promptly. However, that system was better than having to wait in line while standing in a train corridor. Our trip took us through the Japanese megalopolis from Tokyo westward, past all sorts of small factories and small farm communities. We saw lovely peaked, tree-covered mountains on one side of the train or the other during most of the trip. As usual, the countryside was meticulously cultivated; small patches along the railroad track were planted with some convenient crop like corn or pumpkins; and the rice fields, usually arranged neatly in the contours of the land, were often outlined with a planting of soybeans. The forests were as carefully cultivated as in Germany.

The bus trip from Ujiyamada to Shima Kanko was even more breathtaking than other trips because there was something gratingly wrong with the low gear of the vehicle. The young driver dextrously managed to drive in high gear most of the time in the narrow streets of villages and around mountain curves, whizzing gaily along while people leapt into shop doorways or threw themselves against the hillsides to avoid being crushed. Toward the end of the trip in the late afternoon we went surging through low bamboo groves and little villages in a very winding course on a road that seemed barely wide enough for the bus. Nevertheless, we managed to pass all sorts of other vehicles with only a couple of stops to let some other vehicles creep past us while we looked over the side of a sheer drop into fields or streams ten feet or more below the level of the road.

We reached the Shima Kanko Hotel on a remote hill high above an inlet where guests were swimming in the late afternoon sunshine. Numerous flunkies asking for Professor White came out to greet us. We decided against a swim because it would have been such a long hot climb down to the water, and we would have been covered with dust before we climbed back to the hotel. Instead, we sat out on the green bank behind the hotel after dinner, looking out over the calm bay spread out like a hand with fingers stretched open pointing between the pine-covered banks, while enormous black clouds and luminous white thunderheads swept across the sky and an orange, full moon rose gradually above the clouds. We visited for a while with Ohmori, who once again said that he preferred not to use first names with us—that he could not be comfortable doing it. He seemed especially tired and nervous on this part of the trip—very worried whether we would make our connections as planned. We were all quite exhausted by the extent of our travels on this first day but revived by the coolness and quiet of this remote place during the evening.

In order to follow our schedule we had breakfast early even though it was raining steadily. But by the time we were ready to set out for the Mikimoto Pearl Farm at nine or so, the rain had stopped though thick gray clouds still hung over the sky, and we had begun to get radio reports of typhoons off the west coast of Japan so that there was little hope of clearing. At a small dock in the village we boarded a launch that had been hired for us and surged down a narrow bay while threading around the light rafts from which trays of oysters for cultured pearls were suspended. Next to these rafts small boats were moored; from these boats workers cleaned the trays, also raising or lowering them so that they would be in water of the proper temperature. At the Pearl Farm we walked around to see the Mikimoto house with its gray tiled roof and then went down to a demonstration place where we were shown how the operation is done. To start the cultured pearl, they insert a small bead into the oyster along with a special bit of oyster tissue. The pearl takes three years on the average to grow in carefully controlled conditions in the bay. After the demonstration, we were presented with some pearls that had been extracted from the oysters.

Having cruised back to the village, we collected our bags and drove to Ujiyamada to visit the Ise Shrine, to which the Imperial Family is especially devoted. It is in a very beautifully tended woodland where many gray wooden *torii* arched the paths approaching the central Shinto shrine buildings. There the guard turned his back for a while, to allow time enough, Ohmori said, for Lucia to take a picture. However, she did not realize that this was the guard's way of permitting an illegal act, and therefore she took about one second too much in her photography. Unfortunately, therefore, when the guard wheeled around, her "photo opportunity" was lost.

From the Ise Shrine we somehow managed to go by train to Yagi, where we were met by Shinzo Kaji's friend, Matsumura, and his seventeen-year-old American guest, Stanley, a student who was travelling under the auspices of the Friends Service Committee from, of all places, Shreveport, Louisiana. They announced to us that Joannie Sturgis of Cambridge, Massachusetts, was in the region, also with F.S.C., and would phone her schoolmate Nick during the evening. Matsumura took us by local train on a sweltering ride, during which everyone half-slept, to a small village where his home was situated. This part of the Kansai district is very prosperous farming country. The rice fields appear to be more vividly green than in other parts of Japan; the undulating hills are covered with wonderful blue-green foliage; and the village houses, which have fine gray tile roofs, are trimly kept and simply ornamented. After viewing these scenes with dazed pleasure, we arrived at the Yagi station, from which we drove to Matsumura's ancestral home.

It was a very ample establishment with a large entrance hall that rested on an earth floor. From it you climbed up—after, of course, removing your shoes—into a small Western-style living room, then into a long narrow Japanese-style room with Buddhist shrines screened off behind one wall and an inner court garden at one end. We were served refreshing drinks by Mrs. Matsumura, and before supper Mr. Matsumura took us on a walk through the village, past the school he attended as a child and up the hill to a large Stonehenge-like mausoleum of rocks. This was supposed to be some fifteen-hundred-years old and to show that slavery must have existed in Japan because such a structure could have been built only by slave labor.

After exploring the site, taking pictures, and admiring the extraordinarily beautiful mountain neighborhood, we straggled back to the house—once again to be installed in the Japanese living room together. Soon after that we were taken around the inner gardens of the house and shown the extensive buildings behind. It appeared as though supper was about to be served, but we were all so exhausted that we said frankly that we'd prefer having a quick bath. After our baths, we partook of a pleasant supper and visited languidly with Mr. Matsumura and Stanley until we drooped so much that we were shown to our beds in a special guest house—very handsome and delicately built—and there we collapsed with fatigue.

On the next morning Lucia had a glimpse of the family kitchen in the main house off the entrance hall. It was a large room that contained stone sinks along one wall, a big stone table across its middle, and a big iron wood-burning stove. It was a room big enough for a whole family to work and eat in. Mrs. Matsumura was already up serving breakfast and her mother-in-law, a pleasant gray-haired little hunch-backed lady, appeared for a little while. After giving us a hearty meal, the whole family came out to wave us good-bye as we boarded a bus that took us to the railroad station.

With so much of our leisure time taken up by visits to Japanese homes, inns, and shrines, we did not have a great deal of opportunity to see many artistic treasures of which the country is justly proud. Nevertheless, we did see some of Hamada's ceramics at Mashiko, and in Tokyo we had a chance to see some other remarkable works of art. One day we browsed for a brief time at the Ueno National Museum of Fine Arts in Tokyo, and looked especially at the carved, more than mansized wooden Buddha of the Heian period of 600–800 A.D.; at the more realistic, dynamic messengers and escorts of Buddha of the Kamakura period of 900–1200 A.D.; at some horses, boats, and a wild fowl from burial mounds of the neolithic period; and also at a clay figure of a knight in armor which was amazingly representative of this period. We saw a beautiful bronze mirror decorated in a geometric design which was a lovely example of straight lines and curved lines worked into a circular area. It was borrowed from the Imperial collection. Lucia hoped she could go back some day to copy it. Behind the room where the mirror was exhibited was one full of elaborate kimonos. Lucia was especially taken by the summer kimonos of white silk bearing motifs of cherry blossoms, clouds, bamboo, and various flowers. Upstairs, the things she enjoyed most were the Chusan-ji Sutra, written in alternate rows of gold and silver characters on blue silk or fine paper; a high red lacquered chest with double doors from Nara; another flat chest on high legs inset with mother-of-pearl phoenix medallions which alternated in direction. They were distributed with eight on top and seven on the side, and there were nine tiny rosettes of mother-of-pearl in the legs. We saw a fine series of screens—one of islands and mountains in a mist by Beipan, one of the tiger and the waves by Gakan. In the next room there was a lovely, simple print of orchids in the moonlight by Boupon and a series of landscapes by Wang-Gay. In the back rooms we saw some lovely red lacquer boxes of the Edo period between 1600 and 1800 A.D.; some blue and white jars of the Chinese Ming period which had tiny fish-shaped handles; and finally some lovely green celadon jars.

On another artistic expedition in Tokyo we were all taken by Professor Minoru Murai and his wife to see some Noh masks. They introduced us to a very beautiful somewhat made-up young man who was dressed in a *yukata*; he was young Mr. Nomura, son of a famous mask-maker and himself an aspiring actor of Noh. He showed us the elegant small stage in his father's home where Noh plays were performed privately against the background of blue-green beplumed pine trees. When young Mr. Nomura began to loosen up, he explained that he was going to make his first appearance in Noh and sing a minor part. He said he was very eager to show us a series of very beautiful and varied masks carved from wood by his father. They represented young, middle-aged, and elderly women—all showing differences in the molding of the chin, in the cheeks, in the line from the nose to the corner of the mouth, in the shapes of eyes and the folds over the eyes, in forehead texture, and in the way hair might fall on the sides of the forehead. We were shown masks of a jealous woman, of various male heroes, of clowns, of lions, and other animals. Each mask was carefully taken out of a padded brocade envelope and then held up with equal care by the two sides behind the eyes. Some of the masks were very ancient ones, perhaps five hundred years old, and all had to be kept in careful repair. Usually the making of such masks is passed down from father to son, and the Nomura collection was rarely shown to anyone but the actors themselves or to their friends.

The experiences we have reported in this chapter served to deepen our understanding of Japan and to strengthen our ties with many of the Japanese. We came to know Japanese scholars to a degree that transcended the formal and stiff associations formed in classrooms or conferences. We all became friends in a way that contributed more to international understanding than any philosophical lectures could by themselves. Still, philosophical contact was very important in promoting such understanding on an intellectual level, and Morton was pleased to find that some Japanese philosophers wanted to learn more about the kind of philosophy that interested him. By the end of the summer of 1960, then, we had formed emotional and intellectual relationships which became the basis of lasting friendships to be nourished in the next twenty years or so. During that period, as we shall see, even a third generation of our family would visit Japan with pleasure.

NINE

The Japanese Philosophers
Declare Their Independence: 1966

Although we had developed close attachments with our friends—attachments which had been made even closer by their more and more frequent trips to Cambridge, Massachusetts—six years were to elapse before we could return to Japan. There had been some correspondence about a possible trip in 1963, but for one reason or another that fell through, and so it was not until 1966 that we made our next visit. Once again the Harvard-Yenching Institute, then directed by Professor John Pelzel, supplied the major portion of the funds that would finance our travel; and although Morton once again went as a teacher, this time his teaching would be somewhat different from the teaching he had done before.

Instead of lecturing to established professional philosophers, some of whom might, for one reason or another, remain permanently silent during the whole course, Morton conducted a seminar of the traditional kind in which each participant would present a paper at a given meeting. In this way the teacher's role would be less conspicuous; he would, perhaps, lead part of the discussion that followed the paper, but he would not merely lay down the law, so to speak, from on high.

Morton decided to follow this plan after consultation with his closer Japanese friends, especially with Ohmori. The plan arose in part out of a recognition that many Japanese philosophers had greatly improved their understanding of the philosophy then predominant in the States and in part out of Morton's and Ohmori's desire to prod them into being more independent. The idea was that they might in this way develop greater confidence in their philosophical powers and also improve their philosophical English. It might also hasten the day when they would contribute papers in English to philosophical journals, much as their mathematical colleagues did. Of course, Ohmori and Morton knew that Japanese mathematicians would find it easier to do that sort of thing because mathematical terminology was more international in character. There was, the story went, a Japanese mathematician who was able to deliver a lecture to a group of his American colleagues even though he knew only one English word—"therefore." But, granting that Japanese philosophers could not get along with such a sparse English vocabulary, one might hope that they would soon be able to exchange ideas in print with their American colleagues who, of course, would rarely be able to read or write Japanese. For all of these reasons, it was decided to launch the new kind of course.

In retrospect, one might say that in 1952 the Japanese attended an elementary course in the history of American philosophy, in 1960 a more advanced graduate course in the philosophy of history, and in 1966 a real graduate seminar on various topics in systematic philosophy such as *a priori* knowledge and free will. This sort of seminar provided them with an opportunity to present their own views, to criticize the views of the teacher, and, in general, to declare their philosophical independence. No longer would they do nothing but docilely nod their heads in agreement with the lecturer. They had listened long enough, and they were now ready to talk back. The lecturer welcomed this back talk as a sign of his having succeeded to some extent in his pedagogical efforts.

The new style seminar was attended by several old friends, among them Ohmori, Takeo Iwasaki, Makoto Yamamoto, Ryuei Tsueshita, Nobushige Sawada, Minoru Murai (translator of Morton's books, *Religion, Politics, and the Higher Learning* and *Science and Sentiment in America*), Hiromichi Takeda (our man in Kyoto, as we used to call him), and Wataru Kuroda. The list of attendants also included the physicist Father Yanase, whom we had met one year when he had been a visiting member at the Institute for Advanced Study. Shuntaro Ito, Tomanobu Imamichi, Takashi Koizumi, Saburo Ichii, Tatsuo Fukukama, Takashi Fujimoto, and Hyakudai Sakamoto also participated. By the spring of 1966, Morton's *Toward Reunion in Philosophy* and his *Foundations of Historical Knowledge* were familiar to many of these philosophers, and so these books furnished topics on which several of the participants spoke. In keeping with the spirit of the new style seminar, Ohmori emphatically dissented from some of the teacher's views on the distinction between analytic and synthetic statements; and Iwasaki took as his point of departure some views on free will that were advanced in *Foundations of Historical Knowledge*. Politely but firmly both of them expressed criticisms of these views, criticisms which showed that a big chunk of ice had been broken. Because Japanese philosophers had become more familiar with analytic philosophy, closer to the leader of the seminar, and generally more confident in the presence of Americans—and, no doubt, for a variety of other reasons—the intellectual atmosphere had changed dramatically.

The seminar was held in Kyoiku Kaikan, the Education Building next to the Ministry of Education, which was near the intersection called Toranomon. The room was rather bare, businesslike, and eight or nine floors up from the street level. Three long wooden tables were arranged to form a

"U," and the participants ranged themselves around it. The teacher deliberately refrained from sitting in a central position, trying to occupy a different chair at each meeting. The papers were not limited to topics discussed in his books; for example, some papers dealt with problems in esthetics and with parts of the history of Western philosophy that he had never studied carefully. The fare was rich and interesting; the atmosphere convivial but serious; and everyone seemed pleased with the new equality that had developed between Japanese philosophers and the visiting American.

This equality led to candor that was more intense when the Japanese entertained us. One evening while we were at the house of Yamamoto, he reported, with the concurrence of Ohmori, a certain feeling of despair about the state of philosophy in Japan. The nature of this feeling never became altogether clear, but it was connected with a feeling that the first flush of excitement about analytic philosophy was over. After the war—twenty years had elapsed since then—they had been stimulated by developments in the States, but now they had no clear notion of where they were going or what they should do. Yamamoto, who taught at Tokyo University, who had been a protégé of Professor Ikegami, and who had worked at Harvard, expressed this feeling eloquently. He thought that there was no large or deep philosophical framework within which he and his colleagues were working; Ohmori agreed. Morton tried his best to encourage them by saying that they were not alone in feeling as they did, since many American and British philosophers felt the same way. He also pointed out that many interesting philosophical inquiries did not have to be made in the context of some all-embracing system. To this Ohmori responded that Morton was more suited than he himself was to working on technical problems without worrying about the "big picture." Morton countered by saying that a big picture might emerge after technical work had been finished, but Yamamoto and Ohmori replied that Morton was by nature more optimistic than they were. Morton agreed with them as he reminded Ohmori of his main reason for leaving physics and entering philosophy: a desire to find "the metaphysical principle of the universe." Morton also mentioned Yamamoto's attachment to Ikegami and phenomenology, as well as his interest in those two great system-builders, Leibniz and Kant. By temperament and training, he said to Ohmori and Yamamoto, they were more traditional than he in their philosophical tastes. William James, he said, might have called them tender-minded philosophers. They laughed uproariously as they downed their beers which had been spiked with Scotch.

There was even more candor at Ohmori's when we dined there with the philosophers Sawada and Nakamura. These two were highly critical of certain Japanese metaphysicians, saying that they were lacking in philosophical daring and excessively preoccupied with the history of philosophy. But Nakamura went further and said that none of these metaphysicians was a "real scholar," whereas Nakamura thought that Noda of Kyoto was. Someone then poked fun at philosophical pedants who were bereft of ideas. It seemed that Sawada, Nakamura, and Ohmori constituted—at that time—a logical and scientific trio who were in opposition to the more traditional philosophers. And yet Ohmori was inclined to be more charitable toward them, eager to excuse them by saying that they were philosophically honest or that they would soon produce something in systematic philosophy. It was apparent that Ohmori was much more sympathetic than Sawada and Nakamura were toward those who sought the metaphysical principle of the universe in the writings of traditional philosophers.

Getting somewhat fatigued with what seemed to be degenerating into drunken gossip, Morton tried to turn the conversation to a more general question. What, he asked, was the philosophical division of opinion in Japan, and how did it compare with the situation in 1960? He was told that it was not very different. The main tendencies were still Marxism, existentialism, analytic philosophy, and "all the rest"—whatever "all the rest" meant. Someone volunteered that "Marxism is going down somewhat"; someone else announced that "analytic philosophy is about the same." There was some disagreement about how existentialism was faring in popularity, but there seemed to be complete agreement about the fact that philosophy as a discipline was not attracting good students. They all seemed to think that the generation after theirs—philosophers then in their thirties—was very weak. We spent some time talking about why this was so. Nakamura thought that the educational system was at fault, saying that students were forced to specialize too early and were therefore unable to sample philosophy at a sufficiently mature age. He seemed to think that if a student were allowed to wait a bit longer before choosing a specialty, he or she might become wise enough or learned enough to see the virtues of studying philosophy. The others present offered no explanation for the decline of interest in philosophy on the part of good students. When Morton suggested that the lure of money and prestige in industry, commerce, and science might have something to do with it, Ohmori loftily replied that Asians did not value that sort of thing. Morton wondered to himself, thinking that Ohmori was a little too nationalistic, too partial to his countrymen, and given to exaggerating the purity of their motives.

At some point in this remarkably unbuttoned exchange, Morton said that Ohmori was excessively romantic in his personal and intellectual tastes and that he was led, in his wishful thinking, to suppose that his countrymen were more radical, dashing, bohemian, and beat—the last word was then still popular—than they really were. Ohmori replied with great insight that he prized those qualities but that he himself did not have the courage to act on them. Morton could not help recalling that in 1952 the paradoxical

Ohmori seemed like a very advanced, Westernized thinker who was more "Japanesey" than most of his colleagues. And so, in spite of Morton's pleasure about the new intellectual independence of the Japanese in his seminar, he feared that their traditional sentiments might well lead them to return to "feudalistic" ways of acting. He wondered how long American analytic philosophy, logic, and the philosophy of science would remain in vogue among the Japanese philosophers he knew.

Our previous trips to Japan had been supported by organizations connected with American Studies. On this trip, however, even though the seminar would be concerned with philosophy alone, the Tokyo philosophers somehow managed to wangle about 150,000 yen—in those days about 500 dollars—from an organization called "American Kenkyu Shinkokai"—in English "Association for Promoting American Studies." Our friend Ohmori informed us that this outfit was chiefly operated by our other great friend Shinzo Kaji, but, Ohmori went on to say in one of his letters, "I assure you this does not commit you to anything, except maybe to attend a party. Especially the seminar has nothing to do with 'American Studies' at all. Any way, we want the seminar completely free from any consideration other than philosophy. I think this is your intention too."

Behind these remarks there lay something that was evident as far back as 1952, namely, a kind of intellectual gulf between the Japanese philosophers and the Japanese specialists in American Studies. To be sure, many Japanese philosophers had been supported by funds earmarked for American Studies by different foundations and granting agencies, but, nevertheless, many philosophers of Japan had contempt for the so-called "discipline" of American Studies. They found its intellectual standards wanting, and many of them could never understand why Morton, whom they regarded as a member of *their* profession, also worked in American Studies. The Japanese Americanists, especially Shinzo Kaji, seemed to take no umbrage at this condescension of the Japanese philosophers toward American Studies; Kaji was too big a man for that, and so Morton was never made to feel that he was being put in the middle, that is to say, in between the philosophers and the Americanists in an embarrassing way.

On only one occasion was there a glimmering of anything like that, and that was when arrangements were being made for the hotel in which we were to stay in 1966. Because the seminar was exclusively for philosophers and because Ohmori was Shinzo Kaji's junior in age and academic standing, Morton had decided to spare Kaji and to deal with Ohmori about lodgings. Ohmori agreed to keep Kaji informed, and this procedure seemed to be quite acceptable to all parties—or so Morton thought until he received a letter from Kaji in September 1965 (very typically, the Japanese were preparing things well in advance for a visit in the spring of 1966!) In his letter Kaji wrote: "I'm sure I can take care of you better than Ohmori. Please let me do that. It will save his time. I or my secretary can make arrangements for you only by phoning, as I know more people than Ohmori." As soon as Morton received this, he knew that "face" or something kindred was involved. Kaji, the great administrator and our very good friend, wanted to "arrange" things, just as he had in 1960 when it was a question of finding a good Chinese restaurant. Under the circumstances it was necessary to get Ohmori to surrender his job as arranger to his senior, Kaji. This Ohmori did, we were sure, with relief and with a full understanding of everything that might have been involved. He probably realized that Kaji wanted not only to express his friendship for us but also to remind us that the seminar was in some degree associated with American Studies and not an operation of the philosophers alone.

Naturally, the fact that the seminar was purely philosophical did not prevent us from seeing a great deal of our friends among the Americanists. When we saw them, we discovered that, whatever their differences with the philosophers, they too showed signs of nostalgically reverting to older Japanese ways. The highly Americanized Kinuko Kubota told us quite frankly that as she got older, she returned more and more to old Japanese customs. For example, she now preferred to sleep on the floor and not on a Western-style bed. Coming from her, the admission was very significant. Nothing physiological like low-back trouble (some Japanese call it fifty-year old back) was involved. It seemed more like cultural nostalgia in one of the most Western Japanese we knew. The fact that she was a career woman showed how Western she was, and so did her highly developed scholarly interest in American politics. In the States she would giggle, put her hand over her mouth, and say "Amedican Studies" whenever she ate something especially Western or attended some peculiarly American form of entertainment. And she would often attack what she called "feudalistic tendencies." To find her returning to old Japanese ways was therefore even more startling than to find Ohmori doing so. We knew him to be a traditionalist in the clothing of a logical positivist, but Kinuko-san, we had supposed, was very different.

Kinuko-san also complained about the decline of regionalism in Japan, about the fact that when she travelled to the provinces she was disappointed to find so much uniformity in food and social customs. When she went on a lecture tour she resented being put up at Western-style hotels since she preferred to stay at old-fashioned Japanese inns. She added that a growth of what she called "conformism" among the Japanese was dangerous, since Japan always trembled on the brink of nationalism and was always close to abandoning democracy. Paradoxically, therefore, she was for maintaining a variety of traditional Japanese habits as a way of preserving democracy and not because she was a political reactionary. She wanted to turn the cultural clock back so as to keep the political clock moving forward; she believed that the preservation of regionalism and local differences would check nationalism and thereby encourage democracy.

In the same vein she decried the flight of the general population to Tokyo and the decline of other cities. Even Osaka, she said, had ceased to be a serious economic competitor of Tokyo. Nothing stood to Tokyo, she said, as, say, Chicago or Los Angeles stood to New York. To Tokyo all of the aspirants in politics, art, commerce, and intellectual activity wanted to go. There was no division of the kind represented by Washington, Cambridge, and New York, and she deeply regretted this. Once again it was fear of concentration that worried her. It was as if she feared that he who would seize Tokyo would be able to seize the whole nation.

It seemed, therefore, that our best friends were in a pessimistic mood. Yamamoto was worried about the state of Japanese philosophy, whereas Kubota was worried about the state of Japanese social and political life. Yamamoto had compared the philosophical situation of 1966 invidiously with that which had prevailed just after the war, whereas Kubota rendered a similar judgment about the whole Japanese society. She said that when she had returned from the States in 1954 and looked at the people's faces, they had looked happier then than they now did in 1966 in spite of the fact that they had become more prosperous. After the war, relief and hope made for a kind of euphoria, but in 1966 that was gone. We were struck by the prevalence of the romantic notion that the Japanese people and Japanese intellectuals had been happier in adversity than they were in prosperity. We wondered whether this was true of all the Japanese people or whether it was a figment of the intellectuals' imaginations.

While observing this pessimistic mood, we were aware that in 1966 Japan was watching American military forces mired in Vietnam. There may have been some unspoken fear among our friends that Japan would be dragged in to aid its ally, but there could be no question about the fact that some of our friends wisely disapproved of our venture in Vietnam. For example, Minoru Murai said that we should get out and that although he had always been pro-American, it was becoming extremely difficult to defend our policy in Vietnam. When we asked him whether Japan would be likely to serve as a negotiator of peace between America and its enemy, he said that Japan did not have enough military power to serve in that capacity. When asked about Vietnam other friends were elusive, and we could never find out what they thought. They were much more reticent than Murai in expressing the opposition they probably felt toward America's policy.

Mentioning Murai, who was professor of education at Keio, makes this a good point at which to say something about a pedagogical hope of ours that was not to be fulfilled in 1966. The hope was connected with some work we had been doing for a Cambridge organization that was then called Educational Services Incorporated (E.S.I.). During the academic year 1965–66,

Morton had taken leave from Harvard in order to serve as the director of a project under the auspices of E.S.I., a project in which he and Lucia were working on a model curriculum for American high school courses in social studies and history that would lay more emphasis than usual on philosophy and the history of ideas. Part of the project involved setting up a unit on Darwin and his philosophical impact; another unit dealt with the English industrial revolution and the steam-engine; and still another focused on the social impact of that industrial revolution on the English city of Manchester. So, when planning our trip to Japan, we began to think of organizing a unit that would treat the effect of industrialization on Japan, an effect that could be compared by high-school students with what had happened in England. With this in mind we hoped that we might enlist the scholarly aid not only of Murai but also of Edwin Reischauer, by then our ambassador to Tokyo. It should be said at once, however, that this good idea never came to fruition. The time we spent in Japan in April and May of 1966 was too short and too filled with other activities to permit us to work systematically on our model curriculum; and, needless to say, we had failed to realize how little time both Murai and our ambassador would have for this sort of thing.

We called Reischauer fairly soon after we arrived; and we had lunch with him and his wife, along with another American couple, on Morton's birthday, which, as it happens, is the same as the Japanese emperor's—April 29. Needless to say, we did not mention that coincidence since we had planned our own private celebration and feared that if we had mentioned the birthday, Reischauer *might* have felt obliged to do or say something about that at lunch. It turned out that the presence of another couple effectively eliminated the possibility of any talk with Reischauer about our E.S.I. project on the impact of technology in Japan, but it certainly did not prevent us from talking about Vietnam. Reischauer strongly supported the notion of fighting on and was sharply critical of the idea that the Americans should retreat to an enclave in South Vietnam. He said with great emotion that doing that would be worse than pulling out altogether. Of course, he later changed his mind, as so many other Americans had, but at that time he was certainly whooping it up for a fight to the bitter end.

Having opposed the Vietnam venture from the beginning, we were as emotional about our views as Reischauer was about his, but we controlled ourselves, especially because the other couple was there. And after that couple had left, we continued to control ourselves even though we could not mask our view that America should pull out of Vietnam. Reischauer was eager to have us stay longer after lunch, but Haru Reischauer seemed very tired. She spoke despairingly about three or four other arrangements that day, beginning with a call at the emperor's that afternoon. Taking our cue from her, we politely declined Ed's warm invitation to stay on after three o'clock and walked to our hotel. As we did so, we remarked on the fact that while Haru seemed quite tired, Ed was very lively and appeared to be a much more robust personality than he had been while he was teaching at Harvard. He looked as though he enjoyed his work and his power. And well he might have, since he was extremely popular in Japan. Every time his name was mentioned, he was enthusiastically praised by ordinary people and by scholars as a very good and very kind man. He certainly was an enormous improvement over MacArthur. And Haru had managed to overcome the paradoxical disappointment that certain Japanese had expressed about her being Japanese. We had been told that this feeling grew out of fear that, as a Japanese, she would be able to tell Ed things about Japan that he might not have learned himself. This we found only somewhat plausible since Ed had been born and had grown up in Japan as the son of a missionary.

After walking from the embassy to our little Hotel Akahane—the one chosen for us by Kaji—we rested a bit. Then we set out for the Emperor's Palace, having been told that it would be an interesting spectacle to see the turn-out. After riding by cab to the Imperial Hotel, we set forth toward the palace but never got to it because of fatigue and the heat and humidity. We sat for a while in the park and returned for refreshment at the Imperial Hotel, struck by the fact that the crowds streaming from the park toward the Ginza were not in traditional dress, as we were told they would be by the Japan hands at lunch.

After our tea and coca-cola, we took a cab to Ueno Park, where the Tokyo Metropolitan Festival Hall is. There a young French pianist was performing, and Lucia took Morton to the recital for his birthday. The performance was quite exciting: Bach, Haydn, Beethoven, Schumann, Schubert and Debussy. The pianist was a strong, dramatic player who exulted in contrasts and powerful pounding. His music was a prelude to the most exciting and frightening moment of the trip.

Just as we left the hall we discovered a cab, whose driver, after consulting with other drivers around, allowed that he *could* take us to the Hotel Akahane. The first moment of the trip was typical. The driver simply *ploughed* into a group of girls emerging from the concert hall, and they luckily fled from physical harm. He then proceeded to race other cars on a teeming street. At one point Morton said, after consulting with Lucia: *"Doozo, motto yukkuri itte kudasai."* The driver replied in an incomprehensible way, but we decided that he was telling us that *he* was the driver and would choose the pace. There followed one hair-raising episode after another: speed-ups, and zigzags, and short stops, and light-passings, especially on one of the new expressways. By the time we were on one of those, we decided that we could not bear the thought of riding all the way home with this madman, who, by now, was driving with one hand, having lit a cigarette while both hands were off the wheel and the car was slithering around on tram tracks at about forty-five miles an hour. However, we could not exactly get out on a speedway and so, biding our time, we finally saw that we had come to a familiar place—Shimbashi. As soon as possible, we told him to turn in on the left and to let us out—in English. The price was 360 yen, but we gave him 400 yen, and we rushed from the car in relief, without waiting for the change. Unfortunately, he must have felt *rewarded* for his madness, but we just could not wait for the change!

From Shimbashi we walked home after we had figured out from our map how to get there. Lucia had earlier planned a sukiyaki dinner in honor of Morton. It was served in the basement dining room of our hotel, where we first had Scotch to calm our nerves after our ride with the *kamikaze* taxi driver and then went on to saké and beer while feasting. The dinner came to an end toward midnight with much well-wishing and little gifts from the restaurant's waiters and its chef, who presented Morton with a side-order of delicious duck and a bottle of beer. Morton speculated that he was being rewarded for having been born on the same day as the emperor (not, however, in the same year!).

Having said something about our very concrete experiences with a chef, a cab driver, an ambassador, philosophers, and Japanese Americanists, we now offer some more general observations about changes in Tokyo during the years we had been away from it.

(1) The most startling thing was to see the number of new buildings that had gone up since 1960, not to speak of those that had risen since 1952. In 1960 we saw much construction in process but now we saw the products of that activity: massive hotels, office buildings, and elevated freeways covering broad avenues. And the process of construction was still going on. Little men in hardhats were all over the place and the noise of the drill could be heard everywhere.

(2) The kimono had almost disappeared from the larger streets and certainly from central Tokyo—so much so that we were shocked one morning to see a *man* in kimono near Toranomon, the large square between our hotel and Shimbashi station. We saw almost no women in kimono any more. When we attended a performance of *Cosi Fan Tutte* one day, we thought that about one out of a hundred women were dressed in that traditional garb.

(3) Segregated toilets had just about taken over. It was a far cry from the day when Morton discovered, as he turned from a urinal at Tokyo University, that a co-ed had been powdering her nose in a mirror behind him. And while we are on this mundane subject, we might remark on the disappearance of public urination by men who had no compunction in 1952 about relieving themselves on the street. No longer did men remove their trousers so that they could have cooler rides on the railroad in the summertime. And it was no longer common for nude men and women to appear together in

public baths without any self-consciousness. Western prudery seemed to be conquering the Japanese along with Western technology.

(4) The smell on the streets was much more pleasant, partly because of the decline of one of the habits just mentioned and partly because there were fewer open sewers in Tokyo. We recalled our horror at the smell of the Sumida River when we visited working-class quarters near it in 1952.

(5) Foreigners were noticed with less curiosity and wonder in Tokyo. Perhaps the Olympic games in 1964 contributed to this (as well as to a great increase of building in Tokyo).

(6) People were better dressed and looked healthier. The young people were taller and looked stronger.

(7) The tiny taxicab had disappeared from the streets. We recalled that it had been said in 1952 that they used wood as fuel!

(8) There were an extraordinary number of expensive private automobiles on the streets. Many Mercedes were in evidence.

(9) Prices had risen considerably.

(10) An academic friend reported that whereas once he had to work at five colleges in order to earn his keep, he now could do so by working at one.

(11) The decoration of the new hotels, like the Okura, was very opulent. There were no overstuffed chairs of the kind that we saw at the Hotel Matsudaira in 1952.

(12) We ate in several restaurants that served better Western food than any place in Boston.

(13) Television had come to Japan in full force. We were treated to a Japanese soap-opera every morning in our hotel's restaurant.

(14) Bowing seemed to have declined—certainly on the streets. It was seldom that we saw Japanese women bowing and watching out of the corner of an upturned eye to be sure that the other person had come out of a bow first.

(15) Passing out name-cards had declined. In neither 1960 nor this year did Morton have them printed with his name and address in English on one side and in Japanese on the other. By contrast, he had been told in 1952 that it would almost be imperative to carry such cards.

(16) There were fewer people riding bicycles.

(17) The automobile traffic was worse than ever, and pedestrians were much more respectful of cars.

(18) The Tokyo subway was much more extensive than it had been in 1952 or 1960.

When we mentioned some of these changes one night at a dinner-party at Yamamoto's—in response to his asking us about our impressions of Tokyo—our Japanese friends concurred with some of our judgments while remarking that others had not occurred to them. This was, of course, understandable. As returning visitors we kept our eyes open for changes that might be too gradual to be perceived by those who were experiencing them without attending to them or dating them. When we asked *them* what differences *they* would report, Ohmori replied that *the* great difference was that Japan was richer, as he added with a smile that he was not speaking of the academics present. And yet we were sure that they were, judging by Kaji's earlier report that in 1952 he had worked at five different places to earn a living for himself and his family, and even by the spread that Yamamoto's new *okusan* —wife—had prepared for us in their attractive new house.

Yamamoto's wife turned out to be the girl who had played the *samisen* for us one evening in 1960 before they were married. By 1966 they were the parents of a lovely little girl of eighteen months, who appeared at several points in the evening to stare at the guests, at first dumbly, then with chattering animation, and finally in a state of drowsiness.

Yamamoto's house was pleasant but small by comparison to Murai's, which is in a suburb of Tokyo. We were taken to the latter by a cab that Murai had ordered to pick us up, and so he insisted on paying the driver for our expensive ride. That suggested to us that the Murais were comfortable, and our theory was supported when we looked at their house. It was quite spacious and surrounded by a very large garden. The land, they told us, had been bought by Mrs. Murai's father for about fifty yen per square meter (about sixteen or seventeen cents at the exchange-rate of 1966, we estimated) but by 1966 it was said to be worth about $500 per square meter. We were so startled by this report that we wondered whether we or the Murais had made some arithmetical mistake. We dined in an extremely Western dining room after having been ushered into what was described as *her* study. The latter was lined with bookshelves containing many books on music—she is a musicologist—and there was also a *viol,* which she was beginning to play. Dinner was served by a teenage girl—whether a permanent servant or just in for the night we did not know. The meal was chosen with an eye to serving us authentic Japanese dishes—much like the Hotel Akahane's effort to serve us rarities.

We have always liked both Murais very much. They are intelligent and warm-hearted, so we were able to talk to both of them quite freely. At one point when we spoke of the impact of the West on Japanese customs, Murai-san said that he hoped that Japan would retain its traditions without turning to a reactionary form of nationalism. It seemed clear to us that he, like many of our Japanese friends, wanted to keep their traditions without playing into the hands of zealots who wanted to celebrate the emperor's birthday with pre-war fanfare. Like Kinuko Kubota, the Murais were dismayed by the disappearance of old Japanese ways even though they themselves are Westernized. While discussing with him the impact of the West on Japan, we told Murai, who had become principal of the Keio University Girls' High School, about our work at E.S.I.. He was quite excited by our idea of comparing the English and Japanese responses to industrialization; and it occurred to us that if we were to pursue the idea, Murai would perhaps be a more useful collaborator than Reischauer.

Whereas Murai might have been a useful collaborator on *that* E.S.I. project, the new wife of Wataru Kuroda of the Tokyo University Department of Philosophy might have helped us with our work on Darwin. When her husband introduced us to this pretty girl, she quickly informed us that she had written an undergraduate thesis about Darwin's influence on Hardy. During our Sunday lunch at the Imperial Hotel, she announced categorically that "Hardy read Darwin." Her English was quite fluent and stocked with a large vocabulary. She was strikingly different from her husband's senior colleague, Iwasaki, who was so shy in speaking English that we almost dreaded the prospect of having dinner with him one night. Fortunately, he had also invited Tomanobu Imamichi, a member of the seminar who was unusually good at English and so brilliant in German that he had been offered a professorship at a German university, which he had recently turned down. Imamichi managed to fill some of the silences caused by Iwasaki's shyness and his wife's apparently total lack of English. She, however, was very sweet, and after we arrived at her house in a driving rain, she served us tea and slices of rich cake before she and her husband took us and their other guest to an impressive eight-story *Kaikan* for a Japanese dinner. As we left the Iwasaki's house, filled as we were with food that did not exactly serve as an appetizer, we went through a narrow garden walk bordered by very flourishing waist-high bushes and then entered a car that took us to the restaurant. There we were treated to a barbecue prepared by a boy cook and, following custom, sat on the floor at a low table. We were presented with tiny eggs and also half birds that looked like balls of bed springs. Iwasaki, being unable to tell us what kinds of birds these were, much to his own amusement settled for saying that "the bird was either the mother or the father of the eggs." Iwasaki was a very intelligent, very tense, but also very decent hospitable man who suffered from a heart condition to which he later succumbed. During riots some years after 1966 he was taken prisoner by student radicals, who were finally persuaded to release him when a physician attested to his ill health. In 1966, however, he was enjoying himself as a member of the seminar and on this occasion he was taking great pleasure as our host. He watched with fascination — as we did — while all of the foods were dipped into a jar filled with a mixture of soya sauce, saké, and sugar for basting. The basting was done easily since each variety of food was strung on very thin wires and then laid across the charcoal grill in the center of the floor.

Conversation with Iwasaki was not very easy, but we came to enjoy his company. In philosophical exchange he spoke slowly but precisely. Unlike some of his colleagues, he did not strive for effect. There were no attempts—like Yamamoto's—at mixing humor with philosophy; and unlike Ohmori, he would not appeal to complicated mathematics or science when arguing. He was an old-fashioned, clear-headed philosopher who knew a great deal about ethics and the history of philosophy. His death in his sixties was a major loss to Japanese philosophy. He was neither flashy nor pretentious, but he was a serious, honest, and solid man who was a stabilizing intellectual force in Japanese philosophical circles.

Mentioning the departed Iwasaki leads by sad association to a visit that we made to the house of the late Hideo Kishimoto's widow, Miyo. We were taken there in a taxi by Miss Kiyoko Takagi, the daughter of a famous Japanese mathematician but no relation of Professor Y. Takagi, the Americanist. Miss Takagi had been a student and later an assistant of Hideo Kishimoto; and in 1958–59 she had visited Harvard, where she had done some work under Morton's direction on the philosophy of William James. In 1966 she was kind enough to tutor us in Japanese. She had always remained loyal to Miyo Kishimoto and was delegated to take us to Mitaka-ku, where Miyo lived.

The occasion was one of the few on which we saw three generations of a Japanese family under one roof. The house had a small garden that boasted several large flowering azaleas. Besides Miyo and Takagi we saw Jim Kishimoto's wife and her two-year-old daughter, Haruko, who greatly resembled her grandfather, Hideo. Later Jim, who is an architect-engineer, joined us at supper. We had a very cozy time. Little Haruko was very solemn at first, but she became quite chatty at dinner so that we soon found her Japanese was better than ours. When she went to play by herself, she was quite voluble; every once in a while she said "wa-wa-wa-wa," which Miyo explained was Haruko's way of talking English. After dinner when we were back in the living room Haruko presented everybody with colored papers to make origami toys: a samurai hat, a crane, boxes, and other little hats. To Haruko's delight, Morton made an airplane and also a paper mask; and some paper "colored" snow made her laugh loudly, and she became very friendly.

Jim Kishimoto described some buildings in Tokyo which illustrated the most interesting contemporary architecture, notably the Tange building for swimming meets at the Olympic Games, the Sogetsu Kaikan, and the NCR Building near Toranomon.

We were sent home to the Akahane with a taxi driver who had been carefully instructed to drive very slowly and spare our nerves. And, in a footnote to the evening, Miyo Kishimoto phoned Lucia the next morning and reported that Haruko, after we left, began calling Morton "wa-wa-wa" uncle (or "para-para" uncle) and Lucia "wa-wa-wa" aunt (or "para-para" aunt), the English-speaking uncle and aunt.

The apparent affluence of the Kishimotos and other academic families in

1966 stood in contrast with what we learned about the situation of a very nice philosophy professor who had worked at Harvard a few years earlier. He and his pleasantly relaxed wife—a Hokkaido girl—took us for a delightful meal at a tiny tempura restaurant off the Ginza because, they said apologetically, their apartment was "too narrow." They spoke nostalgically about how much they had enjoyed their apartment in Cambridge, especially because of its central heating and large rooms. While discussing academic salaries, the man reported that the president of Tokyo University, who received the highest salary of all of them, earned about $500 a month and that other academics received salaries much less than that, ranging downward to his own pay of something under $200 a month. He said that he could barely manage on that amount and that one of his largest expenses—out of proportion to other expenses—was the payment of $6 a month for electrical lighting and television. He felt that the vaunted economic boom in Japan was superficial, that it hid many underdeveloped things throughout the country such as sewage systems, roads, sidewalks, and housing. He also complained about his academic load, which included eight hours of teaching per week, serving on many university committees, and being the head of the labor union at his institution.

Our friend spoke English extremely well and with a marked British accent. He said he had learned to speak English in middle school, where, however, he had concentrated on learning to read it. His British accent, he said, had been acquired while listening to the lectures of a young Oxford poet whose name, we think, was "Thwaite." Our friend also reported that he himself had, while he was a college student, conducted some high school English classes, which he did "passionately because of [his] attractive young lady-pupils." This man and his wife were different from some of our other academic friends in being more direct and down-to-earth. We had not anticipated as pleasant a time as we had with them; they were lots of fun.

Although they were lots of fun, we were distressed to hear of their straitened circumstances in a year when, we thought, our Japanese academic friends were enjoying a higher standard of living than they had enjoyed in earlier years. We began to reflect on the matter, and it occurred to us that our friend might well have been different from all or most of the others by virtue of not coming from a well-to-do family. And this reflection then led us to recall how many of our friends had grown up in comfortable families. Most of them were probably of upper middle-class origin when they were not children of academics, as some of them were. Some, for example, were children of physicians or of diplomats. In general, it was very rare to find professors whose fathers had been shopkeepers, and it was simply impossible to find any of working-class origin. This led us to realize how different their backgrounds were from those of their counterparts in the United States. And it helped explain not only their gentility but also a certain innocence and even snobbishness that a few of them sometimes exhibited. They may have been poorly paid, but they behaved as though they were members of a priestly class and were treated as such by many of their fellow-Japanese.

The social background and education of our friends and their wives may have served as a partial explanation of the wives' great interest in flower-arranging. It certainly was not the sort of thing, we thought, that would be common among women of working-class or lower-middle-class origin in spite of the highly developed esthetic taste of the Japanese people. The faculty wife most interested in flower-arranging was Reiko Ohmori, who had once conducted a class in it for Lucia and several other Harvard wives when Reiko and her husband had spent part of an academic year in Cambridge. One day Lucia was taken by Reiko to the Fortieth Anniversary Exhibition of the Sogetsu flower-arranging school at the Matsuya Department Store. There must have been two or three hundred arrangements both of natural flowers and branches and artificial materials. Three natural arrangements stood out. (1) A simple one of red Japanese maple and light green fan-shaped leaves arranged in two narrow rectangular vases slightly off center. (2) A rather large arrangement in a blue vase mottled in gray pebble effect; the arrangement consisted of pine twigs, some with pine cones but no needles, some small orange and yellow lily-shaped flowers bunched rather low just above the rim of the vase, and some rather dense twigs bleached ivory. (3) An arrangement from a French correspondent of the school in a handsome gray and walnut vase. In it there were pale purple wild onions which had tiny yellow flowers and dark tapering green leaves a little thicker than daffodil leaves.

Reiko Ohmori was very serious and interested by the displays and seemed exhilarated by them. Her taste was wonderfully subtle, it seemed to Lucia, who had a general impression that she was somewhat preoccupied beneath her wide smile showing unusual dimples right in the middle of the front of her cheeks. She kept introducing Lucia to her teacher—one Mrs. Ito, a plump dark-haired lady who looked sixty but was really eighty. Lucia and Reiko did not stay for beer after the exhibit, but Reiko insisted on taking Lucia to our hotel and then disappeared to do some shopping. She said on parting that she wanted very much to return to Cambridge some day and that she was now too busy with her children to think about flower-arranging. Earlier she had said that her older daughter, eleven, was quite studious; the younger one, eight, quite domestic, but that neither helped much in taking care of the little boy, two and a half, who was very beautiful with a very appealing, gentle face.

We have reported so much on our doings in the company of our friends that one might suppose that we never ventured out without being entertained or shepherded by them. Fortunately, this was not true even though our friends were remarkably devoted. In fact, they were so devoted to us that we occasionally felt that we had to escape from their tender clutches. Prompted by this feeling we took a number of nighttime as well as daytime excursions by ourselves.

One evening, after a record-breaking warm day reaching eighty-four degrees, we walked over to the Okura Hotel for dinner at the Orchid Room, a large open dining room where about equal numbers of foreigners and Japanese were gathered under the tiers of Japanese lanterns. In one corner of the room a robot-like young Japanese strummed jazz of the nineteen-twenties and other light music on a combination piano and electric organ. Near us was a party of two Australians, let's call them Mr. Allbright and Mrs. Allbright, and five Japanese—an elderly man who looked like a robber from the movie *Rashomon,* his gray-haired wife in gray kimono, two rather bland sons, and the plump pretty wife of one of them in Western dress and silver slippers. We heard snatches of their conversation, or rather of the remarks of Mr. and Mrs. Allbright against the background of music that went something like this:

Music: "You mean something to me . . . "

Mr. Allbright: "Of course in World War I England and Japan were allies, and we had a treaty, don't you know; and we got along very well indeed. On the other side were Germany and Russia, but *we* were good friends. Then came the Second World War, which was a great mistake, don't you think? That was really just a misunderstanding. Nothing like that could happen between us again."

Mrs. Allbright: "I always think that there are bound to be misunderstandings between the generations. In all of history this has taken place: the older generation thinks *it* is right and the younger generation sees things differently, and thinks *it* is right. You find this happening over and over again when you read history."

Music: "Oh Ochichornia . . . "

Mrs. Allbright: "Do you ever see any Russians over here? You know we have never seen any of them. Oh maybe I've met one. But I don't like them. You never know where you are with them. Then there are the Chinese, of course. You never know where you are with them either, do you? There are Chinese on the mainland, and then there are some more Chinese on that island called Taiwan. It's a very peculiar situation. But you can't ever really tell where you are with the Chinese."

Music: "Liebestraum . . . "

Mr. Allbright: "It is very good of you to come all this way to have dinner with us. It must be a very long trip for you. Now on Friday we'll meet again, and it will be bosses day, ha-ha-ha, bosses day ha-ha-ha-ha."

Both Allbrights by this time were quite drunk and shouting loudly, while the Japanese smiled and played it very cool except for the old man who grimaced and kept giving Mrs. Allbright expensive cigarettes which she lit one after another; and once in a while with gales of laughter, she threw lighted matches on the table.

The first few days we were in Tokyo we made several other excursions on our own; we seemed to be exhilarated by the long flight and felt as though we had to keep moving. One trip we made was to the park for the Study of Nature, hoping to find something connected with our interest in Darwin. We had spotted this park on our Tokyo map and drove there by taxi. There was quite a stretch of park before the driver found an entrance which led to a tan cement building much like the older Tokyo University buildings. In it Japanese in formal dress were gathering, the women all in kimonos— apparently for a wedding. We thought that it all had the air of a French movie—in that we had wandered into a setting where things were happening in an unexpected way we did not understand. We ambled through a run-down formal garden and past a deserted, dingy tea house. Later we strolled along a driveway and along the main road to another park entrance which was barred. Two school boys in their conventional black suits and visored caps understood enough English to tell us the main park was closed because of some holiday. We then marched down the busy main thoroughfare and recognized a subway station. After puzzling over the subway map on display, we bought two tickets to Tokyo station and were delighted to find that we made the trip easily without incident and recognized the Maranouchi section quickly enough to get off and make our way back to the Imperial Hotel.

Another day we walked all the way from the Akahane Hotel up to Roppongi, around the corner to Toriizaka-machi, past International House, and back to the cross roads at Roppongi, where we found a neat new supermarket at which we purchased crackers and cheese for midnight snacks. Then back to the hotel. It was remarkable that we saw no other Westerners on either of these excursions.

On still another day, finding ourselves around noon at American Express on Hibya-dori, we walked along the moat of the Emperor's Palace grounds and came to the Palace Hotel. We had the bright idea of ascending to the restaurant on the top floor where we had a splendid view of the Imperial grounds and half of Tokyo. When Morton ordered trout for his lunch, we did not reckon on what would happen: a special chef appeared with a serving cart bearing a brazier and a glass bowl containing a lively trout flopping around frantically. The chef with surgical finesse poured vinegar over the trout and turned the bowl over and over until the trout succumbed as we watched with horror. It turned out to be a very delicate repast after all, and Lucia enjoyed a filet of sole with delectable Mornay sauce. Before we left, the place filled up with parties of Japanese businessmen who kept exchanging name-cards at the dining room entrance—a display we had not seen before on this trip when name-cards seemed to be less common.

In one of our more daring demonstrations of independence we chose a really clear and balmy day on which to make yet another exploration. Armed with maps of Tokyo, we boarded the subway at Toranomon and shortly arrived at Ueno Park in the midst of throngs of families on holiday—this being Boys' Day Festival. The children especially wore bright-colored holiday clothes, the little girls tiny beribboned straw hats. We climbed up into the park, following the streams of people past the handsome concert auditorium. First we stopped off at the Museum of Western Art containing the Matsukata collection, which consisted mostly of Rodin bronzes, many of these being mildly erotic ones of Eternal Spring and of the Kiss. There were also several busts—a particularly handsome one of Rodin's father. The second most numerous collection consisted of paintings by Claude Monet, including scenes of the Waterloo Bridge, a village in snow, and of the sea off Trouville with bathers. We also saw a few nice watercolors of fishing boats in port by Paul Signac. Apart from these and one or two minor Renoirs there was a large number of awful chromos. We got tired of these and so decided to go next door to see if there was anything about Darwin in the Museum of Science.

In contrast to the Museum of Western Art, where there was only a medium-sized crowd, the Museum of Science was swarming with families jostling in front of the displays, since here admission was free on Boys' Day. What we could see were large plaster figures of various kinds of dinosaurs and some fossils in thickly packed cases. We wrote down the inscription "ma-h-mo-su"—which used the Japanese syllabary—to ask our teacher Miss Takagi about. We thought it might be "mammoth." On the second floor we saw acres of stuffed animals. After ploughing past the crowds, we escaped again into the outer air—just in time, because we met a procession of about five hundred school girls and boys in uniform marching on the museum entrance.

After the return ride to Tokyo Central station, we had a pleasant lunch in the Crown Restaurant on the top of the Palace Hotel. Then we taxied back to the Akahane where we collapsed in our bedroom.

That evening we were revived by the continuing coolness and clarity of the weather, and so we decided to try yet another hotel's restaurant for dinner—this time the Belle View, as it was called, on the top of the massive New Otani Hotel. The uniformed doorman helped us out of our taxi, very deliberately shouting "WELCOME!" in English. After we ascended to the restaurant, we were given a window-table in a room that was slowly rotating. As it went around and around we were able to take in the dazzling lights of Tokyo while listening to very sentimental music played by two Viennese, one a pianist and the other a violinist. We could see tears in the eyes of some of the other diners as they listened to Strauss waltzes along with other Austrian or Hungarian numbers. Like the Germans, the Japanese are able to combine military efficiency with extraordinary sentimentalism.

We thought that their ability to combine efficiency and sentimentalism was not unconnected with their ability to combine modern technology and flower-arranging, advanced thinking and arranged marriages, militarism and the Buddhistic philosophy of peace, and the many other seemingly antithetical elements of their culture. Sometimes after reflecting in this way, we wonder whether Japan is really different from any other culture in this respect, and therefore whether, if we tried very hard, we would not be able to list analogous "contradictions" in our own country or in any foreign country that we know. And yet, after wondering whether our reflections about Japan's divided culture might not be banal and not worth expressing, we often console ourselves with the thought that the Japanese combination of opposing elements was more interesting. And why should it not be so, considering that Japan had moved from feudalism to a highly developed form of industrial capitalism in so short a time? The very speed of that transformation made it possible for these antitheses to exist side by side in an especially arresting way. Small wonder that a country which was so advanced in technology could continue to have officials clicking sticks in the middle of the night to signal residents of the largest city in the world to put out their fires. Lucia was sure that one night she heard a "clicker," as we called him, outside the Hotel Akahane at about 3 A.M., just as we had heard one outside the Hotel Matsudaira in 1952. The clicker of 1966 made us realize that we were once again visiting "a land of contradictions," but a land in which the contradictions need not be ferreted out by deep thinkers. In Japan these contradictions lie on the surface of social life. And even though in 1966 we noticed the decline of more traditional habits such as the kimono, public urination, and mixed public bathing, as well as the introduction of Western skyscrapers, elevated speedways, and deluxe hotels, we never doubted that we were still visiting the Orient. For all of the Japanese interest in Western habits and ways of thinking, and for all of our feeling that we had become closer to our Japanese friends in a way that was not blocked by our failure to speak Japanese, we continued to feel that there were many things about Japanese life that we did not understand: gestures, looks, tones of speech, and so on. Mystery remained but it was not mysterious why mystery remained. The cultural curtain that continued to separate us from some Japanese was no thicker or harder than the curtain which separates some Americans of one ethnic origin from Americans of other ethnic origins. Indeed, that curtain was not very different from one that can separate people of the same ethnic origin.

TEN

The Fourth Visit: 1976

In the spring of 1976 Morton took a term's leave of absence from the Institute for Advanced Study, the faculty of which he had joined in the summer of 1970. In January, 1976, we began our travelling from Princeton by going to the Huntington Library near Pasadena, California, and then flew from California in March to attend a conference sponsored by Tokyo University's Department of Philosophy. But we also had another very strong reason for going there. Our granddaughter Jenny, who was by then eleven years old, had been staying in Tokyo with her mother since the fall of 1975, and we missed Jenny very much. What a fine idea, we thought, to see her in Tokyo—where, we heard, she had been learning Japanese—and at the same time to see old friends! It was now ten years since our last visit to Tokyo, time enough for many changes to have taken place.

Although in 1960 we had already observed improvements in the economic situation, by 1973 a writer in the *New York Times* could report that "the affluent society" had arrived for one hundred and four million Japanese. He told of a young woman of twenty who had been graduated from a commercial high school two years earlier and who, while working for a dental-supply manufacturer, had recently taken a five-day vacation in Hawaii which had cost her $830. He also wrote about a thirty-seven year old industrial manager who owned a car, a color television set, a stereo system, a washing machine, $7,500 worth of stock, and memberships in two golf clubs which had cost him $7,900. The *Times* writer also reported that another manager in an industrial firm had spent $1,885 on audio equipment, had joined a golf club at a cost of $3, 200, and had nearly finished paying more than $12,000 for a plot of land on which he hoped to build a $38,000 house. Although the Japanese people suffered from inflation, inadequate housing, and pollution in 1973, the *Times* went on to say that virtually every Japanese owned a television set; that over 90 per cent of the thirty million households had refrigerators and washing machines; that the ownership of automobiles had greatly increased; and that in the preceding year the number of people taking business or pleasure trips was four times what it had been in 1969.

All of this prepared us for the effects of technological and economic advance that we saw when we arrived in Tokyo in the cold March of 1976. The ten years which had elapsed had intensified the developments we had witnessed then. Enormous concrete freeways had come to sit over more avenues than they had darkened during our previous visit, crisscrossing each other with a complexity that astonished us. The resulting darkness and pollution in Tokyo reminded us of the effect that the elevated trains used to have on New York. Now the Japanese not only wore surgical masks in public—as they did earlier to protect themselves from smog—but we were told that they would sniff bottled oxygen as they sat in cafés near heavily travelled streets. The need for oxygen may also have explained the new Japanese passion for playing golf. Whatever doubts we may have had about that passion were removed when we prepared to enter the taxi that drove us from the airport into Tokyo. We asked the driver to put our three bags in the trunk of his car and found him, to our surprise, a bit reluctant to do so. We understood his reluctance when he finally opened the trunk and thereby revealed the set of golfclubs that he was carrying. The cab, incidentally, was a Mercedes—a far cry from the alcohol- or perhaps wood-burning vehicles we knew here in the old days. The whole scene symbolized one side of Japan in 1976—a cabbie who drove a Mercedes and played golf!

This time we stayed once again at I. House rather than at some place like the Akahane, not only because I. House was a familiar haunt that we liked but also because it was cheap enough for us to afford while living on our own money. Since I. House was near Roppongi, we were able to witness with amazement the change that had come over that part of Tokyo. Highrise buildings and luxury hotels had been multiplied (beyond necessity); luxury restaurants, luxury apparelshops, and even luxury bakeries had sprouted. Young men and women were dressed as they would be in certain parts of London, Paris, Rome, or New York. They swaggered up and down the streets as they might on the Champs Elysées; no longer were they deferential to Westerners. And as the skyscrapers had climbed "with heaven-scaling audacity" in William James's phrase, so had the prices. No doubt our tastes had become more demanding than they were in 1952, but near Roppongi we found it hard to find a decent dinner for less than $7 or $8; and often it would come to $10 apiece, without drinks, unless we ate at International House, where the food was not terribly exciting but where the prices for food and lodging were subsidized. The prices of ties, dresses, shirts, shoes, and other such items seemed well beyond what we were inclined to pay, even though we were probably better able to afford them than most of the Japanese customers who patronized the kind of shops we saw around Roppongi. The same was true of liquor, of art objects, of taxis, and of all the other luxuries that we would not have hesitated to indulge in during earlier visits when our own income was smaller.

Forgetting about economics, we took delight in the fact that Tokyo was still exciting and safe—except, of course, for the maniacal taxi drivers and their competitors in private cars, who still seemed to speed up when they saw a pedestrian trying to cross the thatched sections of streets. And this feeling of excitement and gaiety was heightened when we thought of our almost two months in Pasadena before coming to Tokyo. In Pasadena we would walk down the fashionable shopping drag—Lake Avenue—at about seven o'clock in the evening and would see at most one or two other couples strolling. How depressing it all was! And how depressing it was to have to drive thirty-two miles over scary freeways to have dinner with friends in Belair. But in Tokyo we could walk to Roppongi in five minutes and feel the way we did as young people in Times Square forty years ago, without being afraid of muggers and dope-fiends. We could also enter the subway with complete confidence and get to the Ginza in ten minutes. There was much to be said for a city the safety of which far surpassed that of New York or L.A., not to mention Houston, Detroit, Chicago, Washington, Philadelphia, and other American cities where we no longer dared to walk the streets at night. Furthermore, our eleven-year old granddaughter could safely ride the Tokyo buses and subways during the day—by herself.

Jenny had dinner with us the night after we arrived, and we observed with pleasure how rosy and mature she looked. She let us know very quickly that she liked her school and Tokyo, remarking with special enthusiasm about her ability to travel freely in this spread-out, complex city. And we saw what she meant about her school when we visited it a few days later. The Nishimachi International School seemed to us to be a sort of Japanese counterpart of the Shady Hill School in Cambridge, Massachusetts. It was run by a Miss Matsukata, a member of the family for which the art collection in the Ueno Park Museum of Western Art had been named. Miss Matsukata was also the sister of Haru Reischauer and the cousin, we think, of Shigeharu Matsumoto's late wife—connections that may explain why Miss Matsukata was running a school attended by so many Western children.

When we visited Jenny's school, we did not have a chance to talk with her by herself. She was taking part in a Japanese language contest, serving as a member of an off-stage chorus which was providing background music for a play about the adventures of a fish! The group staging this play constituted one corporate, as it were, competitor in the contest; and because Jenny was singing off-stage we did not even see her except for a fleeting good-bye. Unfortunately, her group did not win the contest but Jenny good-heartedly took consolation from the fact that it was won by a Swedish friend and classmate, who gave the prize-winning speech in Japanese about her Swedish grandmother. This twelve-year old child was the daughter of a banker and had lived in Tokyo since the age of three, so Japanese was her first language. Tokyo was indeed a cosmopolitan place.

A day or so later we saw Jenny at I. House, from which we all telephoned her father, Nick, who was then in Washington, D.C. We grew sentimental about the fact that Jenny was now travelling around Tokyo just as her father had when he was a teenager in 1960. Her father sounded well and happy on the phone, but our conversation ended all too quickly. After the phone call we all walked downhill from I. House, turned right at the first corner, and headed for the Stockholm Restaurant, recently discovered by us. It was in the basement of a high-rise building erected, we thought, by the Swedish Embassy. In addition to the restaurant, the building housed a street-level store that sold Swedish goods and several offices on its upper floors. The Stockholm Restaurant was a dimly lit but lively place with good cuisine, and Jenny made a big dent in the smorgasbord while we enjoyed wiener schnitzel. After lengthy debate, we all decided to make an excursion to the Meiji Shrine. Jenny was our guide on the subway and then during a two-hour stroll through the avenues and garden paths of the park itself. When our steps began to falter, we fell into a cab that took us to Meguro subway station, from which Jenny led us through her neighborhood. She proudly showed us all the public sport facilities—tennis courts, golf driving range, and swimming pools—across the street from her apartment house. After that tour, we had dinner with Jenny and her mother. When dinner was over, Jenny showed us her photos of Japan, India, and Nepal. And once she started to do her math homework, we said good night and took a bus to Naka-Meguro station so that we could proceed home frugally by subway to Roppongi again.

Our next night out was at the Ohmoris, who continued to be our closest friends in Japan. By 1976 they had moved to the house formerly occupied by Ohmori's late father, a banker who had recently died. He had left his comfortable, middle-class establishment, with a relatively large garden, to his only son, who was now obliged to take care of his old mother. She did not appear that evening in spite of living nearby in a separate house on the same plot. Her absence led us to reflect that we had never met her or Ohmori's father even though we had received lavish gifts from them through Ohmori during the twenty-four years we had known him. Our requests to meet them in order to thank them were never satisfied by their son. He, in spite of some grumbling about high taxes, was put in a substantially improved financial position by his inheritance and by his new $20,000 annual salary. Being proudly nationalistic about Japan's economic improvement, he reminded us that in 1952 the ratio of Morton's salary to that of a Japanese counterpart would have been twenty to one, but now, even though Morton was drawing one of the higher academic salaries in America, it was only twice Ohmori's and that of his friend Yamamoto.

Yamamoto was the other guest—naturally, he came alone, as he did on a similar occasion ten years ago. Apparently the idea of inviting another Japanese *couple* to one's house along with an American couple was not yet *de rigueur* among academic Japanese. On the other hand, Reiko Ohmori, Ohmori's wife, was not dressed in kimono but rather in blouse and long skirt; and she did not, as she did ten years ago, crouch and crawl surreptitiously into the dining room to serve us and then disappear. On the contrary, she actually sat at the table and ate with us, helped in the preparation and service by her two charming and handsome daughters. One was in her early twenties and about to enter college even though she was more interested in tennis than in learning; the other was a high school teenager who was very shy, sweet, and tall—much taller than her older sister. The star of the family was the youngest child, a very bright and precocious boy of eleven who made a brief appearance to be introduced.

Seeing Ohmori, the Bohemian-in-principle, presiding over this bourgeois establishment reminded us of how paradoxically complex he has always seemed to us in certain respects, oscillating between a certain nostalgia for the old *samurai* life of his ancestors and admiration for the sort of Western intellectual life that brought him to Oberlin College for a year as an undergraduate, to Harvard as a visiting scholar, and then to the Institute for Advanced Study as a member in 1973–1974. By 1976, Ohmori's traditionalism seemed to have increased. Some indications of this stand out in our memory. One had to do with some reference to Jefferson's statement that all men are created equal. Upon hearing this, Ohmori said, as he pointed to his chest: "I think that statement has always penetrated just a small distance into me but it has never gone all the way in." And then there was the mocking tone in which Ohmori and Yamamoto referred to a colleague's taste for the "étranger." That colleague had always been notorious for his admiration of Western technology, science, and philosophy; and now both Ohmori and Yamamoto took a lofty view of that attitude. Of course, their remarks were clouded by alcoholic fumes, but through them one could cleary detect their feeling that their colleague was not "Japanese" enough for their tastes—a little "kooky" perhaps in his excessive gazing toward the West and a "Meiji-type," as they called him in patronizing tones.

Another incident at the home of a philosopher whom we had met in Cambridge fortified our suspicions about the increase in traditionalism. Morton was reminiscing about his first Tokyo seminar in 1952, laughingly recalling that when he entered the room, the whole class would rise at a signal from the monitor and would sit only at another signal from the monitor. As he told the story, Morton could not help thinking that our host was offended by what he regarded as Morton's derisive remarks about a custom that the host nostalgically prized.

In spite of his nostalgia, we were not asked by our host to take dinner while sitting on the floor but rather in stuffed chairs around a low table. That was part of our host's ambivalence, we thought. In 1960 we had sat on the floor at his house. This time we ate in what looked like a Western dining room, but we were obliged to exchange our shoes in the entry-hall for slippers which we surrendered at the door of the dining room, where we sat in stockinged feet. Poor Lucia began to freeze, partly because the room was inadequately heated by an electric heater and partly because she did not drink much of the available Western whiskey. When Morton managed enough courage to suggest that she put her coat on, our host apologized profusely and his wife ran out to get a gas-heater, which was trailed by a long rubber tube. The tube was attached to a jet along the lower part of one wall, and another guest, now filled with whiskey and beer, was delegated to light it. We were scared to death lest he blow up the place, but, to his credit, he proved to be a master of this piece of technology and soon we were perspiring!

The evening was, on the whole, very enjoyable in spite of some of the odd moments when our Japanese companions were evincing too much of the traditionalism of which we have spoken. Our host was very sentimental about our old house in Cambridge, which he said he remembered fondly. He talked of the snowy night when Morton came out to help him get his car started; he also talked charmingly of the evening when Morton's colleague Henry Aiken had spilled red wine on our light-colored living room rug and when our host, using some experience he had gained as a student in Germany, proceeded to direct the cleaning operations. "I behaved like a general," he said in a very amusing way, "commanding people to do different things—especially to bring me salt and water, and to rub very hard." At the end, after his success, he went on, "Professor Aiken threw his arms around me and kissed me." "Oz you know," he went on in a way that we shall *try* to recapture by imitating his speech, "we Joppannese are very emotional about everything but even I thowt thot Professor Aiken was going tzoo fah!" That gave us a great laugh.

By now it will be evident how much of our social life was carried on at meals—not a surprising fact. Our next social meal was "arranged," to use one of his favorite words, by Shinzo Kaji. His first wife, whom we had known well and admired, had died since our last visit, and now he was going to introduce us to his new wife. He arrived with her late one afternoon at I. House. She was considerably younger than Shinzo, dressed in a formal midnight-blue kimono; her expression a mixture of the quizzical, the hard, and the humorous; looking like a classical Ukiyoe female. She smiled often, spoke not a word of English, and showed herself very attentive to Shinzo's every wish. At his command she arranged to take all of us from I. House on a long trek by taxi to a Chinese restaurant near the Ginza. There we met Shinzo's nephew, the economist Motoo Kaji, and Motoo's wife, a research sociologist—both of whom were attractive and extraordinarily fluent in English.

The dinner conversation revolved mostly around what changes had taken place in Tokyo in the past ten years. The Motoo Kajis told us that the very expensive fashionable French shops of our Roppongi neighborhood were patronized mostly by young, single men and women who had good jobs and spent all their money on fancy clothes and restaurants—quite different from the traditional Japanese way of regularly putting aside a considerable portion of income as savings. The Motoo Kajis also thought that the increased prosperity of this country during the past ten years had not been cancelled out by "the oil shock" and the recession, but that the prosperity simply was not increasing and was now levelling off onto a plateau. There was also gay chit-chat during the meal, and then we bade farewell to Shinzo and his bride in the underground parking space beneath the restaurant, an enormous maze of a place from which the Motoo Kajis drove us home.

The Lockheed affair that was prominent at the time in both Japanese and American newspapers also came up one evening at the house of another friend. Although he clucked a bit about it, he was really not outraged by it and hoped it would not topple the Miki government if only because that might mean political turmoil and a triumph for the left. He seemed very anti-Communist and very anti-Socialist, but he did not want to condone the taking of bribes even though he was not very critical of what had been done. There was much general talk of how hard it was to define "bribery" and to establish that it had taken place, and there was an implied hope that the short memory of the public would permit the whole "unfortunate" incident to slip away without much effect—a hope that the *Mainichi* English newspaper thought would not be fulfilled since that paper believed that President Ford's handling of the matter might "lose Japan" for the United States just as Vietnam was lost to it.

When our good friend, Goro Mayeda, invited us to his house for another evening party, he told us that he was about to retire from his professorship in classics at Tokyo University. When he told us this, we were reminded once again that Japanese teachers at Tokyo University give up active duty at what we would regard as the extremely young age of sixty. Consequently, Morton was somewhat shaken by the thought that if he were a professor at Tokyo University, he would be leaving his professorship only a year later, in 1977. Because of Mayeda's impending retirement, he was in the process of bringing his books home from his university study, and so, he told us, his house was in a chaotic state for which he wished to apologize in advance. Going on in his very rapid and excellent English, he said that his wife was feeling very uneasy about entertaining us under the circumstances. Nevertheless, he told us, there would be no opportunity to see us except on the night in question, and he hoped we would join in a modest family sukiyaki supper, along with our friend Kubota-san. Using his rich English vocabulary, he asked us to "avert our eyes" from the chaos at his place.

We arrived there with Mayeda-san after a somewhat hectic taxi ride. Mayeda's house, which looked out on a charmingly narrow road that ran beside what looked like a canal rather than a river—a walled-in canal—reminded us of a house in Amsterdam. The house was also walled-in, as almost all such suburban one-family dwellings are, however small their yards may be; and we entered by a gate that immediately opened onto a tiny court in which what we would call a mayberry bush was starting to blossom (we had a lovely one in Cambridge, planted by us in our semi-Japanese garden there under the influence of what we had seen on our first trip to Japan). The door opened to Mayeda's knock and we were greeted by his beautiful wife and his two children—a boy of about sixteen and a girl of fourteen, both handsome and engaging—the boy tall, dark, long-haired, and very quiet, the girl cute and giggly, as Japanese girls can be. We reminded all of them, after exchanging our shoes for the customary slippers, that the last time we had seen them as a family was in Karuizawa in 1960, when the boy was an infant and the girl not yet born. As the girl laughed about this reference to a time preceding her existence, we reminisced about how strange we four Americans—Nick and Steve were with us—had seemed to the local villagers; and about how a large group of children simply stared at us from a distance as we had tea on the porch, unwilling to come closer in order to be introduced, but glued where they were with fascination. Mayeda repeated what he had said in 1960: that the children had probably never seen foreigners of our complexion, dress, and general appearance before and that was why they stared at us for so long.

We were next ushered into a tiny living room, where there was about enough space for a two-seated couch and two other comfortable chairs, all of it in that plush brown that we associate with our own childhood, sort of itchy and hairy, and characteristic of many Japanese "academic" houses which have introduced Western-style rooms. The evening was damp, raw, cool, and London-like; mist was hanging over the canal and so we felt quite cool, as we had in other homes. But this time the heating system, though it was the same gimcrack combination of gas-heaters and electric ones, was more effective, mainly because the rooms were smaller. Mayeda told us that his house was pre-fabricated and reinforced in some special way so as to be earthquake-resistant—or at least resistant to the hundreds of small quakes that hit Tokyo annually. We reported to our friends that our granddaughter Jenny had told us of a small quake that she felt at her school one day. The class was being taught by a recent arrival in Tokyo—an American woman—who remained standing alone in the assembly-room while the more knowing Tokyoites, the children in the class, all dove under the grand piano! Jenny said it had been very exciting and wished that it had gone on longer—a reaction that is not peculiar to eleven-year old children, since William James reported the same desire when he experienced the great San Francisco earthquake.

Soon after Mayeda told us about the construction of his house, our long-time friend Kinuko Kubota arrived, smiling her sweet smile. Her hair had become silvery gray, but she showed the signs of her age only in her appearance since her mind was as keen as ever. She told us once again of the death of her old mother, who gave us an ink-drawing because she thought the man depicted in it resembled Morton; and then Kinuko-san went on to say that when she went through her mother's hand-bag at the time of her death, she found a picture of her mother with both of us, taken many years ago when she and Kinuko had visited us in Cambridge. Kinuko was surprised and we, of course, were very much moved by this discovery. Kinuko also told of how delighted her mother (and she herself) had been to get Lucia's recipe for vichysoisse.

While all of us were chatting in the living room, Mrs. Mayeda and her children were elsewhere, presumably preparing the materials for the meal. At her request, made in Japanese to her husband, we entered the tiny dining room which was almost filled by the table and its occupants—the family of four and three guests. Once again we witnessed a Western-style arrangement, so different from the low tables and the sitting on the floor in all our friends' houses when we were invited in the past.

The lady of the house spoke no English at all, and the children, who surely understood it, were silent out of shyness. Meanwhile, Mayeda himself and the rest of us chattered on as he opened a bottle of German white wine that was quite good—reflecting, we thought, his experience abroad. Here there was none of the whiskey, the beer, and the carousing we had had at Ohmori's, for Mayeda was much more of a school-masterish, German-style professor, very restrained and very unbohemian in his tastes, just as Miss Kubota is, in spite of her cosmopolitanism and her long experience with the Japanese mission at the U.N..

The evening at Mayeda's was interesting not only for its conversation but also because our dinner was on a Western-style dining room table and the sukiyaki was prepared mainly by Mayeda himself, with his wife running back and forth to the kitchen at his command. We were given the traditional raw egg, which was broken so as to provide a cooling liquid into which to drop the ingredients of the meal after they were lifted out of the hot pan in the middle of the table. As soon as parts of the meal were declared done by the master of the house, they were pushed to the side of the pan and we were asked to "dig in" with our chopsticks. This method of eating is a very sociable, homey, and jolly one, inviting conversation and laughter around a common source of nourishment; so a good time was had by all at the table-cum-hearth. The end came when we began to feel tired and asked that a cab be called. Instead, the host walked out with us and Kubota-san to the end of his street, hailed one, and when the cab stopped, not only did we all get in but Mayeda thrust 1,500 yen into Morton's hand and ran away so that Morton could not resist it. As the cab sped off, Mayeda shouted goodbye and responded to our shouted protestations about the money that it was *his* responsibility to get us home just as it had been his responsibility to get us to his house. This meant that he had spent about 3,000 yen or $10.00 on transporting us, but there was no stopping him. Indeed, had we thrown the 1,500 out of the cab, we would have insulted Mayeda or lost the money on the dark street. True, we had entertained Mayeda in Cambridge, and there we had picked him up and driven him home in our own car. But, lacking a car, he felt obliged to substitute the cab for it, and he would, as the saying goes, brook no resistance. As we shall see, an even more startling example of this sort of thing took place when we went to Natuhiko Yosida's house, because he and his wife Hiroko lived in Yokohama—to which distant place he took us by cab and from which he had us carried back to I. House by a pre-paid cab driver. Once again protest availed us not at all. Japanese hospitality has its own iron laws, and transporting dinner guests is one of them!

Although Japanese homes had become more and more accessible to us after 1952, there was an occasion in 1976 when one of our friends revived the older custom of entertaining us in a restaurant without his wife present. Takeo Iwasaki decided not to repeat his earlier attempt at having us meet with a wife who knew almost no English; therefore, he arranged to take just the two of us out to lunch on a cold, rainy, blustery day in the middle of March. Morton felt a sore throat coming on and so he made an effort—with almost full knowledge that it would fail—to get Iwasaki to take lunch with us at International House, even going so far as to suggest that he could, if he wished, reimburse Morton since Iwasaki was not a member of the I. House club and therefore could not sign for meals. Morton felt that he could not inform Iwasaki of the nascent cold since that would bring excessive pressure on our sensitive host. But when our host said that he had made a reservation at a restaurant, we had to capitulate, sore throat or no. Iwasaki apologized for the absence of his wife, and off we zipped in a cab to a place in Meguro, the section in which Jenny and her mother lived.

The restaurant was one of the those magnificent Japanese establishments in which several men and women greeted us with much bowing and scraping at the spot where one removed one's shoes. We were led up a brilliantly polished wooden staircase to a private room overlooking a rainy, gray, but nonetheless magnificent garden that dated back to the days of a Tokugawa shogun who had lived, Iwasaki told us, about two centuries ago. The restaurant was called Happoen.

In the extremely large tatami-covered room with its lovely *tokonoma* and elegant flower-arrangement, all of us sat on the floor. We sat on one side of the table while our host sat on the other with the window overlooking the garden on his right and our left. Iwasaki struck us as having aged a good deal in the ten intervening years, now showing rather deep circles under his eyes and seeming, for a while at least, quite nervous. His lip twitched slightly as he began to speak to us. When the waitress entered, she quickly went down on her knees, asking Iwasaki in Japanese what we would like to drink; he then asked us in English whether we would like beer or saké. In spite of Morton's cold, we decided to ask for beer, not only because it was only mid-day but also because we had some vague recollection that Iwasaki was not much of a drinker. Immediately upon our asking for beer, he seemed relieved and informed us, in what by now is a much-repeated form of humor among our friends, that in Japan one must, in order to be a philosopher, drink much alcohol—witness Messrs. Ohmori and Yamamoto—but that he, Iwasaki, was not up to their standards. This produced a few chuckles and we leaned back on our back-supporters—a device which seems to have been invented for visiting foreigners who lack the traditional Japanese capacity to sit erectly at a low table with only a cushion under them. The device—a sort of legless chair—was a godsend to Morton, who was never able to manage the proper sitting posture and who was always sticking his legs under the low table because he could not tuck them under him; he would be leaning on one arm or another before the meal was over. Lucia had no trouble at all imitating the authentic Japanese posture on these occasions.   The repast was delicious and very Japanese, all the way down to octopus-meat which came, we were told, from very small members of that species, dwarfs, we gathered from the waitress, who assured us with gestures and horrid faces that were supposed to represent our common notions of the big octopus that we were not being fed parts of *that*. Raw fish, tempura, and tiny fish of the size of gold-fish appeared in dizzying order, followed by soup, and God knows what else. Consequently, we were faced with the usual Oriental smorgasbord, not knowing, as it were, what soup to begin with and what nuts to end with.

The conversation was at first desultory, partly because of Iwasaki's unsureness about his English and partly because of his shyness. Inevitably, we discussed the great changes between Tokyo today and Tokyo ten years ago, not to mention Tokyo twenty-five years ago. Iwasaki amused us by telling us that when our friend Bill Frankena of Michigan was teaching in the Stanford-Tokyo Seminar in American Studies, Bill spoke English so slowly that Iwasaki developed great confidence in his capacity to understand the language. However, when he went to the States shortly thereafter, Iwasaki said he could, at first, understand *nothing* because, he realized, nobody in the States spoke as slowly as Frankena had spoken.

Suddenly, however, Iwasaki said: "To change the topic completely, I want to *ahsk* you *abot anoddza mattah*. What *hoppens* in your country when, as in the case of my wife and me, the children are married and leave *za* house of *za* parents?" Of course, he was touching on a problem which is newer in Japan than it is in America, the decline of the extended family in which the grandparents remain under the same roof as their children and grandchildren, or at least on the same plot of ground. In Japan an older *son* would be obliged to take care of his widowed mother in that way—witness the case of Ohmori and his mother and that of Miyo Kishimoto, who lived near her older son in her own cottage on the same plot. But parents like the Iwasakis who had only daughters were in a different position; and therefore Mrs. Iwasaki was, according to her husband, much distressed by the departure of her children even though he said that they saw the girls and their husbands every Sunday. We pointed out that this was a far better situation than what the Iwasakis might experience in America, where one daughter might live in Michigan and another in Seattle while the parents lived in New York. We do not know how much consolation that gave Iwasaki, but it occurred to us later that some of the special unhappiness that isolated Japanese grandparents might feel could derive from their system of un-romantic, arranged marriage. If two people had not been in love when they married, they might not develop the kind of attachment in later years which is supposed to occur after the cooling of sexual ardor. Therefore, two people whose children had left the house, who lacked affection for each other, and who also lacked *intellectual* community—as would be likely when the man was a Japanese *academic*—might well find themselves uneasy and without much interest in one another.

As we left Iwasaki, we felt very sad for him. When we heard of his death, we could not help recalling that gloomy day in Tokyo when he unburdened himself—almost tearfully—as he looked out of the restaurant window at the pouring rain and the gray sky. It was one of the few occasions on which a Japanese had spoken to us about so intimate a matter. We had always thought of Iwasaki as reserved, shy, laconic, and very much under control; and so the most controlled of our Japanese friends, it would appear, may have unburdened himself to us more than any of his more loquacious countrymen. We have sometimes wondered whether his heart condition and ultimately his death could have been connected with his tendency to keep strong emotions bottled up; and in retrospect we felt very badly about not having encouraged him to speak more freely to us. On the other hand, Goro Mayeda was also taken away by a heart attack, and he was almost the opposite of Iwasaki in temperament. Mayeda chirped while Iwasaki rolled his eyes in silence, yet both departed by the same route.

Among the more outgoing Japanese philosophers—more like Mayeda then like Iwasaki—was Natuhiko Yosida, who was just about to take up a membership at the Institute in the fall of 1976. We came to know him when he had visited Harvard a few years earlier and were immediately struck by his brightness. He had no hesitation about using first names, spoke English extremely well, and later showed himself to be a first-rate philosopher in the analytic tradition. Since he had already been elected a member of the Institute, he felt some special obligation to us. He and his wife met us at the airport when we arrived, and they insisted that we come to their place in Yokohama where he teaches at the Tokyo Institute of Technology. At his insistence, he picked us up in a taxi at International House, saying hopefully that it would take about twenty minutes to drive to Yokohama. Actually it was more like an hour and a half during rush-hour traffic over a maze of superhighways interspersed with dashes through narrow, winding streets. The Yosidas lived in a huge high-rise apartment—close to the top and at the end of a long open-air corridor—where we blew in around eight o'clock and were greeted by Hiroko Yosida, who is a very lively, good-natured woman. The arrangement of the apartment was all Western-style with books lining the walls. Soon after we arrived, Yosida ushered in another couple. The husband was an astrophysicist and the wife was a piano teacher; both of them spoke English very well. The subjects of conversation now escape us, except for a long discussion of the merits of contemporary pianists. To illustrate some point, Yosida played a tape recording of Glenn Gould's rendering of Beethoven's Fifth Symphony. But suddenly in the midst of our happy feasting and conversation we realized it was very late and that International House might lock us out if we arrived there after a certain hour. Frantically, the Yosidas hurried us into a taxi and, like some of their compatriots, insisted on paying the driver without our knowing it. When we got to I. House we offered to pay the fare but our driver shook his head, and we then knew that the usual thing had happened. There was not escaping the determined hospitality of the Japanese!

Almost all of our old friends vied with each other in their efforts to entertain us in the prosperous days of 1976, either by inviting us to their homes or to restaurants. For some reason, they rarely took us to concerts or plays, probably because attendance at those entertainments would have diminished the amount of time for conversation and catching up. Among those friends who wanted very much to catch up were the Wataru Kurodas. When they came to take us out one day, they struck us as having changed very little. He was slightly stouter, rosier, and more relaxed; she was even more flawless in her geisha-like elegance. Wataru—he, unlike Ohmori, wanted to use first names—continued to impress us as both bright and shy, and his wife seemed to speak English less militantly than she did when we first met her ten years earlier. She had given up her studies of Thomas Hardy for a full-time job as "a homemaking woman with a homely wit." They were now the parents of a nine-year old son, whose photograph showed a lively, mischievous-looking boy in his soccer uniform. After picking us up at I. House, they sped us to a first-class French restaurant on an avenue west of Tokyo Tower near the Prince Hotel. It was situated in a building that looked like a Victorian mansion which was built only a few years ago to capitalize on nostalgia. To the sound of intermittent *samisen* music and Mozart as background entertainment we feasted on French delicacies. Needing a good dose of fresh air afterwards, we walked back through a funeral assemblage which was gathered at a Buddhist Temple to honor the deceased, a fabulously wealthy, self-made business man. Then we walked around Tokyo Tower toward I. House. Since the sun was still shining, Kuroda lined us up in the International House garden for farewell photographs.

When we were not being rushed about town by our hospitable and now more affluent friends, we had time to observe the habits of poorer people who made life so comfortable for us in I. House, our Japanese home away from home. At the front desk in the main lobby there were three little maidens dressed in black who—as in past years—performed the services there as a *group*. Also in the main lobby there were two very pleasant, venerable gentlemen who discreetly walked about the lobby, coffee shop, and main restaurant, keeping a sharp eye on everything that went on, and behaving in general like two floorwalkers of a department store. They kept things running smoothly and flawlessly from the point of view of a constantly changing stream of guests. Another mark of the service was the hypersensitivity of the immaculate, doll-like waitresses and waiters to every need of the guests they served at table. They tried eagerly (and usually successfully) to remember whether the particular guest took coffee at breakfast, or tea, whether he liked two boiled eggs, or only one, and how many pieces of toast he ate. Almost all of the waiters and waitresses were very eager to use their correct but limited English; they politely declined to play the game of letting us use our incorrect and limited Japanese. Another thing we noted about the service at International House was the choreography of the cleaning women. They also worked in teams of three or four. When we crossed the main lobby at breakfast time, the team would be rhythmically vacuuming the whole surface with toy-like shiny, Hoover vacuum cleaners; the team members would all be wearing spanking-white kerchiefs, blouses and full skirts, and black stockings and shoes. We also observed the remarkably indefatigable devotion of the chauffeurs who drove the fancy automobiles that were parked every day at the front entrance, ready to be commandeered by their owners. The elegant, shiny-black limousines, with white linen slipcovers on their upholstery were, of course, a badge of prestige. A further mark of prestige was the right to expect the tireless exertions with which the chauffeurs brushed their limousines with feather dusters and polished them inside and outside all morning and all afternoon as long as their owners were attending meetings at International House.

The teamwork and tireless activity of these dancing teams reminded us of an earlier visit when Lucia went to the hairdresser's and was astonished at having *four* beauticians crowd around her to do "a wave and set." We observed something similar at I. House one day when we saw two stalwart young houseboys carrying a long, slim pole which could easily have been carried by one of them alone; they even used four hands on that pole while fishing a pane of glass out of the garden pond. The pane had fallen from a Japanese lantern perched on a stone in the middle of the pond. Their mission accomplished, they returned sedately through the garden back to the house. Numerous social values are probably served by these working arrangements, values beyond the sociability and family-like solidarity that they encourage. They may well contribute to the extremely low crime rate in Japan by keeping certain people off the streets; and they certainly diminish unemployment.

Teamwork was also present in the world of scholarship. Morton discovered that a group of three Japanese scholars were working on a translation of his book *Science and Sentiment in America*. Murai himself had translated Morton's *Religion, Politics, and the Higher Learning*, but by then he had become enough of a mandarin, so to speak, to assign parts of such a task to academic dependents. This scholarly team consisted of former students of his, since he was a professor to whom they continued to defer in the German—or at least what used to be the German—manner. By this we do not mean to say that Murai *ordered* these three young professors to undertake the translation since he is rather mild and does not strike one as a managerial type. We suspect that because he was too busy to take on the job himself, he merely "suggested" that they help him with it and they did. The consequences of their doing academic work as a team were not altogether salutary. When they met with Morton, they all put questions to him about what he meant by certain passages in the book. The grilling began after a pleasant meal in the main dining room of I. House when Morton and the troupe of translators went to the lobby and commenced the business. It was not easy and, in fact, was made especially hard by the fact that Morton was coming down with a cold. The questioning was done mainly by Tanaka-san, a very boyish man of indeterminate age who was assigned the chapters in the middle of the book and the epilogue. He produced a very large notebook and simply went over problematic words and phrases one by one, saying things like "P. 201, line 14 from the bottom" and then asking his question well before Morton could get to the puzzling passage. Many of these questions concerned idioms, metaphors, and literary allusions, all of which a Japanese might well fail to catch. The most amusing query was about Morton's reference to something being as "American as apple pie, indeed, as apple pie in the sky." Here there was a need to explain *two* Americanisms and why they were linked as they were. However, if Mr. Tanaka had gone to the library of International House, he would have been able to put his hands on a dictionary of American idioms or slang in which "pie in the sky" was adequately explained; and if he had consulted the big Webster, there he would have found an entry on "Lochinvar" which would have made it unnecessary for him to ask Morton why he had called Josiah Royce a philosophical Lochinvar out of the West. Such questions were asked for almost four hours during which Tanaka and his teammates just about knocked out Morton without satisfying their curiosity completely. It was agreed, therefore, that they would either telephone him before he left Tokyo or write to him about things which in their opinion demanded his attention. The meeting was closed with many pleasant "sayonara"s, but Morton left it with a qualified view of the value of team-translation.

Since Morton's cold had grown worse during this session and since Lucia was suffering from "Tokyo tummy," our activity after that had to be curtailed considerably. Our ailments forced us to cut out a dinner at Murai's house and one at Miss Kubota's later that week, but we found time on the weekend for a lunch that we gave to Miss Takagi and Miyo Kishimoto on Saturday and for a Sunday lunch with Jenny before a trip to the Tokyo Tower, Japan's effort to out-Eiffel the Eiffel Tower by several feet.

While eating with Miyo Kishimoto and Miss Takagi we were struck most of all by Miyo's youthfulness and energy. Then about seventy, she was dressed in a smart green and black checked pants suit. In the course of the luncheon, she showed us photographs of three granddaughters, children of her older son, with whom she still lived in a little house he had built for her alongside his own house. Every day her granddaughters would come in to see her, or else she would go over to the main house to help with the household. She is such an agreeable person that you can imagine the arrangement works very well. When we saw Miyo in 1966 she was considering taking up Ikebana (flower-arranging) as a profession, but she abandoned that, she said, in favor of singing, which she had done as a young girl. In 1976 she sang with a regular chorus with whom she had recently given a concert. A photograph of this group showed all the other members of Miyo's chorus to be young women of college age, and she laughingly said that she was the grandmother of the chorus. After telling us about her special interest in water-color painting, she reported that Bill, her younger son who lives in the U.S., had been divorced from his American wife and had been remarried to a very pretty Japanese girl. Bill was then teaching art at Deerfield Academy in Massachusetts, not very far from our summer cottage in Vermont.

Our trip with Jenny to Tokyo Tower turned out to be more of an undertaking than we had expected. Jenny had said several times that it was her ambition to go all the way to the top of Tokyo Tower (she had previously managed the first half of the ascent), so since this Sunday was a brilliantly clear day, we decided to take a taxi to the tower on the spur of the moment.

We arrived there in a traffic jam, and long queues were lined up three-deep on the main floor of the tower because what seemed like a million people had, like us, taken advantage of the splendid weather. The huge crowd behaved very quietly, and finally we were transported half way up the tower in a jammed elevator. The view was splendid enough at several hundred feet above Tokyo; but we pressed on, bought more tickets, queued up for another elevator, and finally emerged on the top platform. From here we could see about a hundred miles of packed buildings covering the earth in all directions. It took some time studying our maps before we triumphantly located in the near distance the locations of Jenny's Nishimachi International School and our International House.

Because our indispositions had forced us to cancel a planned trip to Kyoto and Nara, we had a hectic but amusing time trying to recoup the money we had paid in advance for our tickets on the famous "Bullet Train," which speeds at more than one hundred miles an hour from Tokyo to Kyoto and beyond. Morton had recalled that Yosida's secretary had bought them for us earlier in the week for a little over 21,000 yen, which amounted to about seventy dollars, and so it seemed desirable to try to get some of that money back. It was after dinner on Sunday, March 21, when we first decided to cancel our trip, and we were scheduled to go the next day at about 10 A.M. So the question arose: could we cancel *now*? At the front desk of I. House there was much learned consultation, of which we comprehended nothing, but the consensus opinion—given to us by the clerk best able to speak English—was that we could get some of our money back if we cancelled at least two hours before departure time. Well, then, what to do? Two hours before departure time the next day would be eight o'clock on a Monday morning, and the traffic at that hour would be indescribable. We would have to be up by at least 6 A.M. to have breakfast and to get an early enough cab; then there would be the interminable lines at windows in Tokyo Station, not to speak of the problem of *what* window to go to for a refund when they were all labelled in incomprehensible Japanese. We concluded that if we waited until Monday morning, we might as well say good-bye to our seventy bucks.

Therefore we asked the man at the front desk to find out how late the Tokyo Eki (station) would be open that Sunday night. (We inquired about 9 P.M.) He got on the phone; it was about fifteen minutes before he could penetrate the waves of busy signals; and then he learned that the station closed at 11. Consequently, we asked him to call for a cab, which came in about ten minutes, directed our driver to "Tokyo Eki" and then were hit with a torrent of Japanese which, we inferred, was a request for the part of the station we wanted to go to—it being about a mile long, it seemed. Suddenly, we remembered the name of the Bullet Train in Japanese, "Shinkansen," and when that magic word was uttered, we apparently satisfied the driver.

Fortunately, the streets of downtown Tokyo were relatively deserted on a Sunday night, and we got to the Eki a little before ten. We were told that the Shinkansen windows had green lettering above them, so we headed for one of them. There we found, naturally, two chaps who knew almost no English. So we produced all the various tickets for the round-trip and kept shouting, in the manner of Perry Miller, "No go tomorrow. Want money back," until they finally, after looking at the tickets, got the point. However, they were saying—as we gathered—that *they* could not refund any money and that we would have to go to what they managed to indicate was the "Tsentrol Awfice." But where was that? Well, all they could do was sputter and point, so we followed their fingers with a deep fear that it would be so long before we got to our destination that we would have reached it after the magic hour of eleven. We made a couple of mistakes even though Lucia had the good sense to get our guides to write "Central Office" on a chit of paper in Japanese. We kept showing that to people who kept pointing, and finally we reached our last two men. (There are always at least pairs of people, and this was fortunate because if one of them was unable to understand, the other might be able to get the point.) They looked and one shook his head, but the other smiled and at that point we knew we had crashed through the linguistic barrier when he opened up his cash-till and refunded all our money except for about 8 per cent of the 21,000 yen. We returned home by taxi feeling luxuriously that we had a lot of extra money in *our* till.

It should be added that we arrived at our decision not to make the trip to Kyoto by consensus. We had in our desk two cancelled tickets from Tokyo Tower and decided to vote secretly on them—to write "Yes" or "No" after a lengthy discussion in which neither was sure what the other really wanted to do. This voting showed the following result: unanimously "No"! Later, when Morton saw Hiromichi Takeda, "our man in Kyoto," who was to be our guide, he allowed that *he* had had a cold too; so that it may be said that if *he* had voted, the result would have remained unanimously in the negative. Naturally we regretted our not being able to see all those lovely palaces, shrines, temples, and gardens but we had seen them three times before; and we could not help thinking of our discomfort on one earlier trip to a holy place when we ran around cold floors in stockings, looking for nonexistent toilets!

So, after a few days of rest and recuperation in I. House, we faced what had loomed as the greatest chore of our stay, namely, Morton's lecture and conference; but it turned out to be a very pleasant informative occasion. It was sort of an old home day in which he delivered part of a paper on the philosophical foundations of the Declaration of Independence under the title "Self-evident Truth and Natural Rights" to about thirty-five Japanese scholars and Lucia. However, he put at the beginning of his talk a sort of sentimental set of reminiscences of his connection with Japanese philosophers, remarking at one point while his *Science and Sentiment in America* was not an autobiographical work, it did in some sense reflect two aspects of his personality—the sentimental and the rational—as it did the two components of American philosophy upon which he had focused in his book. Therefore, he went on, he was going to indulge his sentiments, his feelings, and emotions by expressing from the bottom of his heart the gratitude we all felt—Lucia, our sons, Jenny, and he—toward our old Japanese friends.

Morton gave this talk on self-evident truth and natural rights rather than a more technical one on free will and possibility after he had been informed by the organizer of the meeting, Wataru Kuroda, that he was not familiar with some of Morton's recent papers on the latter subject and therefore he for one would not be able to follow such a talk very well. Indeed, even when Morton outlined the talk he *did* give, Kuroda asked that copies be made for distribution so as to improve the discussion; but Morton resisted this idea, saying that he would speak *very* slowly and that he was not in a position to provide a finished text. For all of the going back and forth of Japanese and American philosophers since the war, in 1976 there was still a great gulf, part of it linguistic but part of it something else which reflects the difficulty that philosophy has in moving across borders and cultures. Progress had been made, but there was still a long way to go. Nevertheless, there had been a deepening of emotional sympathy which had done much to improve communication.

Because Morton chose to speak slowly he exhausted virtually all of the time of the formal meeting—so that no time was left for questions—and not without what seemed to be the encouragement of Kuroda. Morton felt that the Japanese were definitely relieved by the fact that they would *not* be obliged to exchange with him publicly before their colleagues, lest they reveal some egregious misunderstanding for which they could be sneered at or pounced upon in private. Therefore, the meeting moved to another room of I. House, where a magnificent supply of alcoholic beverages was laid before us as well as a splendid table of delicacies that could have served as a supper.

At first, there was coolness and typical Japanese shyness, exhibited in the way in which the group of thirty-five or forty (augmented by the arrival of a few who did not come to the lecture) spread into a circle that was almost as great in area as the room itself. But as soon as the Suntory Whiskey and the beer made their impact, there was a noticeable increase of noise and several approaches to Morton by commentators and questioners, often speaking very informatively. And very quickly there was a call for quiet by the head-man, Kuroda, who called upon Iwasaki-san to make a few remarks. Shy, diffident, and even frightened by his inadequacy in English, Iwasaki first spoke in Japanese and then translated what he had said into English for our benefit. It was a touching but brief expression of gratitude and of welcome.

The party became noisier and noisier, the drinking and munching went on, more and more people asked obscure questions and made unclear remarks—some of them very difficult to understand—yet by accepted standards for these occasions in Japan, there was "exchange." Morton had the feeling that he had been understood by many but by *how* many he really did not know. Unfortunately, Ohmori came in only toward the end of the talk because, he said, he had had much business connected with his being dean now. This was unfortunate because he is candid and might have said how the lecture had gone over *if* he had heard it. Kuroda was cordial at first and later was even enthusiastic, reporting that Professor Tsueshita, a specialist on British empiricism, had spoken very highly of what had been said about Locke. Morton was sure that there were several people there, like Yosida and a chap named Imamichi, whom we had met at Iwasaki's in 1966, who could have discussed the paper in private very intelligently. But once the atmosphere became jolly, there was a tendency to avoid making the speaker "feel tired," since all of them knew that he was overcoming a cold and that he had thrown himself into the lecture rather vigorously even though he had spoken slowly. Nevertheless, there *was* discussion and exchange, and he felt that he had made some contribution to the advancement and diffusion of knowledge and even more certain that he had struck a blow for understanding at a more emotional level. This became evident when Kuroda called on our old friend Sawada to make a second set of remarks.

Sawada spoke entirely in English and began rather wittily by saying that he supposed that he had been called on to make the *second* speech because he was, after Iwasaki, the oldest Japanese philosopher in the room. We judged that Sawada was then about sixty, and Iwasaki about sixty-two or sixty-three. Sawada responded with a surprising amount of feeling and even ease about how much they appreciated the speaker's remarks and especially how much they agreed with him about the changes in attitude among Japanese philosophers since the days when Ikegami, the phenomenologist, ruled Tokyo philosophy. Indeed, Sawada paid the speaker the compliment of saying that he had played a great part in bringing about the change, reminiscing with warmth about how so many of them had attended seminars at our house at 28 Coolidge Hill Road in Cambridge and how they had learned much there. He concluded in what seemed like an earnest tone by asking both of us to return to Japan in the future.

We had mistakenly thought that this would be the end of speech-making but as soon as Sawada—who had been asked to "close the meeting"—finished, Morton was asked whether he would not reply and say a few words. Obviously, he could not refuse, so he thanked all of the participants for coming and all of our friends for their kindness and loyalty. Pointing out once again that our connection with Japan was now a matter of *three* generations, with Jenny now here, Morton said he hoped that the connec-

tion would continue forever—and with this he ended. Next Lucia was unexpectedly called upon to speak, and Morton thought she rose brilliantly to
the occasion—much to *her* surprise but not to Morton's. He congratulated
her on having the good sense and sweetness not only to thank the group but
also to extend an invitation to all of them to come to see us in Princeton.
Soon thereafter the festivities closed with handshakes, "sayonara"s,
"good-bye"s, and "au revoir"s. It was a genuinely successful pair of
feasts—one of science and one of sentiment.

The lecture, conference, and reception had been on a Friday night; and on
Saturday we rested our stomachs after having eaten on Friday the usual
unidentifiable tidbits like rice-cum-seaweed sandwiches, unknown fishes,
and other comestibles that can have odd aftereffects on foreigners, especially
when washed down by draughts of beer or Suntory. But we had ourselves
laid on a stomach-taxing luncheon and dinner for the last Sunday of our
stay—the former for the Ohmoris, the Kurodas, and the Yosidas, and the
latter for Jenny and her mother. The Japanese couples were those to whom
we were most indebted: Ohmori had been the prime mover of the trip and
our host at a fine party; Kuroda, the chief organizer of the conference and
our host at another fine party; and Yosida, the supplier of secretarial assistance and also our host at a fine party. Besides, we liked all of them and all of
their wives, so we asked them to come to I. House on Sunday at noon,
planning to go from there to the Stockholm Restaurant down the hill. We
puzzled for a long time about our choice, thinking that some might find it
too Western whereas others might like it for that reason. In any case, it
honored American Express cards, it was close, and we liked it, so we took
our fetchingly outfitted party—Mrs. Ohmori and Mrs. Yosida in lovely
kimonos and Mrs. Kuroda in a handsome, chic Western frock—to this dark,
Scandinavian rathskeller near Roppongi, presided over by a tall handsome
Norwegian and specializing in smorgasbord.

We asked Ohmori to transport the ladies in his car while Morton walked
down the hill with Kuroda and Yosida. When the three men arrived, the
others were all sitting in a dark cocktail lounge that reminded us (as it had
earlier, too) of Haakon's Hall in Bergen, Norway; so we could just imagine
raucous toasts and much chewing of venison-bones before roaring fires. But
here in the Orient there was a splendidly lit bar, whose shelves were lined
with whatever liquor could be found in the best bar in Manhattan, also a
quietly efficient bartender and a beautiful white grand piano that separated
the lounge from the main dining room.

Because we had all elected to partake of the smorgasbord luncheon, we
sat at two tables for four, Morton with Mr. Ohmori, Mrs. Yosida, and
Kuroda, and Lucia with Ohmori, Yosida and Mrs. Kuroda. There seemed
to be general enthusiasm for the Swedish fare, judging by the number of
returns to the smorgasbord table, especially on the part of Mrs. Kuroda,

who, it will be remembered, was a specialist on Thomas Hardy though she had never set foot outside of Japan. We had a vague impression that the place was too un-Japanese for Ohmori, but there was much merriment over luncheon and then a general brief farewell at the lounge at I. House, since we expected *not* to see any of our closest friends again before leaving for Los Angeles.

In the evening Jenny and her mother arrived for our second farewell meal, and though they had spent the day at a seaside resort, they were ready to go out on the town again rather than stay at I. House's quiet dining room, so this time we picked Sereyna's (near the Roppongi cross-roads) about which various people had raved. It turned out to have excellent shabu-shabu, served up with delicious Kobe beef, which Jenny said they almost never ate—indeed they almost never ate beef of any kind because it was so expensive. The restaurant was quite vulgarly elaborate and ornate, and we had in the center of our table a large copper pot with a round cover that had a sort of smokestack in the center out of which steam poured when the gas fire had heated the pot to boiling. First we "fell to," boiling the thin slices of beef for a moment; then Jenny heaped into the broth Chinese cabbage, mushrooms, bean curd, soya, spaghetti, and something like watercress. We were ushered to another part of the restaurant in a nest of writhing dark brown ugly sculptures for the dessert course. There we finished our meal with a delicious green-tea ice cream.

On the way to the Roppongi subway we were struck again by how flourishing Jenny looked. She seemed quite pleased and happy to be in Tokyo. Her latest assignment at school, about which she was most enthusiastic, was a play about a dwarf-king who is miserable because of his size. The plot now escapes us, but Jenny played the part of one of "the protesters" and had to do a lot of shouting. On the next weekend there would be two public performances of the play at a neighborhood auditorium in an impressive public community center. We were disappointed to miss seeing Jenny's latest production and very sad to be saying "sayonara" to her at the Roppongi subway station, into which she and her mother descended together without a qualm at nine o'clock at night while we walked back through crowded Roppongi and along the dimly-lit Toriizaka-machi street, a quarter of a mile back to International House.

These two Sunday meals were delightful but tiring—as so many of our social meetings were—and therefore we regaled ourselves for the most part on a rainy Monday, the day of our departure, by resting. We were very happy in reflecting on our good times but very sad to think of departing a place we liked so much, not to speak of taking leave of Jenny for a few months and of our Japanese friends for what could be years. We took breakfast as usual at I. House but check-out time was 1 P.M. and our plane was not to leave before 9:45 P.M., so what to do on a rainy, gloomy day? We arranged to extend our time of departure to 3 P.M., a great concession to us because the hostelry was expecting to be packed that night in anticipation of an announced strike by railroad workers which would force people to stay in town so that they could get to work the next day.

Because we could not face eating supper at I. House after taking lunch there, we packed our bags, checked them in the cloakroom, and locked the door of our own room at three for the last time. After that we wasted time in the lobby, looked into the library, ambled around the neighborhood, and finally took an early supper at the Stockholm Restaurant again. The Norwegian headwaiter, very delighted to have us eat there so often, remarked that it was too bad that they did not serve breakfast there. A handsome, tall, blond man, he opened up a bit about himself. He told of having lived in Tokyo for about a dozen years, of being a Norwegian from Oslo and not a Swede, of not liking Norway at all. He had, he said, tried to go back there for a while but could not—he was, we guessed, in his late thirties—readjust to his family or to Oslo. He did not say whether he was married but reported how he lived in Japan, owning a seaside house, having a flat in Tokyo, being able to sail or ski at his whim when he had time. He seemed to speak perfect Japanese and, as "maître d'," to run a tight but happy ship whose entire crew was Japanese. (He even told us of having lived for one year in Brooklyn, just across the Brooklyn Bridge, and of liking *that* more than Oslo.)

We finally said "sayonara" to him too, trudged up the hill, and sat down to await Professor Tsueshita, Morton's one-time seminar student at Harvard, who was desperate to drive us to the airport. He had been scheduled to take us to Kuroda's house in Kamakura, but when that visit had been cancelled, the poor man had been deprived of the opportunity to "do something" for us, and now this drive seemed like his last chance. Being nervous, he arrived at 7 P.M. after having agreed to come at 7:30. But since at 7 we were sitting aimlessly and anxiously in the lobby of I. House after our early dinner, his early arrival was a godsend. Our bags were scooped up by various members of the I. House staff—the elderly floorwalking manager, the young chap who looked like a naval captain, the tall white-coated bellhop, the black-dressed little girls—and then after we had our bags put in the back of Tsueshita's car, they all lined up and bowed and waved in the old touching way that was so common in the Japan of a quarter of a century earlier. It was very affecting.

After we got into Tsueshita's car on that drizzly night, he headed for the superhighway that runs almost directly from Roppongi to the airport. At times we were nervous because *he* was. In spite of having ample time, the rain and the traffic obviously made him tense as he kept murmuring about this being the worst kind of driving weather. We looked at each other with some degree of concern as he tried to break into speeding lanes of cars that included those fearless and pushy Tokyo cabdrivers. Somehow luck was with us, and the trip went off without incident. Tsueshita dropped us at the JAL entry, and then went to park his car, promising to return. Meanwhile we checked in with our tickets and Tsueshita did return. Together we mounted a staircase to a large hall for departing passengers and their friends. We were all for letting the poor man go home and for proceeding, on our own, through the rest of the formalities. But he began to make us feel that something was "up" when he refused to leave and began to say things like "I shall go to look for others; I *think* there will be others; I *know* there will be others. Please wait here for a while."

What had happened, of course, was that Tsueshita, by scooping us up from I. House so early, had gotten us to the airport too early for a group of wellwishers he knew would come. Therefore, he had to keep us from entering the maw of the so-called "sterile" area for-passengers-only before the wellwishers arrived. In short, he had to stall us, which he did successfully since all of a sudden we were surrounded by many good friends, as we had been on other occasions when flying from Japan.

We had not expected such a group to see us off because we had thought it was agreed that this time we would depart without their making the long trip from Tokyo to Haneda airport. Nevertheless, we suddenly saw a delegation crowding behind Tsueshita—Reiko Ohmori with her younger daughter, Mrs. Yosida, Mr. and Mrs. Sawada, and finally—to our astonishment—little, shy Iwasaki, the elder statesman now of all the Tokyo philosophers. There were many warm exchanges about how delightful it had been to be together, many reminders that they were all to come to Princeton as soon as possible. Reiko Ohmori pinned a corsage of yellow fuchsias that she had made on Lucia's shoulder, and Mrs. Yosida pressed a small package into Lucia's hand as she begged us to leave word in Princeton—if we should be away when they would arrive the following August—as to who would be there to give her the advice she would need about the Institute, concerning which she was already harboring vague fears. Before much more could be said, the loudspeakers began to blare in Japanese and English that the passengers for Japan Airlines Flight 62 should proceed to the "sterile" area. Again and again we promised to write and called out "sayonara"s as we were swept along by crowds of passengers. Soon we could not distinguish our friends from the rest of the waving, cheering mob in the waiting room.

Earlier we said something brief about the introduction to Morton's talk "Self-evident Truth and Natural Rights," but that introduction expresses so much of what we both felt after almost twenty-five years of contact with the Japanese that we conclude this chapter by reproducing it in spite of its excessively stiff and autobiographical character:

> "As many of you know, I am the author of a book called *Science and Sentiment in America*, and although that is not an autobiographical work,

its title in a certain respect represents two aspects of my own personality
and my own philosophy for I am, as some of you know, a man of
sentiment as well as a man of science or reason—exhibiting these two
qualities which I think all women and men—even philosophers—
exhibit in one degree or another. And therefore, with your permission,
I shall begin this talk with a brief expression of certain personal feelings,
or sentiments, or emotions which I have as I face this group of distinguished scholars and friends.

It is now almost twenty-four years since the day Lucia-san and I first
arrived in Japan in the summer of 1952, and we did not dream at that
time that our relations with your country and with Japanese scholars—
both philosophers and students of American life—would become as
close as they have become. For since the time we first arrived in Japan,
we have made four separate visits to your country: in 1952, in 1960, in
1966, and 1976; and in those twenty-four years many of you have visited
us in Cambridge, Massachusetts, or in Princeton, New Jersey. You
have become friends of ours, of our sons, and of our granddaughter,
and you have expressed your friendship to all of us in more ways than I
can possibly summarize without taking up the whole time of this conference. For all of this I wish to thank you from the bottom of my heart
on behalf of all our family: my wife, myself, my son Nicholas, my son
Stephen, and my eleven-year old granddaughter Jennifer, who, if she
were here delivering this talk, would be delivering it in Japanese. My
one great regret is that, in spite of having had such close connections
with Japan, I remain incompetent in your language and my one great
hope is that before I become incompetent in all languages, I shall become competent enough to deliver a talk to you in your language.
However, I hope that in spite of my incompetence in Japanese and because of your great competence in English that I shall be able to make
myself understood to all of you even if I do not persuade you to agree
with me. My hope is based on the fact that some of us have had enough
contact over a generation to be able to sympathize with each other and
to understand each other even when we cannot agree about the truth of
certain statements in philosophy or history.

Before I conclude these personal remarks and turn to the more scientific or rational part of this paper, I want to tell you how differently I
feel today from the way in which I felt twenty-four years ago, when I
first addressed a specialist's conference in philosophy at the Todai
Alumni Club. The subject of my paper was, as I recall, "The Right to
Believe," and I tried to develop in it views which were expressed in
print four years later in a chapter of my book entitled *Toward Reunion in
Philosophy*. It was a very hot, humid day in July and I was a very nervous young American philosopher about to face a very professional au-

dience. Several of you will recall that I was one of five American professors from Harvard and Stanford participating in an American Studies Seminar: one professor in American literature, one in American history, one in American economics, one in American political science, and one in American philosophy—myself. The distinguished chairman of the Committee was the late Professor Hideo Kishimoto, who became a very good friend of mine in later years and whose passing all of his American friends deeply regret. But on that hot July morning in 1952, just before I was to deliver my paper, Kishimoto-san whispered to me: "You will have the most difficult problem of all of the American professors for the Japanese do not believe that there is such a thing as American philosophy." Naturally, this was a somewhat depressing thing to be told just as I was about to face a distinguished critical audience, especially as I looked at the rather stern face of the late Professor Ikegami. Nevertheless, I began my lecture—I could not do anything else—and hoped for the best. And somewhere in the middle of the talk I began to feel that my audience was beginning to relax, to be a little more friendly to the young American philosopher. At last, I thought I saw Professor Ikegami smile and I even thought I saw him shake his head in approval of perhaps one of my statements. From that moment on I felt, not that I had persuaded anyone completely of my thesis, but that I had won at least the respect of some of my Japanese colleagues, and that I could communicate with them in a friendly, cooperative way even when we could not agree.

This feeling was intensified when my wife and I came here and some of you came to Harvard, to my house at 28 Coolidge Hill Road, Cambridge, and to the Institute for Advanced Study. And therefore I appear before you today with a greater confidence in our powers to understand each other, something as difficult as it is rare in philosophy. Naturally, I do not expect total agreement but I feel that a generation of communication between us has brought about greater intellectual and emotional community than that which existed before. Therefore, I no longer feel as I did when I addressed the Japanese philosophers in 1952 for now I know that I face a very different kind of audience. Even if we disagree now, we shall know what we are disagreeing about. And even if we diverge scientifically, I know that we shall be close in sentiment because we are friends.

No doubt this speech will strike some readers as excessively sentimental but to them we can only say that it expressed some of our feelings toward our friends. A generation of sporadic but frequent contact had forged a very strong personal link between us and the Japanese we knew.

ELEVEN

Japan Visited for the Fifth Time: 1979

Our fifth trip to Japan began in early May 1979, but it was made under auspices that were very different from those under which we had made our earlier trips. It will be recalled that in 1952, 1960, 1966, and 1976 private American sources had footed most of the bill, but the trip of 1979 was supported in a manner that clearly showed the great strength of the Japanese economy. The so-called Japanese miracle had spread into the world of culture and education with the establishment of something called The Japan Foundation in 1972, and the miracle seemed even more wondrous when that foundation proceeded to invite Western scholars to come to Japan without any obligation to lecture or to teach. This time Morton crossed the Pacific as a sort of V.I.P.; he was given a *per diem* that was ample enough to take care of the expenses of both of us; and was also presented with a first-class round-trip air ticket to Tokyo that could be exchanged for two economy tickets without requiring the payment of too great a supplement. Of course, the Japanese inflation would make it difficult for two to live as cheap as one in Tokyo, but we would live quite comfortably by our standards.

The official brochure of The Japan Foundation contains as an epigraph the following statement: "the goal of the Foundation is to contribute to mutual understanding and the enhancement of world culture through the expansion of cultural exchange," a statement we have excerpted from what is referred to in the brochure as Article 1 of The Japan Foundation Law. The same handsomely printed pamphlet—which is written in very good English—contains a photograph of the foundation's headquarters in Tokyo, a squat but very new building of about ten stories. Another part of the pamphlet for 1978 reports that the foundation's sources of revenue are earnings from "endowment, government subsidies, and some private contributions," and that the endowment in 1978 had reached the sum of forty billion yen. The total budget for that same year was 4,910 million yen, no mean sum, as any American student of the yen's value can easily discover. In short, we were under the wing of a very affluent sponsor, a fact which was also brought home to us upon our arrival in Narita Airport, which had been opened to planes after many protests and demonstrations by Japanese students and farmers against the government. The affluence of our sponsor was immediately made evident by the very expensive Japanese car that was made available to us for our trip into town. And our devoted friend Ohmori who, as usual, had come to meet us, laughingly reported that the driver of the limousine in which we all rode had had the honor of driving the great Mr. Henry Kissinger on one occasion. It was all a far cry from 1952, and it made us believe without hesitation in the Japanese miracle. Each year things had gotten better and better. Indeed, as Emerson, the idol of so many Japanese, had once said, *things* were in the saddle in the Japan of 1979. We were not particularly impressed to learn that our chauffeur had driven the car of Mr. Kissinger, whom we knew as a second-rate academic flunky when he was at Harvard and as a dubious character in Washington. But academic travellers to the Orient cannot always be choosers, and that was how Morton justified accepting the invitation of The Japan Foundation, which, so far as he knew, was not a front of the C.I.A. nor of any Japanese counterpart of that organization.

The main force behind the invitation was our old friend Kinuko Kubota. She conceived the idea of Morton's coming as a Fellow of The Japan Foundation because, as she generously said, it was high time for him to come to her country without any formal duties. She sweetly argued that he had done much to foster Japanese-American intellectual exchange through previous trips to Japan and by sponsoring the visits of Japanese scholars to Harvard and later to the Institute for Advanced Study. In her successful campaign to wangle the invitation Kinuko-san was ably assisted by Makoto Saito, a professor of American history at Tokyo University, who, like her, had once been a member of the Institute for Advanced Study.

In pressing for the invitation, Miss Kubota must have come down very hard on the word "exchange" in the phrase "cultural exchange" that appears in the epigraph of the brochure on The Japan Foundation. Nevertheless, when we got to Japan and visited the offices of the foundation, we came to feel that although the word "exchange" appeared ostentatiously on its flag, the purpose of the foundation was actually conceived as if communication was to run only in one direction, and that was from Japan to the rest of the world. If The Rockefeller Foundation thought that it was sending cultural emissaries from America to Tokyo in 1952, The Japan Foundation was now reversing the flow.

This policy was made more ironical by the foundation's explicit announcement that there should be "greater emphasis on mutal exchange rather than the mere presentation of one's culture abroad" and that Japan's conviction was that only through these exchanges can we—all the nations of the world—"improve the quality of our lives and preserve our respective cultural legacies." We emphasize the irony of the foundation's actual policy because we quickly felt its effect when we visited the Tokyo office of the foundation. Having been to Japan so often, we were hardly in need of extensive sightseeing tours, but that was what the foundation seemed eager to provide for us by generously assigning to us pleasant young guides who would cart us about Tokyo and Kyoto in limousines or taxis. Therefore, one business-like stern administrative officer of the foundation and his brisk female secretary were somewhat surprised to hear that we had on many occasions attended performances of the Kabuki, the Bunraku, the Noh, and so on. Therefore they were not able to introduce us to Japanese culture or to have their guides and escorts shepherd us to many Japanese museums, shrines, temples, cultural events, or festivals that were absolutely new to us. Of course, we went back to the National Museum in Tokyo to see that once again—though an important part of it was closed—and when we were in Kyoto we revisited Katsura and Sugakuin. But we did not beg to visit celebrated Japanese politicians or Shinto priests or Zen Buddhist monks. In consequence, the stern executive officer once remarked that Morton ought not to spend so much of his time seeing the Westernized scholars who were his best friends in Tokyo.

In response, Morton tried his best to point out that cultural exchange was not a one-way street and to suggest politely and obliquely that his own contact with Japanese scholars with whom he discussed questions of common interest had probably done more to foster international understanding—the ultimate aim of The Japan Foundation—than any visits he had ever made to Shinto shrines. Pursuing that theme, he tried to persuade the administrator of the value of making supplementary grants to Japanese scholars invited to America—whether in philosophy or in American Studies—grants that might be necessary when American funds were insufficient. Somewhat reluctantly, the administrator agreed that such a thing would be possible, though he added that applicants might appeal to other Japanese sources, like the Ministry of Education. He was very firm, however, in insisting that his foundation would not set up any regular grants for Japanese scholars who would be coming to the States. Instantly Morton agreed, saying that there might well be years when there was no candidate worthy of support and that it would be of dubious value to have a standing fellowship for which one *had* to find an incumbent. The administrator liked that and therefore Morton dropped the subject with the understanding that if there was ever a candidate he felt strongly about, he might encourage such a candidate to approach The Japan Foundation, perhaps through the intercession of Kubota or Saito. This might limit the thing to Americanists and exclude philosophers, but half a loaf would be better than none.

After seeing this foundation executive, Morton had occasion to visit with our old friend Shigeharu Matsumoto, who had ceased being the director and had become the chairman of the board of International House. He was almost eighty and had just lost his lovely wife, but he was still alert of mind and still shrewd. After hearing about what the bureaucrat at The Japan Foundation had said, Matsumoto remarked that the whole purpose of International House had been to foster cultural exchange, and yet it had not benefitted from The Japan Foundation as much as it should have because of the foundation's policies just described. He too thought that understanding is best brought about by exchange and not on a one-way street, and he had pointed that out to The Japan Foundation. Shortly afterwards, another Japanese friend expressed exactly the same view on the subject of The Japan Foundation. So, clearly, there was some strong feeling that the foundation was not altogether on the right track. Matsumoto, being a politician, pointed out that although the statute of the Diet establishing the foundation had been formulated in very broad terms, the politics of the situation demanded assurances that it would in fact be operated along the questionable lines followed by the tough administrator. In other words, the foundation was sold to the Diet as a device for spreading Japanese culture even though lofty internationalistic language about cultural exchange was used in the legislation. Miss Kubota, on the other hand, thought that the foundation was veering toward a broader interpretation of its mandate. Who knows? The fact that the foundation had invited Morton lent some support to Kubota's view, but in 1979 the Japanologists of the world seemed to have more to gain from The Japan Foundation than the Japanese philosophers or the Japanese Americanologists.

In reporting our views about what appeared to be the actual as opposed to the stated policy of The Japan Foundation, we do not wish to seem ungrateful for what the foundation had done for us. Nevertheless, the behavior of some of its employees revealed a certain change of tone and spirit that were consonant with Emerson's remark about things being in the saddle. This change was evident in other aspects of Japanese life, from which we were protected to some extent by taking refuge once again in our dear I. House, in 1979 an even more desirable retreat from the hurly-burly metropolis that Tokyo had become. While we were at I. House we were insulated to a degree from the company of businessmen who haunted the luxury hotels and who gorged themselves while they were on expense accounts. In 1979 a double room with breakfast at I. House cost between forty and fifty dollars a night, which was much more than it had been in 1960, but a pittance by comparison to the price charged by Tokyo hotels for comparable accommodations.

Naturally, inflation had moved beyond what it had been in 1976, and this was blatantly evident in the neighborhood around I. House, namely, good old Roppongi. It surpassed what it had been in 1976 as a brilliantly neon and sign-painted area with wall-to-wall coffee shops and restaurants, mostly tiny ones. We could not tell how full they were, but we could observe on the streets crowds and crowds, day and night, of young people, probably a combination of students and young office workers. Since prices both in shops and restaurants were very high, we kept wondering how young people could afford such sums. It was never made clear to us by anyone, but later in Kyoto, Takeda suggested that young people swarmed into Roppongi because it was the part of town where film stars and "communications personalities" congregated. The Yosidas agreed, adding that most of these young people were supported by their parents and spent their total income on food, clothing, and entertainment. Roppongi was a miniature Ginza for the young, who filled it nightly in search of music, dancing, sex, alcohol, and any other kind of fun that it could provide. For example, there was in Roppongi a tiny Greek restaurant in a basement where the waiters would begin to dance after they had served you; and you were expected to throw plates at their feet while they went through their routines in the tiny area surrounded by the tables.

We were led to this place, oddly enough, by a list of restaurants given to us by the American Embassy. The author of the list commented that the place was lively and served good food. Both those things were true, but we hardly expected that its owners would give us a pile of plates that we were expected to send crashing around the feet of dancing waiters who deftly avoided being maimed by the flying glass. We suspected that this was all ultimately connected with some scenes in the Greek film "Never on Sunday" where plates also fly at dancers. But it certainly seemed weird when we thought of the Tokyo that we had known in earlier years. The plates were all being thrown by people in their twenties or younger, who cheerfully spent the 8,000 yen that a relatively cheap meal for two commanded in this noisy, windowless den; and *that* number of yen came to something like thirty-five dollars. The female patrons looked like typists and department-store salesgirls, the males like young white-collar workers. How could these kids afford these prices? We did not know; but there they were, eating lamb and hurling china that we surreptitiously hid behind our backs because, puritans that we were, we did not have the stomach to break it. When the manager saw us merely *watching* this spectacle, he brought us another pile of plates, thinking that we had run out of our supply. Meanwhile, Lucia urged Morton to put his spectacles on lest a piece of flying glass become lodged in one of his eyes.

While on the subject of nightlife in Tokyo, we must mention another, more sedate but equally strange nightspot near the Ginza. We were taken there in the second phase of what could have become a long pub-crawling evening, had we been younger. The first phase occurred in an elegant traditional Japanese restaurant to which we had been invited by our friends the Yosidas. The Inoues were also there. We have already mentioned Yosida, a very good philosopher of science who attended a seminar of Morton's at Harvard and later spent a year as a member of the Institute under his sponsorship. Inoue, a student of classical philosophy, greatly admired our son Nick and his work. Their wives were very bright and very agreeable. All four of them were in their late forties or early fifties, we *think*—and this emphatic qualification we must always make when guessing the age of a Japanese.

In Phase One of the night all six of us had had a delightful meal while sitting in the usual way on the matted floor of a beautiful, simply appointed room. We had been served by two handsome women crawling around the table in the old-fashioned Japanese manner. But as soon as the after-dinner conversation was over and our feet had been re-shod for Phase Two, we went down into the blazing, neon-lit crowded street in search of another establishment. We reached it after a short walk and a short elevator trip up to the fourth floor of a building, that is, to what a New Yorker would have called a loft. We were immediately ushered into a room whose dimensions were about thirty feet by ten—certainly no bigger—with patrons sitting at tables around the periphery and with a pianist and an electric guitarist in one corner. A shiny microphone was standing near them and into it a comparatively tall, middle-aged Japanese was singing. He was crooning a sentimental Japanese ballad and seemed for all the world like a professional singer as he poured his soul into his number. While he did, two attractive women came to the table and began to take orders from our Japanese friends. Soon our glasses were filled with drinks, in most cases Suntory whiskey. And, in the Japanese manner, those glasses were never allowed by the waitresses to be very far from filled. Other delicacies were also put on the table, including tiny clams and a variety of unnameable tidbits of reddish-brown hue. All of this seemed a little premature in light of the recency of our large meal, but it was probably presented as a normal accompaniment of the drinks.

As we sipped those and began to speak about the place, we learned that the crooner who was virtually at our elbows was a patron of the establishment. Hearing that was only mildly surprising to us, since it is not unheard of in Western nightclubs for a drunken patron to offer a ditty to the crowd in this way. But as soon as the crooner went back to his seat he was replaced by one of his male comrades at the microphone. When we asked *our* comrades what was going on, we learned that *all* of the entertainment in this place was self-entertainment! The patrons and only the patrons did the singing, accompanied by the house pianist or the house guitarist. This was amply demonstrated in the hour or two that followed our arrival. One Japanese after another came up to the microphone, was supplied with a little fat song-book that contained the words of the number he or she wanted to sing, and away the self-entertainer went. One pretty girl belted out an American song whose vintage was so recent that neither of us was able to identify it, but the girl sang lustily without understanding a word that she was singing. She had memorized the English words as well as the tune! A tall, handsome Japanese man periodically abandoned his drunken girlfriend to seize the microphone and regale us with sentimental, slow, minor-key Japanese songs of such predictable structure that we could anticipate the next note that was to come from the singer's lips. Indeed, we anticipated so well that he kept turning to Morton and kept offering the microphone to him. In this the crooner was joined by our hosts, who urged both of us to get up there and add to their merriment by singing "You Are My Sunshine" or, for some reason, "Tea for Two." Both of us declined, and declined even though an English song-book had been pushed into our hands. Fortunately, this book contained nothing recognizable by us, and so we were never drafted successfully. However, Professors Inoue and Yosida rose to sing as a duet; they sang us a famous old Japanese college song. And their wives also did a duet, but we never heard what kind of a song it was—probably a typical one about lost love or a distant, long-forgotten home on the Japanese range.

Our experiences in the plate-throwing cellar and in the self-entertaining loft were very different from what we had known as Japanese amusement in earlier years. Prosperity had brought with it a taste for forms of entertainment that we were never shown in 1952 or, more likely, forms that did not exist then or in 1966. This is certainly not to say that the Japanese were not capable of bacchanalian carousing in those earlier years. We could well remember the wild party in 1952 when we were entertained by, of all people, the head of the Tenrikyo religion—said to be a Japanese cousin of Christian Science. On that memorable occasion the American professors and their wives danced into the early hours of the morning with the help of geisha girls and men who looked like wrestlers. But that wildness was supposedly in the Japanese manner and not in imitation of what was supposed to be the manner of twentieth-century Athens or New York. Besides, when we were entertained by the Tenrikyo patriarch, we were not entertained in a Roppongi cellar or a Ginza loft; we were in some holy hall near Nara.

Enough has been said about The Japan Foundation and about our adventures in the nighttown of Tokyo to show some of the effects of the new Japanese opulence. If more evidence of that were needed, we could point to the shiny new taxicabs that made New York's look like New York's garbage-trucks, to the Dior, St. Laurent, and Givenchy dresses that filled the windows of shops in Roppongi, to the men's suits that seemed to come from London's Savile Row rather than from New York's Park Row of fifty years ago, to the self-assured looks on the faces of bankers and brokers in the financial sections of Tokyo, to the lights of the Ginza that shone more brightly than ever in spite of a shortage of oil and gasoline, to a vast number of other things that we identify with "modernization" and "Westernization."

By an interesting coincidence, one of our scholarly tasks while we were in Japan was to discuss American intellectual attitudes toward the modernization associated with urban life, a subject we had treated in our book *The Intellectual versus the City*. We led discussions of that subject on two occasions, first in Sapporo and then in Kyoto; and while doing so we could not help thinking that some Japanese thinkers might well have developed attitudes toward urbanization which were not unlike those of American thinkers from Thomas Jefferson to Frank Lloyd Wright. Naturally, in our ignorance of the history of Japanese thought, we could not be sure that there were Japanese counterparts of Jefferson, Emerson, Thoreau, and other American anti-urbanists, but, as we have indicated earlier, some of our friends, for example, Miss Kubota, expressed feelings about modernization that were not very different from those that we had discussed in our book. The chances were, we thought, that there was such a strain in the history of post-Meiji Japanese literature, sociology, and philosophy.

Having speculated that there might be such a strain in Japanese thought, we ought to add that there was one familiar complaint about the American city that did not seem to be as justified as it would have been if it were levelled against Tokyo in an earlier day—and that was the complaint about urban air. In 1979 Tokyo's air seemed to be much cleaner than it had been in the days when people wore surgical masks and sniffed oxygen in cafés. There seemed to be much less smog in 1979 because, we were told, factories and cars were stringently required to use devices that would prevent pollution. The cleanness of the air now rivalled that of the streets in all parts of the city that we visited. We did not see as many of the elderly streetsweepers who used to wear kerchiefs on their heads, so we thought that they might work at night in order to make New York look like a pig-sty by comparison with Tokyo. New York also suffered by comparison when one looked at the new buildings of Tokyo. Office buildings and apartment houses had been squeezed in everywhere in all conceivable shapes and sizes, but they never rose as high as they would in the American metropolis. The colors of Tokyo's newer buildings were all shades of gray and white though occasionally one would see structures made of rather large ugly bricks of an attractive terracotta color. The buildings were rarely like the chunky, monotonous, and rectangular objects that jut into the New York sky. They were more irregular, having different kinds of setbacks and often carrying amusing little turrets of different shapes that housed water towers or other devices that were needed for other public utilities. When reflecting on the air and architecture of the new Tokyo, we concluded that there might be less cause for anti-urban feeling in Japan than America.

The city of Sapporo did not strike us as favorably when we first saw it.

When we arrived there, we were reminded of certain towns in the most western part of the American middle west. Sapporo is quite flat, its streets are organized on a grid-pattern, and in the distance one can see plains beyond which snowcovered mountains loom in a Wyomingish way. As we drove from the airport, the countryside seemed drab and gray. Only the barest signs of spring were evident whereas Tokyo's cherry blossoms had come and gone. What little of the town we saw as we drove to our hotel was architecturally dull, and we were taken aback by the hotel itself. It was a vulgar high-rise called "The Sapporo Prince," which brashly introduced itself by way of imitation-Victorian décor in the lobby. A sickly brown was the dominant color; bellhops were scurrying all over the place in pillbox hats; desk clerks were forever ringing bells; people were ambling in and out; taxicabs were rushing up to the main entrance and away from it; and we later learned that the hotel was a Maytime favorite of honeymooning couples! On the way up to our room, one drunken patron grandly said "Konnichi-wa" (*Hello*) to us in the elevator after he got on with his wife or girlfriend. And when we entered our room, we discovered even more signs of Victorian or Meiji decoration: telephones that were reminiscent of, say, 1890; lacy curtains; and a swinging double door of the kind that used to open into barrooms—one that merely covered one's torso and that looked like a pair of swinging shutters that protected the inner part of the bedroom from intruding maids or waiters. We should emphasize that the decoration and the appointments were not really late-nineteenth century. The hotel was very new, having been erected for the Winter Olympics which had been held in Sapporo a few years earlier. The furnishings were imitation-Victorian and pretty awful.

As soon as we were left to ourselves, we took a short rest and proceeded to the dining room on the top floor, where we commanded a stunning view of Sapporo and of the surrounding countryside. The menu was very elaborate and, as usual, very expensive, featuring French wines at exorbitant prices. The service imitated that of the best European hotels. The table just next to us was occupied by three Japanese businessmen, one of whom even went to the New York extreme of having a telephone brought to his table, no doubt in order to impress his companions or us. We ordered something modest like hamburgers and coffee, returned to our rooms, and awaited our driver, who was to bring us to the American Studies Center. There Morton was to speak on behalf of both of us for about twenty-five minutes on the intellectual versus the city with paragraph-by-paragraph interpretation that would take about the same amount of time—ali this before we would exchange ideas with the audience.

Before entering the handsome, recently built auditorium, we were ushered into the office of the director of the center, which is connected with the ICA (International Communication Agency), the renamed successor to

USIA (United States Information Agency). That change in name was bemoaned by the Japanese interpreter, an employee of the American embassy in Tokyo who flew up on the same plane to carry out his mission since, we gathered, they did not have anyone in Sapporo who was thought to be his equal as an interpreter. The reason why he disliked the change in name was a good one—"ICA" is often confused with "CIA" and that does not make the ICA very popular with the Japanese.

The director of the Center for American Studies had been recently transferred from Korea, where he had also been in the diplomatic service. He was a short, stocky, fair-haired man in his thirties, we should say. He was not altogether smooth in his manners but somewhat abrupt and nervous. He relied heavily on an unnamed, attractive Japanese adjutant who seemed to have made all of the arrangements. We spent only a few minutes in the director's office, long enough to be told that although he would come to the beginning of the talk, he would not be able to remain to the end because he had to return to his house in order to make the salad for the dinner that he was giving us afterwards—he was, we inferred correctly, a bachelor—and to which he had invited a number of philosophers from the university, philosophers who wished to talk with Morton. We should repeat that although some Japanese philosophers are very much interested in American philosophy, they often do not consider themselves in the professional academic field that goes by the name "American Studies." That is why a separate gathering was being held during which they could talk with Morton about philosophy. Indeed, they had planned a luncheon for us on the following day and were therefore disappointed when we told them that we would be flying back to Tokyo. We had decided while we were still in Tokyo that we would require an intervening day of rest in Tokyo before going on to Kyoto. We did not feel like staying on in Sapporo nor like touring the Hokkaido countryside in that bleak season.

Since we are running ahead of our story, we must take the reader back to the auditorium in which we were to meet with specialists in American Studies. When we first entered it, we thought that the audience would number no more than a dozen because the middle of the room contained an elevated wooden platform that rose about six inches above the floor, and on that platform there were about twelve folding metal chairs for the expected audience. Strangely enough, the audience was going to sit on a higher level than the speaker, whose chair was on the floor itself. Although there were about twelve when Morton began to speak, there were more than thirty by the time all of the latecomers entered. We were greatly relieved, more for the center than for ourselves. They had gone to all of this trouble to import us from Tokyo for a reasonable honorarium, expenses, and fare, so we hoped we would draw a decent crowd. Our hopes were fulfilled when the latecomers made Morton feel that he was giving a lecture rather than conducting a seminar, though we may well have exaggerated the need that our hosts felt about the size of the audience.

The audience having risen to a respectable number, the moderator, a certain Professor Hanada, who told us that he had attended Morton's 1952 seminar in Tokyo, began to introduce the lecturer. We thought he would never stop. He had material in front of him that exceeded what the lecturer had in front of him. Hanada spoke in Japanese and a simultaneous interpretation was whispered into our ears by the Tokyo man, Mr. Tominaga. Hanada's introduction was full of reminiscence, praise, and much droning about Morton's collected works. Morton was flattered but slightly unnerved because the talk was to begin at what was called "1600" and continue to "1800"—from 4 P.M. to 6 P.M.—and there was supposed to be time for the lecture, for interpretation, and for comments and questions. Nevertheless, Professor Hanada had to mention his earliest acquaintance with Morton's work by way of buying, when he was a student in Toronto, the French edition of Marvin Farber's collection of essays, *Philosophic Thought in France and the United States*. That volume had appeared in 1950 and contained Morton's youthful effort, "Toward an Analytic Philosophy of History," which was mentioned at the top of Hanada's page and followed by a list of all of the lecturer's books, which list Hanada proceeded to read! Somehow all of this stopped at last, and the lecturer was allowed to speak. We do not know what time it was then but we had the feeling that it was only a few minutes before 1800.

Morton began by thanking Hanada and by pointing out that his talk, which was based on the article by him and Lucia entitled "The American Intellectual versus the American City," was not by Morton alone. In fact, Morton said, we should both be giving the talk but since speaking in unison might prove difficult, Morton was going to do it himself. He presumed that this effort at humor got through to those who knew English because he heard laughter or saw smiles, but he did not know what the interpreter did with it because when it came through in Japanese, Morton did not get the response he would have expected. This sort of thing had happened before in Japan, so Morton went on without too much disappointment. Soon he abandoned his prepared manuscript and merely took to looking at it occasionally for cues that would help him give structure to the talk. His performance ended about twenty minutes before the magic hour of 1800 when we were expected to leave for the director's salad and the assembled philosophers. Therefore, the number of questions was limited. It was even more limited because the speaker did something that was at once nice and unfair to Lucia. He asked her to rise and take a bow—which was gracious—but then he called on her to make a few comments. This shocked her—quite properly because she had not been scheduled to do so—but Morton thought that she managed to acquit herself splendidly in spite of being totally unprepared for this. There were a few questions and comments from the audience. One question was from a philosopher who wanted to know about Charles Peirce's views on the city in spite of acknowledging that Peirce had never written about the city. The other was a comment from a man who must have been a professor of American literature. He maintained what is often maintained in response to our thesis, namely, that all our critics of cities were genteel Wasps who did not know about the realities of American life. This is not true, and we indicated why. A few more hands soon went up, but Hanada, no doubt out of kindness to us and concern about the director's waiting salad, adjourned the meeting and off we went—in the inevitable limousine—to the director, his salad, and the Sapporo scholars.

The Japanese invited guests were virtually all Sapporo philosophers, as we have indicated. Many of them knew us, either because they had attended Morton's seminars or lectures in Tokyo or because they had been to Harvard while he was there; and one of them was a specialist in classical philosophy, Katto, who knew our son Nick. Fujimoto, the Peirce scholar, who also knew Nick, was there. Hanada the moderator reappeared. Another guest was Ohatta, who had been a member of Morton's 1952 Tokyo seminar. Then we saw Utsonomyia, who had shepherded Nick, Steve, and the two of us from Tokyo to Kamakura in 1960. We were ashamed not to have recognized him at first, but he gently reminded us of his labors in our behalf, and when he did we instantly saw the boyish face of 1960 behind that of the middle-aged philosopher he had now become. He was a lowly assistant at Tokyo University when he was given the job of guiding us, but now he was a full-fledged professor at a major Japanese university. We felt a little older when we reflected on the time that had passed. We felt still older, but very proud, when Katto announced that he was a pupil of Inoue and that Inoue was a student of Nick. And the climax of this part of the story came when Fujimoto told us that they were eager to get Nick to come to Sapporo as a visiting professor of philosophy.

It is time to say something about our American host. He loudly welcomed us as we entered his Western-style house that was filled with Korean art treasures, as he called them. It seems that while he was stationed in Seoul, he bought quantities of painted screens, bowls, scrolls, statues, and knickknacks, hardly one of which electrified us. By contrast, the Japanese were even less talkative than usual. We had heard from an embassy man in Tokyo that one of the purposes of this gathering was to give them an opportunity to talk philosophy with Morton; but there was hardly any philosophical chat with him, perhaps because the philosophers realized that he was fatigued but more likely because of the director's food and drink. He was a generous host, who offered us many kinds of alcohol that we supposed he had brought from the States in a diplomatic pouch. But this alcohol may have also served ultimately to diminish the amount of philosophical talk. One man who sat near Lucia was soon reduced to a series of non-words—"uh"s and "ah"s and sounds approaching groans and sighs whenever he was asked a question; and Utsonomiya's long face became longer and longer as he swallowed his drinks. By contrast, Fujimoto, more gifted in English than most Japanese, kept up a lively patter. But it was a man called Suzuki, perhaps the only non-philosopher among the Japanese guests, who was most articulate and most interesting in his comments about the state of American Studies in Japan.

The meal, which was served, strangely enough, on an upper floor of the director's peculiarly designed house, was moderately good; and so was the salad that forced him to leave the talk early. Mr. Suzuki—probably Professor Suzuki—drove us back to the hotel and that was the last we saw of a Sapporo scholar for in the morning at about ten we boarded a flight for Tokyo, once again with Tominaga the interpreter. We had been scheduled by the embassy for a later flight, but somehow our experiences in Sapporo suggested that we get out earlier, primarily to escape the luncheon that had been planned for us without our consent. There was interest and even excitement in our first trip to Hokkaido but the next trip there—if there is one—should be more leisurely.

Our trip to Sapporo was originally supposed to be followed by a trip to Kyoto, with no intervening time in Tokyo. This schedule was planned by Kinuko Kubota without reflection on the fatigue it might engender, and so we revised it. From Sapporo we flew back to Tokyo for a breather. We wanted to stay in Tokyo longer, but International House was booked to the point where they could allow us only one night between our Sapporo stint and our Kyoto stint. Valuing even this small a breather, we took the room for one night and on the following day boarded the fabled "bullet-train" for Kyoto.

As usual, The Japan Foundation arranged for us to be picked up at International House by a car, a chauffeur, and an escort. This time it was a Miss Maruyama, who led us through the vast Tokyo Station to our train after putting our bags in the hands of a disappearing porter. But the extent and complexity of Tokyo Station are such that even a professional Japanese guide can get you to the wrong railroad track, and Miss Maruyama did just that. She had us climb up one staircase only to be corrected by the reappearing porter, who saw us make our mistake. Fortunately, he was able to shout in time to Miss Maruyama that she was leading us astray. Smiling with flustered embarrassment, she had us run down one staircase and up an adjoining one, led us to our seats in the train, and then waved us on our way to Kyoto in the spotless train called "Hikari Number 115." "Hikari" means light, and our speed was as that of light from the point of view of an American railroader. We travelled comparatively slowly through Tokyo itself, but when we left the environs of that vast metropolis, we began to pick up speed, and soon we were moving so rapidly that we could not read the large English signs on skipped stations. We were on our way to the famous rival of Tokyo in Japanese history—Kyoto, the town of culture, the so-called Boston of Japan as opposed to its New York, which was, of course, the sprawling city of Tokyo.

Indeed, Tokyo sprawls so much that it is hard to know where it ends. And if there ever was a megalopolitan area, it is the stretch from Tokyo to Kyoto with Nagoya intervening. The combined population, we had read somewhere, of Tokyo and the adjacent cities of Kawasaki, Yokohama, and several others was then over twenty million souls; Nagoya had a population of more than two million. On the trip to Kyoto one can almost never look out the window of the bullet train without seeing factories, rice paddies, or residential houses. On one's left one sees a good deal of water as one rides from Tokyo to Kyoto, and on one's right there are high mountains. At a certain point, not very far from Tokyo, one can see, if one is lucky, "Fuji-san." Although we did not catch a glimpse of it on the trip down, we had the good fortune to see it on the way back, resplendent and imposing, with a ring of clouds around its middle, as it dominated a cluster of smoking factories.

When we arrived in Kyoto, we were, of course, met by the inevitable representative of The Japan Foundation. In the manner to which we had become accustomed on this trip, we were than escorted to the Kyoto Hotel, where we had stayed during one of our earlier visits. Although Kyoto itself appeared to be much less changed than Tokyo, that was not true of the hotel that bears its name. When we first stayed there in 1952, it was modest and relatively small, and its lobby was filled with the sort of overstuffed furniture that we had found in the Hotel Matsudaira. But in 1979 large structures had been attached both to the front and the back of the old building so that the Victorian lobby and dining room were now in the middle of the renovated building. As a result of these additions, a tunnel-like driveway had been formed, and it separated different parts of the hotel. Through that driveway, taxicabs and fancy private cars would come in order to pick up passengers, often honking and spewing the fumes of their exhaust. Well-uniformed doormen would whistle, open doors, and close doors, all in a manner that out-Wested the West, one that made the similar activities outside the Plaza Hotel in New York seem peaceful and quiet by comparison. In the lobbies and restaurants there were hordes of tourists of many nationalities and races. Among the guests there were a couple of African princes dressed in colorful gauze and gold-threaded blouses and in pajamas of pale blue and purple hues. They sat next to us one night while we were dining in one of the restaurants of the hotel. Indeed, the fact that this establishment now had several restaurants instead of one was another change associated with the great transformation of Japan, a transformation which had also affected the sedate and spiritual city of Kyoto. In one of these restaurants we sat next to a group of Germans who constantly hectored the sweet little Japanese waitress. We also heard a good deal of French spoken, and we saw many non-Japanese Orientals whose nationality we could not identify even after hearing them speak. There was no escaping the fact that even the Boston of Japan had been jazzed up beyond the wildest dreams that we could have entertained during our earliest visits.

As we sat in the lobby of our hotel, we reminisced about a visit to Kyoto in 1960. At that time we stayed in the famous Hiragiya Inn and lived in the Japanese manner, sleeping on the floor, taking meals in our rooms, bathing in the great wooden tubs, and so on. It was then that Ohmori, who had also stayed at the Inn, played Go and Japanese chess with Nick and with Steve. It was then that he taught them—to our dismay—to smoke cigarettes in a manner that would supposedly allow them to pull smoke into the upper parts of their respiratory systems without letting it enter their lungs; they had learned from him to inhale partially, and we feared the next step would be the real thing.

In our earliest trip to Kyoto, we also recollected, we had started to buy old Japanese wood-block prints under the guidance of Shinzo Kaji. He took us to a small shop where the owner would sit on an elevated, stage-like platform from which he would display his wares to us at remarkably cheap prices by today's standards. Once Lucia saw a hole in one of the prints which the proprietor described as a "womhole." It took us the longest time to realize that he was referring to what we would call a worm hole. In any case we owe most of our prints by Toyokuni the First to that little man in Kyoto.

Kyoto was the town where, as we learned, older Japanese customs were more commonly followed than they were in the brash upstart of a city called Tokyo. One night in an earlier year we saw what this meant when we invited the philosopher Professor Noda and his wife out to dinner. We took them to a restaurant on Kawaramachidori (the street where the Kyoto Hotel also stood). But since the entrance to the restaurant was quite narrow and since the sidewalk also was, we all had to line up on the sidewalk before entering. In the Western manner Morton tried his best, as the host and as a man, to go to the rear of the line, but he fought a losing battle with Mrs. Noda, who stubbornly insisted on claiming that privilege for herself, the Japanese woman of Kyoto! And, speaking of Kyoto women, in 1979 we vividly remember our first glimpse of a bevy of young geishas when we arrived at the Kyoto station one afternoon in the summer of 1952. We had always thought of them as nighttime figures, but there they were, in full regalia at high noon, surprising us no end.

Naturally, on several of our visits to Kyoto we had gone to the Katsura Imperial Villa, built in the sixteenth-century and especially famous for its garden, designed by the master Enshu Kobori. We had also gone to the Sugakuin Imperial Villa, built in the early seventeenth century as a retreat for the emperor, and the scene of so many remarkable gardens. On one of our earlier visits to Katsura, in 1960, our good friend Hiromichi Takeda told us an amusing story about his arrangements. It is necessary, or at least it used to be necessary, to make application for tickets in order to visit Katsura. Moreover, one must give the names of those who are to visit. Takeda-san, it seems, had forgotten the first names of our sons, so he was in something of a predicament when filling out the necessary forms. He knew our names and duly inscribed them on the document, but what to do about Nick and Steve, who were anonymous to him? He decided to tell a white lie—if the reader will forgive that pun. He called one of the boys "Abel," but then, wishing to go on to what should have been "Baker" by American custom when preparing such a list, he was stumped. He had forgotten "Baker" and wrote down "Benson" instead. Why "Benson"? When asked that question, he replied that it was the only Christian name beginning with "B" that he could remember at the time; it was the name of the Berkeley philosopher Benson Mates. For a good while afterwards Nick and Steve were known to us as Abel and Benson!

When we were in Kyoto in 1979, we had time to see only Katsura and Sugakuin, but this time we were not taken there by Takeda but rather by two couriers of The Japan Foundation. They were directly employed by another outfit with the following imposing name: "International Hospitality and Conference Service Association." It seems that this association was connected with the Ministry of Foreign Affairs, but we could never disentangle the threads that tied all these bureaucratic entities together. In Kyoto the hospitality association provided us with guides as it had in Tokyo. We gathered that it employed both undergraduates and graduate students, as well as educated adults who have a good command of English and who are eager to improve their English (or some other foreign language) by talking with foreign visitors. These young people were hired to show visitors the most interesting sights and to be companions during these excursions. All of them were capable, attractive, and considerate, and lived up to the requirements of a country that can boast of being one of the most hospitable in today's world. Our best guide of the lot was Mr. Ueyma, a young married Okinawan who was a graduate student in Spanish at Kyoto University and who expected to return to Okinawa University to teach Spanish after two years of study in Kyoto. His wife and baby daughter had remained in Okinawa with relatives, and they would remain there until he completed his graduate work.

Ueyma and a colleague served as guides to Katsura and Sugakuin. Katsura once again struck us as the most exquisite of country palaces; in 1979 it was even more carefully cultivated by teams of gardeners—both men and women—than ever before. They weeded and pruned meticulously, serving, we suspected, as low-paid but devoted retainers whose activity served to implement the Japanese desire to maintain full employment. The Katsura gardens showed the remarkable effects of their work but, alas, we could not see the main building of the palace. It was enveloped in a canvas tent under which complete repairs were being done, so that we missed seeing the very fine decorations and details of workmanship in the interior of that building. By contrast, Sugaquin was never, in our memory, more glorious. Our trek around it was quite splendid and lengthy, through several acres of park and up and down a mountainside in summer-like heat. Again hordes of gardeners were swarming to keep the grounds immaculate. This trip, however, proved so strenuous that we cancelled a projected excursion to Nara for the next day, an excursion which the local representative of The Japan Foundation had said would be combined with attendance at a performance of a Noh play.

Nara we had visited in previous years. There we had seen the great Todaiji Temple, which housed Daibutsu, the huge bronze Buddha; and we had been to the magnificent Horyuji Temple, built in 607. We had also seen Yakushiji Temple as well as Shin-yakushi-ji Temple, both of which were almost as old as Horyuji. And, of course, we had been to many other remarkable temples, gardens, and museums in both Nara and Kyoto. For this reason we felt justified in deciding to rest instead of marching excessively. Instead, we lounged around in our hotel room and afterwards explored the nearby mall where several streets now have glassed-over roofs (like the central mall of Milan) and where there are infinitely many tiny shops full of Japanese knickknacks, none of which attracted us in the least. We did find one very good shop of artists' supplies, recommended to us by the Takedas, where we were able to buy the celebrated Japanese watercolor brushes, some of which we expected to use ourselves and some of which we meant to take back as gifts to friends who painted.

After purchasing the brushes, we threaded our way back through the alleys of the extensive mall to the main avenue Kawaramachidori leading back to the Kyoto Hotel. Like the mall, the avenue was crowded with Japanese shoppers who seemed to have plenty of money to spend, though this was difficult to judge. At any rate, the shops were full of consumer goods, as the economists say, but since we did not see things that were especially attractive, we were glad to shoulder our way back to the hotel and leave the busy shopping street to the jostling, chattering crowds.

While making our way back, we decided to stop for what we thought would be but a few minutes in a bookshop that displayed English books in its windows. And there we had an amusing experience. Two young men—of high school age, we judged—approached us and began to address us in somewhat stilted English. "Lady and Gentleman," one of them said, "will you be kind enough to converse with us in English." At first, we were taken aback, but then one of us said something like: "Of course; we cannot converse with you in Japanese." One of the young men then said that they were studying English at school and that they had very few opportunities to talk with "native English-speakers." So the exchange continued for quite a while until one of them saw one of us holding an English novel. Morton seems to recall that it was a Hemingway novel, but whatever it was, this boy had read it and discoursed about it in a remarkably intelligent way. We were so impressed that we stayed in the shop for much longer than we had expected. Instead of feeling—as we did at first—that we had been accosted by two young nuts, we felt that we had had a delightful time. The forthrightness and inoffensive boldness of these boys was not only impressive in itself, but also, like so many other experiences in 1979, it was evidence of the great transformation in Japanese behavior. In 1952 the fathers of these two boys would have never dared to do what they had done so appealingly, even if the fathers had known as much English as their sons. We said good-bye (forever) to the two boys and they said to us: "Thank you very much, lady and gentleman. We were delighted by your good English."

Upon returning to the Kyoto Hotel, we took a rest, had dinner in one of its excellent restaurants, and then watched television in our room. We were amazed by the amount of time given over to *sumo* wrestling. After watching these enormous men bumping each other around with their big bellies, we switched channels and looked at three lovely Japanese girls who were dressed in stunning gowns while shouting into three microphones. From their rock we went to baseball on another channel, and after that we caught a gangster movie. After another flick of the wrist we encountered some kind of contest that was conducted by a middle-aged Japanese woman who was throwing her audience into fits of laughter. All of this was interrupted by ads for cereal, laxatives, toothpaste, the Japanese version of alka-seltzer, and all the other sorts of fascinating things that American viewers know about. So if it were not for the faces we saw and the language we heard, we might just as well have been in a Holiday Inn somewhere in the United States. With a certain amount of depressing exhilaration, so to speak, we turned the damned thing off and turned in to get some rest because on the next day our performance in Sapporo was to be repeated at Doshisha University in Kyoto.

Kinuko Kubota had arranged for us to discuss American intellectual attitudes toward the American city with a group of Japanese scholars interested primarily in American Studies. The meeting was to take place at Doshisha University, which has a close connection with Amherst College. Our transportation was, as usual, taken care of by the young guides employed by the International Hospitality and Conference Service Association. One of them accompanied us to a Doshisha University building that looked like a well-worn Victorian brick elementary school in New York. We arrived there about five minutes before the appointed time for the afternoon seminar, but unfortunately our young guide was completely unacquainted with this university, not to say this building, so we scampered around making inquiries. Finally, we managed to find the second floor office of the historian Shoichi Oshimo, an extremely gracious man whom we later came to know well when he was a member at the Institute for Advanced Study in 1980–81. With characteristic shyness and understandable nervousness, he greeted us and then introduced us to his assistant; together the two of them led us to the large airy room in which the seminar took place.

The meeting was attended by perhaps a couple of dozen mature scholars and students interested in the field of American Studies. As he did in Sapporo, Morton delivered to them a short talk that was—thank goodness—not preceded by the sort of windy introduction that he was given in Sapporo. In his Kyoto talk he presented an abbreviated version of the argument that we had first presented in our paper "The American Intellectual versus the American City," an argument later amplified and documented in our book *The Intellectual versus the City: From Thomas Jefferson to Frank Lloyd Wright*. Continuing to think, as we had earlier, that the very rapid urbanization of Japan might well have led to some similar responses on the part of Japanese thinkers who might have been disappointed by the transformation of Japan, we asked the Japanese scholars whether in fact there was any parallel in Japanese intellectual history to what had taken place in the history of American thought.

The discussion that followed was very interesting and very lively. One of the most illuminating responses to the question put by us came from a Professor Ueno, a highly placed administrator of Doshisha University. Ueno spoke English extremely well, and he formulated his points with great clarity. In essence, he maintained that Tokyo and other large Japanese cities differed from large American cities insofar as Tokyo, for example, was the result of fusing many, many small neighborhoods which even today retain a distinctive character. Apparently, Ueno though that this difference made the big Japanese city less likely to draw the sort of fire that certain American writers had directed against New York, Boston, or Chicago. Whether Ueno is right we do not know, but we were certainly struck by the wit and perspicacity with which he spoke as well as by his great familiarity with Japanese and American history. He was indeed an impressive figure. Others at the meeting spoke intelligently but not so memorably; still others preferred to withhold their comments until they met with us later at dinner. We had experienced this shyness before on such academic occasions. Many Japanese scholars of great ability were afraid to expose themselves on such occasions for fear of making what might be thought to be a horrible error in the presence of their colleagues and invited speakers; and this fear was obviously greater when they did not have full command of the language in which they were expected to express themselves.

After the seminar we were taken to dinner at an attractive Japanese restaurant. Our party was made up of Professor Oshimo, who was the host, and a number of other scholars who came from a variety of fields. We met, for example, a professor of theology who had studied at Yale while working in a factory to support himself, a bright young female professor of linguistics, an amiable, middle-aged, skeptical-looking economist, and a self-contained man who specialized in American Studies. We also met an American expatriate who told us at some length about having become a collector of rare Oriental art objects. To his own surprise he had, by imperceptible steps, come to the point where he was the owner of so good a collection that it was about to be exhibited in Seattle and Pasadena museums.

Lucia's most interesting conversation was with the theologian, who talked at considerable length about a model Japanese city which had been built and organized fairly recently. It was the city of Kurashiki, near Okayama, which is situated on the northern shore of the Inland Sea, about an hour and a half's trip to the west of Kyoto by the bullet train. Kurashiki was intended to be a "New Jerusalem," in the (predictable) language of the theologian, and to be admirably well planned as an ideal community in accord with Japanese ideals of living. The theologian and his wife had evidently spent some time there assisting with the organization of the city and he was enthusiastic about the charm of living there. Lucia did not have a chance to hear more details about it because of the shifts in dinner-table conversation, and so she could not ask him why he and his wife had left such an idyllic place. Unfortunately, moreover, our time in Kyoto was too short to permit Lucia to pursue the lead given to her by this versatile theologian. When she bade farewell to her religious dinner-companion that evening, she expressed the hope that we might one day visit the New Jerusalem of which he had spoken so enthusiastically.

On the next evening we entertained Hiromichi and Hiroko Takeda at our hotel restaurant, using that occasion to repay them in a small way for all of their hospitality over the twenty-seven years of our friendship. Takeda, a member of Morton's first seminar in 1952, commuted to Tokyo from Kyoto in order to attend it. He taught philosophy at a college in Osaka and did so with a distinct scientific and logical bias. He came from a well-known medical family but decided not to continue in the tradition established by his father. When he entered philosophy, however, he maintained a connection with his family tradition by favoring such scientifically oriented movements as logical positivism and pragmatism. He had a weird interest in collecting electric refrigerators and—we seem to remember—typewriters. We cannot forget our first visit to his house in Kyoto. After introducing us to each of his five (then young) daughters he led us into the kitchen where he had lined up five refrigerators which, he informed us, were waiting there for the daughters to receive when they were married. Some or perhaps all of these chilling devices might—we seem to recollect—have been bought in California by Takeda and then shipped across the Pacific. Of course, this was done thirty years ago, well before the days when he might have picked up much better ones in Kyoto. Still they were a tribute to Takeda's love for his daughters and for scientific technology, the sort of thing that may have led to his being called a "Yankee" by his more traditionally minded philosophical friends.

Hiromichi must not be thought of as a Japanese version of the engineers who figure in nineteenth-century English novels and who bear names like "Mr. Mechanic." He was a very warm-hearted man who was a promoter of one of the most rollicking drinking parties that Morton had ever attended. In 1952 Takeda and the other seminar students had invited him to be the guest of honor at a gathering of students in a Tokyo beerhall. The place had several stories which were distinguished—if Morton's memory serves him well—by the kind of alcoholic beverages they served. The ground floor was for beer only, and on that floor the impecunious students held the party. However, as soon as the steins of good Japanese beer were brought to the table, several of the provident philosophers proceeded to pull pint-bottles of inevitable Suntory whiskey out of their pockets. Then, to Morton's astonishment, they poured whiskey into their steins of beer. Of course, Morton was served first and all eyes were upon him. What could he do but accept the concoction with gratitude? And when the steins containing this powerful alcoholic mixture were raised, Morton raised his and gulped down its contents along with the rest of his *macho* companions. This went on for several rounds until everyone was, as it were, on the ropes. On that night Morton had to be carried home, but he earned the (undeserved) reputation of being a strong drinker, a reputation that declined, of course, with each succeeding visit to Japan.

Takeda and his wife, a lovely looking and charming woman, always entertaining us lavishly when we visited Kyoto; and he would usually accompany us on our trips to the great sights of Kyoto. Together, they would invariably meet us when we arrived at the Kyoto Station and also see us off, usually with tears and doleful waves, when we left—except, of course, when we were the guests of The Japan Foundation and were obliged to be taken to and from the station by our official escorts. Feeling very warmly toward the Takedas and being so obliged to them, we invited them to our elegant restuarant in the Kyoto Hotel. When they arrived, they both looked very handsome and even noble in a classic Japanese way despite their almost militant Westernism. We saw marks of old age that had begun to appear on their faces and signs of the same in their gait, and they must have observed similar things about us. But the occasion was in no way melancholy or sentimentally nostalgic. It was jolly, animated, and celebratory of our long friendship. We all talked of our children and grandchildren with much pleasure. Four of their daughters, they told us, had been married and so we asked whether the four of them were using the refrigerator their father had reserved for them. That brought a big laugh, but we felt sure that the old G.E.s or Westinghouses had gone the way of the Fords that we had seen in Japan during our earliest visits—replaced by efficient and handsome local competitors. After the meal, as we were leaving the dining room, we passed a table at which we spotted Ueno, the star of our seminar at Doshisha University. Since Takeda knew him, Morton and Takeda stopped for a minute to speak with Ueno while the shy Hiroko bowed and quickly withdrew in the manner of a Japanese wife. Since Lucia could not leave Hiroko alone, she withdrew with her to the mezzanine outside of the restaurant. Soon all of us rejoined each other but only for long enough to exchange sad farewells. Hiroko was tearful, but the invariably cheerful Hiromichi gave us directions to stores that sold artists' supplies and informed us that he would soon see us in Tokyo since he would be attending a lecture that Morton was to give there before our departure from Japan. When he came to that lecture, he brought us a package of handsome water-color paper as a gift, knowing that we were interested in water-color painting.

We cannot leave the subject of Hiromichi Takeda without telling two stories about him. One day when he was shepherding us about Nara in 1952, we believe, we met the famous Zen philosopher Daisetz Suzuki in the dining room of the Nara Hotel. As soon as Takeda spotted Suzuki, he quickly removed the cigar from this mouth because, as he said, he did not want to be seen by so ethereal a philosopher while smoking a cigar. As he tried to hide the cigar, he broke its wrapper and so he looked mournfully at the damaged object which he surreptitiously placed in an ashtray while introducing us to Mr. Suzuki. Once the meeting with the famous Zen Buddhist was over and we had resumed the drinking of coffee, Morton showed Hiromichi how to repair his cigar by wrapping a moistened piece of Kleenex around it. Upon being helped in this way, Hiromichi exclaimed: "Cigar bandaid!"

The second story has to do with Takeda's generosity as a guide in the Kansai area. At some point between 1952 and 1979—the year escapes us—the wife of one of Morton's Harvard colleagues was talking to us about a trip that her parents were about to make to Japan. In the course of the conversation, the question arose as to how they might best see the sights of Kyoto, and we immediately thought of our friend Takeda and wrote to him about the impending visit of the elderly people. When they got to Kyoto, Takeda in his generous way did for them what he had done for us on many occasions, and they were so grateful to him for his help and guidance that they wanted to give him something. Naturally, he would not accept anything from them for himself and so they arranged to contribute to what was called a scholarship fund for the education of his daughters. It was all very touching, we thought: Takeda's generosity, the Americans' desire to respond, their problem of how to respond, and the very Japanese way of resolving the problem by way of an intermediary—in this case a corporate intermediary, the five Takeda girls.

When we left Kyoto for Tokyo on the day after our party with the Takedas, we had to gear up for more lectures and several farewell meals. These lectures by Morton were not obligatory so far as The Japan Foundation was concerned, but he felt a moral obligation to give them when asked to do so by his friends. One was delivered before a group of specialists in American Studies, the other before a group of philosophers. The first was on a theme developed earlier in Morton's *Philosophy of the American Revolution* (1978); the second, on one that would be developed in his book *What Is and What Ought To Be Done* (1981). Throughout the first lecture Kinuko Kubota beamed; she was now the president or president-elect of the American Studies Association of Japan. The second lecture, to the philosophers, brought out many of our old friends. The discussions that followed each lecture were instructive and vigorous. Punches were not pulled even though Japanese politeness reigned. Much had happened to change the style of Morton's exchanges with his Japanese colleagues. Of course, they still deferred to him somewhat as their teacher, as someone who was (in some cases only a little) older than they, and as a foreign visitor. But he felt proud to think that they were now assured enough to argue with him forcefully and forthrightly, for he thought that he had made some small contribution to their education and to their progress as intellectual historians and philosophers.

The last week of our stay was full of farewell parties. There had been official parties after the lectures, but they were supplemented by a dinner party at the house of Ohmori, yet another one at Kinuko Kubota's place, and a luncheon with the Murais. In response to some of these we gave a dinner for four former members of the Institute's School of Historical Studies and one member-elect.

The evening at Ohmori's was, as usual, very interesting and also alcoholic. Ohmori resolutely continued to call Morton "White-san" and to prefer that he himself be called "Ohmori-san," thus showing himself to be, as it were, the last *samurai* among our friends. He brought out the most expensive liquors, including a bottle of Chivas Regal Scotch which had belonged to his wealthy father. He poured himself drink after drink and chided Morton for ceasing to be the drinker he once was. Ohmori also chided him for failing to learn Japanese after so many years of contact with Japan, and Morton sadly acknowledged that he was blameworthy in this respect. Soon, however, his mood brightened, especially when Father Yanase, another guest, managed to steer the conversation in another direction. Yanase, it will be recalled, is a physicist who had been a member of the Institute many years earlier. By 1979 he had become chairman of the board of Sophia University in Tokyo. He is a very charming Jesuit and extremely gentle in his manners. He told us that he was distantly related to Reiko Ohmori and very gallantly remarked that her beauty was typically Japanese. It pleased us greatly to hear his praise of her as she strikes us as a very attractive woman. She told Lucia that she had wanted to come to the reception for both of us after Morton's lecture to the philosophers, but that responsibilities at home had prevented her from doing so. To make up for this, she took lunch with Lucia just before the lecture. She is a very sweet person who writes poetry that is full of tenderness, as we know from the translations that accompany those she has sent to Lucia. The poems usually appear first in Japanese; then they are transliterated into Romaji; and finally they are translated. In English one of them is called "To a Letter of Mrs. White"; it reads as follows:

A letter from Mrs. White full of the sympathy
Every time I read tears come into my eyes
I read it repeatedly again and again.

The subject of poetry leads naturally to our dinner at the home of Professor Makato Saito, not because he is a poet, for he is a historian. Rather the poetic link is with his father, who is one of Japan's great historians of English literature and an authority on Keats. The old man attended the dinner and was really quite remarkable. He shook one's hand with the force of the Commendatore in Mozart's *Don Giovanni*, spoke English fluently, and proudly displayed his remarkable library of English literature. The Saito house showed evidence of considerable wealth. We ate in an entirely Western dining room, complete with impressive oak chairs and table. The silver service sparkled, there were several servants in attendance, and the meal was sumptuous. Afterwards, the conversation was lively, led as it was by the old man of the house who spoke with great admiration for his friend the English poet Edmund Blunden, a long-time resident of Japan.

Makoto Saito once told us a story about his family which was both interesting and sad. When Makoto came to the Institute as a member 1978–79, he brought with him his son, a young man in his early twenties; Mrs. Saito stayed at home, no doubt in order to take care of the nonagenarian as well as another child. It seems that her son had wished, upon leaving college, to go into the world of business and in fact had started working in a firm or in a bank. However, although his father reluctantly approved of this, his grandfather was outraged by this break with the family's academic tradition. So, as we understand, the boy was urged to go into the academic business. But he did not wish to take up his father's subject or his grandfather's. Instead, therefore, he entered the field of African studies. Makoto Saito reported this boy's great fear of his grandfather, adding that he could understand this since even he, in his late fifties, could quake in the old man's presence. The story reveals the power of family tradition and parental authority in Japan today, power that continues to be very great in spite of having declined considerably since 1952.

If there was one Japanese power or faculty which had not declined over the years, it was that of our friends to demonstrate their affectionate feelings for us. On the contrary, that capacity had grown stronger over a generation and was manifested in two farewell gatherings toward the end of our visit in 1979. One gathering was at the home of Kinuko Kubota, who brought us together with some of our Japanese friends of longer standing, among them Ohmori and Miss Takagi, both of whom had been assistants, as Kinuko had been, in the seminars of 1952. All of us sat on the floor eating and reminiscing, comparing 1979 with 1952 and other years, and recalling happy times as well as our memories of departed friends. Kinuko served us while she was wearing slacks, and *not* in kimono. Her friends kidded her about her "hippy" attire, but she took their kidding in her typically amiable fashion. When the party was over, we left with mixed emotions: with great pleasure and with the uneasy feeling that some of us might never meet again. The latter emotion we suppressed, of course, but we could not deny its existence when we reflected on the distance between Japan and our home.

The second farewell gathering took place in the lobby of International House on the day of our departure. The Ohmoris, the Yosidas, and the Kurodas came there to bid us good-bye for a reason that was not unconnected with Japan's economic development and with the august auspices under which we had made our visit. The economic changes in Japan had required the construction of Narita Airport, which was much further from I. House than old Haneda had been. Consequently, our friends could not be expected to come to Narita as they used to come to Haneda to wave their handkerchiefs to us as we boarded our plane. Morever, the V.I.P.s who came as guests of The Japan Foundation were virtually obligated to travel in high style to the airport; naturally, with a chauffeur and an escort. However, in deference to our friends, Wataru Kuroda was allowed to ride with us as a sort of representative of the friends. He would be coming to the Institute as a member in the fall of 1979, so he was delegated to see us off and to glean as much information as he could about the Institute and Princeton while we all rode for what seemed like an interminable amount of time to Narita. Our guide was a rather boring man who looked like a bodyguard, and so we were relieved as well as happy to have Kuroda with us. After we changed our yen into dollars, we were led to the "sterile" area, and at the barrier said good-bye to Kuroda and through him expressed our gratitude to all of his countrymen who had made our fifth trip to Japan so happy. We told him how much we looked forward to seeing him in Princeton, and on that optimistic note we shook hands and exchanged farewells.

TWELVE

Looking Backward and Looking Forward

Perhaps we make a mistake in not letting this book end on the previous page, for with that page our narrative ends. But what more may be said, it might be asked, after the tale has been told? Something of further interest we think, and that is why we go on a bit, hoping that the reader will accompany us while we emphasize some of the significant threads of continuity as well as some of the more important changes that we witnessed in our almost thirty years of journeying to the Japanese. We also intend to do something that may be less evident in what we have already written, and that is to mention a few morals that we have adumbrated in passing but which we hope to stress by setting them down together here.

We believe, in other words, that the story we have told has interest in itself as a record of events and experiences, but we think it worthwhile to stand back from the record and ask what conclusions may be based on it. What worth do we attach to our travels apart from their affording us the usual delights that tourists often experience when moving about in strange lands? What notable persistent traits did we find in the behavior of our friends and in Japanese life? What notable changes? And what conclusions of a more practical kind come to our minds as we reflect on our long though episodic contact with these remarkable people whom we approached with great curiosity but considerable trepidation in 1952 after so horrible a war as the one we Americans had fought with them?

Though we resolve to take up these questions in the order in which we have asked them, we cannot resist immediately suspending this resolution so that we can now say something of the greatest importance. Never, in all of the years of our contact with the Japanese of our acquaintance, did we hear one complaint about the American use of the atomic bomb; never were we made by them to feel in a more acute way the shame or the guilt that we had felt before coming to their country. We do not know how to explain this silence. Perhaps it was connected with what is sometimes called the reserve of the Japanese and therefore with an enormous capacity to mask the hostility they might have felt toward us. Perhaps it was the product of their feeling that the bombing of Hiroshima was deserved punishment for the bombing of Pearl Harbor—a feeling that surely could not be justified by the *lex talionis* of Western morality. Obviously, Hiroshima was immensely more than one eye and more than one tooth for the eye and the tooth of Pearl Harbor. To us it seemed a miracle, therefore, that we were treated as well as we had been from the moment we arrived at Haneda Airport in the summer of 1952 to the moment we left Narita in the spring of 1979—a moral miracle which our Japanese friends had performed.

Now we return to our resolution and try to answer as best we can the large questions we asked earlier. First: "What worth do we attach to our travels apart from their affording us the usual delight that tourists often experience when moving about in strange lands?" Descartes said in his *Discourse* that travel, by acquainting us with the customs of other nations, helps us judge more justly of our own, and our Japanese travels confirmed his wisdom. We became conscious of something about the United States while living in a country which was not heavily influenced by the same religious traditions. Some of our Japanese friends were Christian but not militantly or ostentatiously so; therefore, we labored under no obligation to censor the expression of our own irreligious attitudes. The Tokyo academic circles in which we travelled were much more liberated in this repect than most we had known in the States. We felt that we were breathing a very different intellectual air: we were made more conscious of the burdens that militant organized religion imposes on nonbelievers in America who wish to speak freely.

Another thing that we were made conscious of was the gentle manner of intellectual exchange by comparison to what we were used to in America. We realize that we may have been dealing with our Japanese friends and acquaintances while they were on good behavior in the presence of foreign guests and that, for all we knew, they went at each other's throats when arguing among themselves. But we found that their intellectual debate was characterized by a politeness and gentleness we had rarely encountered in America or in other Western countries. Perhaps Japanese professorial behavior is, in general, more controlled than the behavior of other Japanese for we were certainly aware of the militancy of the radical Japanese students we saw snake-dancing on American television screens in 1960. In short, although we knew that violence was conspicuously present in Japanese history, we found much less aggressiveness in philosophical controversy than we had known in the States.

What we witnessed during all of our time in Japan was as far as possible from violence and terrorism. For all we know, the sociable, lively, and tolerant conversations we enjoyed with our Japanese friends may have masked poisons that lurked in the body politic. In any case, we were the soothed beneficiaries of highly civilized behavior, and we valued it without feeling that it was dull or boring. We felt about it much as we felt about the low crime-rate of Tokyo by comparison with that of New York; we could not help musing on the irony that Tokyo, the largest metropolis in the East, was at once the most peaceful and the least Christian of all the metropolises in the world. We leave it to historians or social scientists to explain why this was so; for us it was a source of relief and probably one of the reasons why we returned to Japan so often.

On our journeys to Japan we were introduced to parts of Japanese culture that have been central to it not only in the twentieth century but also, historians tell us, as far back as the seventh. During most of Japanese history, learning has been held in high esteem, even among government leaders and the military *samurai*. And along with great respect for learning there went devotion to the arts and to esthetic experience in many of its forms. Since we were so closely in touch with Japanese scholars, we learned more than the average tourist about ideas that were prevalent in Japan during the thirty years that began with 1952. But because Japanese philosophers and Americanists were so generous and solicitous about our becoming acquainted with the various art forms in which their country excels, our visits were enlivened and made much more enjoyable than would have been possible if we had been touring Japan on our own. In short, our journeys kept us in close contact with the humanistic values of the society. This made us want to return to Japan again and again, as we were lucky enough to be able to do. Frequent exposure to these more artistic and intellectual parts of Japanese culture balanced our awareness of the rapid and profound material changes that accompanied the accelerating industrialization of Japan from 1952 to 1979. We witnessed the continuing development of modern Japan and the growth of its technology, but over the years we also saw how adroit our friends were at arranging the arduous intellectual programs of visiting American scholars so that they and their wives could enjoy and learn to appreciate traditional fine arts that required no understanding of spoken or written Japanese. With equal adroitness our friends applied themselves strenuously and with strict discipline to their professional work and then easily shifted over to light-hearted relaxation and enjoyment of everything from artfully prepared meals to sophisticated Noh plays and wood-block prints. We think that our friends were among the most cultivated spirits in the Japan we visited. They were not warlords, not tycoons, not bureaucrats; they lacked great wealth and power. They were intelligent and often brilliant, decent, and noble representatives of their culture who probably did more to foster international understanding than any admiral or any manufacturer of cars or television sets.

"What notable persistent traits did we find in the behavior of our friends and in Japanese life?" This question brings us into the territory of social scientists who profess to speak with authority about national character, so we must be careful. One notably persistent trait of those we knew was subtlety, a trait that may be called "cunning" by those who do not like the Japanese. The subtlety we prized was a concomitant of the gentleness of which we have spoken. It was illustrated when one of our friends quietly persuaded military officers to abandon their control of a shrine; when schoolmasters were persuaded to take down pictures of the emperor in military uniform; when Morton was told that Japanese philosophers did not think that Americans had a philosophy, told in a way that gave no offense while it alerted him to dangers that he might wish to reckon with in a lecture. This mode of communication persisted in all the years we knew the Japanese. The indirection they used reminded us of the intelligent parent or teacher who diverts a child from foolish activity by calling its attention to something else and not by issuing inflammatory prohibitions. And yet this subtlety did not destroy candor. The expression "frankly speaking" was often on the lips of our friends, and certainly one president of Tokyo University was frank when he remarked on some of the failings of the Occupation as well as on past American attitudes toward Japanese immigration, whereas another was equally frank when he indicated his disapproval of Premier Kishi's politics. One of our friends pulled no punches when he chided us for not learning Japanese, but his punches were not body blows; they were more like delicate jabs to the head.

We do not think it far-fetched to speculate that the subtlety we found among intellectuals who nevertheless made their point has its counterpart in the Japanese skill at miniaturization in technology. The capacity to produce an excellent but tiny part of a calculator or automobile that works well, we surmise, is related to the ability to make a fine philosophical point effectively without shouting. And so maybe the small Japanese car is not only a response to the shortage of oil in Japan but an expression of a skill that is conspicuous among its people.

The persistent qualities we have so far noted are related to the quiet and controlled side of the Japanese we knew; they were qualities that did not seem to be linked with the expression of tender emotions. Yet we encountered tenderness that often verged on, if it did not reach, sentimentalism. We recall mass academic singing that brought tears to the eyes of some of our more austere Japanese friends. And, as the reader knows, they would collectively bid us good-bye by waving handkerchiefs or scarves in a way that affected us deeply. We vividly remember one such demonstration of feeling as our train pulled away from the Hiroshima railroad station in 1952. Well-wishers had lined up on the track and, while we watched sadly from the rear car of our train, their handkerchiefs slowly went up and down, up and down until we were out of sight. The same thing happened as we left by ship from Takamatsu on the island of Shikoku in 1952. And, as we mentioned earlier, the touching farewell ritual was maintained even when we departed by airplanes that allowed us only peepholes through which we could see the waving. Somehow, we felt, the degree of emotion expressed at the time of departure may have been connected historically with the long isolation of Japan and, of course, with the difficulty of crossing the Pacific in the days before the airplane. We suspect that such emotions have changed somewhat now that the time of travel has been cut to what it is. Surely the Japanese of 1982 do not think that their friends' leaving Japan might be a matter of leaving it forever now that one can hop to New York so quickly. Today the main barrier to travel across the Pacific is money and not time so — who knows — maybe the sad sentimental good-bye may disappear once the Japanese build cheap "bullet airplanes" which scholars may be able to afford as easily as businessmen now do.

Since we are not trying to write a treatise on the Japanese soul but to collect some impressions of the Japanese we knew and to volunteer a few hypotheses on the culture as a whole, there is no point in going on about traits that remained fairly constant during our thirty years of contact with our friends even though others could be mentioned. It is time now to say something about the changes that we witnessed.

At several points in the previous chapters we have had occasion to reflect on changes we had observed upon our periodic returns to Japan, especially in Tokyo and Kyoto. In Chapter 9 we reported some of them when coming back in 1966: many new buildings; fewer kimonos; fewer unsegregated toilets and baths; fewer unpleasant smells (Henry Adams said as far back as 1886 that "Japan possesses one pervasive, universal, substantive smell—an oily, sickish, slightly fetid odor"); better taxicabs; more expensive private automobiles; fewer bicycles; higher prices; more opulent hotels; better restaurants; more television; less bowing; fewer name-cards; heavier traffic; more subways. And by 1976, Japanese cabdrivers were playing golf while secretaries were taking expensive trips to Hawaii. Most of these mundane changes were directly related to growing industrialization, an improving economy, and Westernization, and there is no need to labor them.

But what psychological changes had taken place? What differences did we observe in our friends? The most important was a growth of intellectual independence, about which we have said enough in earlier chapters. Yet there was another kind of independence bred in a generation younger than that of our friends. Their children, one of our Japanese colleagues reported in the mid-seventies while he was in Princeton, were no longer as deferential to Americans as he had been when he first came to the States as a student after the Second World War. They swaggered up Fifth Avenue with assurance, just as they swaggered up the Ginza. They were no longer apologetic and self-denigrating; they held their heads high. And this, our friend told us, startled him. He was, he allowed, incapable of that sort of behavior even though he was proud of it when he saw it in young people. There are Americans who regret this change and who would prefer to see the Japanese as they once were—smiling, bowing, and waiting for orders. But these same Americans would also prefer to see blacks and Hispanic Americans return to their former obsequiousness, just as their predecessors in American society would have liked to see Jews, Irishmen, and Italians hold their tongues and know their places. Yet almost everybody now realizes that those days are gone forever, and just as well. Our Japanese friends, we think, were distinguished by their capacity to become independent without becoming arrogant or obnoxious. We do not know whether this is true of all of their commercial compatriots who buy up companies and empty out New York and Paris boutiques with their cash, so we cannot recite about them.

What we do know, however, is that the capacity of Japanese scholars to become independent and productive is testimony to the value of supporting the international exchange of students. We believe that our contact with the Japanese not only made us and them happy but also advanced the causes of scholarship and peace. Now we live under an American administration which is more indifferent than any we can remember to the sort of contact we have had with Japanese scholars and their families since 1952, and perhaps it is just as well. For if this administration *did* send too many American scholars to Japan, unfortunately they might be even more suspect than the band who travelled to Tokyo in 1952, when it had to be emphasized that they were not agents of the State Department. The solution is one that is favored, for reasons radically different from ours, by the present administration—support by private sources. Over twenty-seven years our travel to Japan was periodically financed by American foundations alone until a Japanese foundation lent a hand in 1979, a method of support we think should continue in the foreseeable future. That is one of the main practical conclusions we draw from our experiences. Another, as the reader might imagine, has to do with American education. We think that there should be a great effort to improve and increase the amount of training that Americans receive in the Japanese language, for it is highly likely that Japan will become an even more important country than it is now. It is a pity that the Japanese language is so difficult, unlikely that the Japanese will simplify it by using only a syllabary, and virtually unthinkable that they will write anything scholarly in Romaji. Nevertheless, the rest of the world will have to contend with this and give linguistic instruction accordingly. Even businessmen now think that they should learn Japanese to increase their sales, so why should scholars not do it to improve their souls?

Stressing something we said earlier, we might add that the flow of scholars between America and Japan should take place in both directions. There should be a two-way scholarly shuttle across the Pacific, and we should abandon the arrogant idea that we are the only ones who should send intellectual missionaries abroad and admit ignorant intellectuals to our shores. A day may come when American philosophers will sit at the feet of Japanese who have something to teach them, not about Oriental cults but about an international philosophical discipline. Let those who think this is impossible take a look at American industry, especially the automobile and electronic industry. Henry Ford is probably writhing in his grave as he hears of American captains of industry who trudge the streets of Tokyo in search of instruction, advice, and money. In spite of the great differences between automobiles and scholarship, we predict that American professors—not only specialists concerned with Japanese culture and language; but humanists and scientists of all kinds—may one day trudge the streets of Tokyo with similar purposes in mind.

We do not say this because we think that Japanese thinkers are our superiors. We say it because we think that they are our equals and that we had best recognize this obvious fact. In 1952 they did not know a great deal about American philosophy, literature, politics, economics, and history, but the Stanford and Harvard professors who came to Tokyo that year knew even less about Japanese philosophy, literature, politics, economics, and history. Leaving aside the amount of learning or information that either group may have had, the Japanese were certainly equal to us in intelligence and sensibility, and such equality provides the most important basis for fruitful scholarly communication.

We should make clear that we are not interested in cultural exchange as an instrument of foreign or military policy; we are not urging American scholars to serve as advance men for military strategists. Indeed, we think that if scholarly ideas are discussed and friendships cultivated between intellectuals of different lands over a sufficiently long period of time, there may be no need for military strategists in the world. Intellectual exchange for military or political reasons is never very effective and, when it is seen for what it is, will produce the opposite of what it is supposed to produce. The aim of intellectual exchange is the advancement of philosophy, history, the sciences, and the arts; and it was our main goal during our long association with the Japanese. We think that all of us did something to reach that goal together during the thirty years that were so pleasant and instructive for us and, we hope, for our Japanese friends.

Index